Reinventing Britain

Constitutional Change under New Labour

edited by
ANDREW MCDONALD

Global, Area, and International Archive
University of California Press

BERKELEY   LOS ANGELES   LONDON

The Global, Area, and International Archive (GAIA) is an initiative of
International and Area Studies, University of California, Berkeley, in
partnership with the University of California Press, the California
Digital Library, and international research programs across the UC
system. GAIA volumes, which are published in both print and open-
access digital editions, represent the best traditions of regional studies,
reconfigured through fresh global, transnational, and thematic
perspectives.

University of California Press, one of the most distinguished university
presses in the United States, enriches lives around the world by
advancing scholarship in the humanities, social sciences, and natural
sciences. Its activities are supported by the UC Press Foundation and
by philanthropic contributions from individuals and institutions.
For more information, visit www.ucpress.edu.

University of California Press
Berkeley and Los Angeles, California

University of California Press, Ltd.
London, England

First published in Great Britain in 2007 by Politico's Publishing,
an imprint of Methuen Publishing Ltd.

Library of Congress Cataloging-in-Publication Data
 Reinventing Britain : constitutional change under New Labour /
 edited by Andrew McDonald..
   p.   cm.
 Includes bibliographical references and index.
 ISBN-13: 978-0-520-09862-6 (pbk. : alk. paper)
  1. Constitutional law—Great Britain.   2. Law reform—Great
Britain.   3. Labour Party (Great Britain).   4. Great Britain—Politics
and government—1997–   I. McDonald, Andrew, 1962–
KD3989.R45   2007
342.41'03—dc22   2007029743

Manufactured in the United States of America

16 15 14 13 12 11 10 09 08 07
10 9 8 7 6 5 4 3 2 1

The paper used in this publication meets the minimum requirements
of ANSI/NISO Z39.48-1992 (R 1997) *(Permanence of Paper)*.

Contents

Part IV: Meaning

Foreword

Rt Hon. the Lord Falconer of Thoroton QC

Lord Chancellor and Secretary of State for Justice

The government came to power in May 1997 committed to a programme of radical social change – to a renewal of our country. We wanted to break free from the class-based politics which had shaped much of British political life in the twentieth century. Our ambition was to leave behind the politics of division and to nurture an egalitarian society. A society of equal citizens, each of us with rights and responsibilities; each of us with the freedom to pursue our ambitions and to fulfil our potential. A society no longer dominated by elites.

This egalitarian spirit has animated our approach to the economy, to welfare policy, to education and to culture. And so it should be of no surprise that it is egalitarianism that has shaped our approach to constitutional reform. Britain is no longer a society in which it is acceptable that hereditary peers should dominate the House of Lords. Whitehall does not always know best. The public wants to be able to scrutinise government decisions and to take a view for itself on what is in the best interest of our nation. We understood that by 1997 the country had changed – and that it wanted its democracy and its government to change in ways that reflected a modern, meritocratic society.

The constitutional reforms of the last nine years have been radical and far-reaching. Each has been an expression of our egalitarian ambitions, and each has been an expression of our progressive values. We have sought to reshape our public institutions so that they are credible in the twenty-first century; to give citizens greater access to decision-making; to make government more accountable to the people; and to clarify the relationships between the three arms of the state. Ours is a consistent agenda – one shaped by principles which resonate with the country.

After almost a decade of determined reform there is still much to do. Some parts of our original programme remain to be completed – most obviously, reform of the House of Lords. And some new problems have arisen, not least the need to balance human rights with the risks posed by international terrorism. We are determined to address these challenges and, in many ways, we are better placed to do so today than we were in 1997. Consider, for example, the difficulties of shaping counter-terrorism policy in a society which was not guided by a human rights law. We are making a transition – a rapid transition – to a society in which the citizen's rights have explicit protection. The transition is not without its difficulties, but it is a profound transformation of our society and one of which we should be proud.

As our reforms develop and mature, I am conscious of two obligations which demand greater priority. The first is the need to focus on making a success of our new institutions: to nurture them and to foster the new relationships between arms of the state *and* between state and citizen. New statutes and new organisations are all well and good – but the toughest challenge comes in effecting a change to our civic culture and to the culture of government.

The second obligation is to promote greater understanding of our new constitution. It is in that context that I welcome this excellent collection of essays. Collectively, they represent a stimulating analysis of what we have done, why we sought to do it and how we have carried it through. There is a range of perspectives and interpretations here, a diversity of views which is sure to provoke debate. I welcome that diversity, even if I do not necessarily agree with all of the opinions expressed here. But what shines through is the quality of the analysis and the clarity of the argument. This is a collection which will, I feel sure, contribute significantly to understanding of these reforms – in the UK and overseas.

Having read this book a reader might be tempted to ask where and when the reform programme will come to an end. My reply is simple: I do not have a fixed endpoint in mind. We want a constitution that gives expression to the values and aspirations of the country. That is not a finite task: as society changes, so must we modernise the constitution. There will, of course, be times when the changes needed will be more modest, when the pace of reform will slacken. But it is far better that we embrace constitutional change than neglect it, allowing our democracy to ossify and to become irrelevant to, or discordant with, contemporary society. It is through change that we are able to foster those constitutional values which we as a country hold so dear – democracy and the rule of law.

March 2007

Preface

The proposition behind this book is a simple one. Since the election of the New Labour government in May 1997, the British state has undergone radical change. For the previous seventy years, constitutional reform had been on the margins of British politics, pursued fitfully – or coincidentally (as with the country's accession to the European Community). But in the last nine years, we have seen the institutional architecture of the state remodelled and the relationship between citizen and state refashioned. New legislatures have been established; Britons have been given new rights; and the country will soon have a new Supreme Court, free of any link to Parliament.

Vernon Bogdanor has said that these reforms amount to a 'quiet revolution'. Note the adjective as well as the noun. It is not that the reforms have been covert: they have been accompanied by referendums, by parliamentary debates and by periodic conflicts and controversies. But they have not been front and central in British politics. And if they have only commanded fitful attention at home, they are even less understood overseas.

The authors of this volume share two assumptions. First, that the reforms are of fundamental importance for the future of the state and its citizens. And second, that the reforms could and should be better understood at home and abroad. This book is our contribution to that end.

We do not all take the same view of their significance, nor of their future trajectory. We take the view that that adds to the value of this collection; we come at the subject from quite distinct perspectives and reach different conclusions. Two of us have worked on the reform programme as public servants; one of us runs a think tank on constitutional issues; another is a political commentator; two of us are lawyers; five of us are political scientists. Half of us live and work in Britain; half of us are based in North America.

And so there is a diversity of views in this collection and the expectation is that many readers will use it selectively. But it has been conceived as a whole and the book may, with advantage, be read from start to finish. The spine of the book – around which it has been organised – is in Chapters 1, 2 and 5. A reader wishing to get a grip on what has happened, why it has happened and how it has happened may want to focus first on these three chapters – by Robert Hazell and myself, by Peter Riddell and by Kenneth MacKenzie. Further exploration of the origins of the programme comes in the chapters by Mark Bevir, who traces the intellectual origins of New Labour's public sector reforms, and Joseph Fletcher, who examines what the public in the 1990s wanted from any changes. The second half of the book stands back from the programme and considers four of its most significant features. Kate Malleson and Ailsa Henderson each focus on a particular element of the programme – the judicial reforms and devolution respectively. Craig Parsons looks at the British reform story alongside the contemporary changes to the European Union – and asks how the European developments have influenced the British story. And in the concluding chapter Jack Citrin considers what impact the reforms have had on public attitudes towards the nation-state and our notion of Britishness.

Two points on scope. First, this is a book about Great Britain and its constituent nations – England, Scotland and Wales. And so it leaves to one side the peace process in Northern Ireland and the constitutional reforms that have followed. That is not to suggest that they are unimportant, nor to deny that they have implications for the UK as a whole. But the Northern Irish story is a distinct one: the reforms since 1997 have their origins in the peace process which had been running under the previous Conservative administration. Whereas British policy towards Northern Ireland has been conducted on a bipartisan basis, the rest of the reform programme has been a source of party controversy.

Second, the pace of constitutional reform remains brisk and so I should note that these essays were prepared in the summer of 2006 and do not reflect subsequent events.

I should like to express my thanks to those who have made this book possible. The contributors met to present and discuss their papers at a conference at the University of California, Berkeley in April 2006. This was funded by the University's Institute of Governmental Studies (IGS), the Institute of European Studies and the Center for British Studies. My own presence at Berkeley in 2005–6 was supported by the Department for Constitutional Affairs and by the Fulbright Commission, which awarded me a fellowship for the year. I will always be grateful to those who had the imagination to support this work and to my many friends at the IGS who made it such a stimulating and congenial place to spend a year. In particular, I want to acknowledge the contribution of Nelson Polsby. It is with sorrow that I note that he did not live to see the publication of this book, which he did so much to encourage. Finally, I thank my fellow authors of this volume for the quality of their work, for their persistence and for their good humour.

Andrew McDonald
Berkeley, California

Part I

The story

1

What happened next: constitutional change under New Labour

Andrew McDonald and Robert Hazell[1]

> The year 1997 has altered Britain for good: politically, institutionally and emo-
> tionally. Corrupt politicians were exposed. A Tory government was shattered at
> the election. A Labour government started to reform the constitution. One of
> the last remnants of Empire, Hong Kong, was handed back and Establishment
> figures cried. Then Diana – the mother of single mothers – died, and the
> country's image changed as millions cried. Scotland embraced Home Rule and
> said it was willing to pay for it. Wales followed if only just – with significantly
> higher support for a Scottish-style parliament than the pup of an assembly on
> offer. Londoners will confirm that people like radical democracy. Labour and
> Liberal Democrats started to co-operate and consider proportional representa-
> tion. British citizens, the term is starting to sound genuine, are to have their
> rights in court. And the government declared that it wanted the European single
> currency to succeed and Britain to join.
>
> Anthony Barnett, *This Time: Our Constitutional Revolution*[2]

Just nine years after it was written, Anthony Barnett's breathless attempt to
capture the mood of 1997 already sounds like a period piece. The death of the
Princess of Wales may have moved the nation to tears, but it was not the
constitutional landmark his book claimed it to be. And few would suggest that
Britain's entry into the euro is now imminent. Instant history is a perilous
business and it is now clear that some of Barnett's observations were wide of
the mark. But his basic contention has been confirmed: 1997 held out the
prospect of profound constitutional change. This chapter will tell the tale of
what happened next.

The central proposition of this chapter, indeed of this volume, is that the story of the last nine years is an extraordinary one. The British constitution has undergone the most radical change in eighty years: power has been devolved from Westminster, citizens have been able to take human rights cases to domestic courts for the first time and the country is to have a Supreme Court. Our purpose here is first to describe what has happened. Beyond that, we will assess the stability of the changes: have we witnessed irreversible changes and do they collectively represent a new constitutional settlement? We will not attempt to answer the question 'Have they worked?' because we cannot yet know what their full effect will be. But we will consider the further changes which may yet follow – either as a consequence of the reforms already made or to complete the agenda which Barnett described in 1997.

Most of the criticisms of the reform programme fall into two categories. The first charges that it is an exercise in vandalism, imperilling Britain's historic constitution by means of piecemeal changes which have not been fully thought through. The second chides the government for a lack of radicalism and urges it on to even more fundamental change, preferably to be secured in a codified constitution. Neither charge is directly relevant to the task before us in this chapter, but we will consider whether the reforms may be regarded as a unified programme stemming from a single plan and we will show how Britain has been moving incrementally towards a codified constitution.

There is a third critique which addresses the governmental reforms more obliquely: it dismisses them by arguing that New Labour's style of government has undermined them. To tackle this thesis properly one would have to determine whether the government's policies and politics have been majoritarian in intent or impact, whether the conventions of Cabinet government have been eroded and whether its criminal justice and anti-terrorist legislation have weakened civil liberties. In short, one would have to assess the whole of the government's record. Our objective here is more modest and our focus is more precise.

We will first provide a short narrative of the reforms, taking the story from New Labour's landslide victory in May 1997 to the summer of 2006, early in its third term. The core of the chapter is a thematic analysis of the reforms. We conclude by drawing the themes together and by considering the future priorities of the programme.

What happened next

To appreciate fully the extent and pace of constitutional change from 1997, one needs three points of reference.

The first is Britain's record of constitutional reform over the twentieth century. From 1928, when the franchise was extended to women for the first time, until the Callaghan government of the 1970s, constitutional change did not occupy centre stage in British politics. The country's institutional architecture had been reshaped by the Parliament Act 1911 (which established the primacy of the Commons over the Lords); by the Anglo-Irish Treaty of 1921 (which divided the island of Ireland, creating the Irish Free State and leaving the six counties of the north as part of the UK); and by the introduction of mass suffrage in 1918–28. The subsequent decades did see further refinements to the suffrage, the introduction of life peers to the House of Lords and the curtailment of the Lords' powers to delay legislation. But governments did not seek to change the fundamental architecture of the state. This is not to say that the constitution did not change over this period. For example, the latter half of the century saw the development of extensive powers of judicial review and, in 1972, the introduction of a species of higher law with Britain's accession to the European Economic Community. But these were not the result of conscious, purposive action by the government to bring about constitutional change. Britain's entry into the EEC did have profound constitutional implications, but it was not conceived as an exercise in constitutional reform. The most radical constitutional bill brought before Parliament in the latter half of the century was the Callaghan government's Scotland and Wales Bill; and this ended in failure which, in turn, precipitated the fall of that administration in 1979.

The second reference point is the Labour–Liberal Democrat constitutional agreement of March 1997. The origins of Labour's conversion to the constitutional reform agenda are discussed more fully in Chapter 2 but for present purposes it is important to note that Labour had been in informal talks with the Liberal Democrats for the previous three years. This ultimately resulted in their agreement to co-operate after the general election on a common programme of constitutional renewal. This was remarkable in its ambition and range, taking in reform of the House of Lords, a referendum on proportional representation for Westminster, introduction of a domestic Bill of Rights and devolution to Scotland, Wales and London. The two parties affirmed their commitment to the programme – and where they had differences (over the speed of movement on proportional representation and the pre-legislative referendum for Scottish devolution) these were side-stepped in the text. Appendix A catalogues the commitments made and shows how they were echoed (with a few exceptions) in New Labour's general election manifesto.

The third reference point is the mindset of the new government: it came to power determined to implement its programme. This, it might be observed, is true of any new administration. But there was a particular edge to New Labour's commitment. This was a party which had been out of power for eighteen years, which had wearied of the charges of betrayal which critics had levelled at the Wilson and Callaghan governments and whose leader had spoken often of the need for sustained achievement over two successive terms. The programme had been crafted accordingly: it was one which was intended to be delivered in its entirety. Some had criticised the manifesto's economic and social policies for lacking ambition and radicalism. Neither charge could fairly attach to the constitutional pledges and yet they, in common with the rest of the manifesto, were to be delivered come what may.

For all the detail in the cross-party agreement and in the manifesto, the programme began with that rarity in modern political life, a complete surprise. Within days of its election the new government announced that it would grant the Bank of England operational control over monetary policy. The government would establish a new accountability framework for the Bank and in future it would be the Bank's responsibility to take interest rate decisions and to hit an inflation target. The changes were to come into effect immediately but they were buttressed by statutory changes in the following year. At a stroke, the incoming Chancellor had surrendered political control of one of the principal tools of economic management.

This aside, the rest of the constitutional programme got off to a more predictable start. But the pace was extraordinary. Elected on 1 May, the government introduced the legislation for the Scottish and Welsh devolution referendums immediately after the Queen's Speech on 14 May. The bill was passed before the summer − and the referendums were both won in September. White Papers on the government's proposals for Scotland and Wales had been published in July; and the devolution legislation was passed before the end of the first session (a long session, running from May 1997 to November 1998). In all, twelve constitutional Bills were introduced in the first session, so that the European Convention on Human Rights was incorporated into domestic law, London was authorised to hold a referendum for an elected mayor and political parties were made subject to registration for the first time.

Despite this pace, the government still faced charges that it was dragging its feet. As early as May 1997 there was press criticism that freedom of information was not to come at the start of the programme. Some feared that the government would not stay the course; others (especially among the Liberal Democrats) wondered whether Labour was genuinely committed to delivering a more pluralist democracy. Devolution was known to be 'unfinished business' from the Callaghan government and Labour's commitment to it was unshakeable, not least because it had been so closely identified with the last Labour leader, John Smith. But what of the rest of the agenda, with which many in the party felt less affinity?

The answer came over the next two parliamentary sessions. Having carried all before it in the first session, the Government met sterner opposition to its programme – and it began to make compromises which provoked criticism from some reformers. But the commitment to fulfil the manifesto pledges was unquestionable and it was clear that the government remained willing to spend political capital in doing so.

The toughest parliamentary challenge was always going to be Lords reform: one way or another the government had to fashion a majority for its proposals in the Upper House (where it was heavily outnumbered) or it would have to resort to use of the Parliament Act, a device which was both cumbersome and time-consuming. Ultimately it made progress through an extraordinary compromise deal with Lord Cranborne, Conservative leader in the Lords. This saved ninety-two hereditary peers pending the completion of the reform at a later date.[3]

Enthusiasts for voting reform gave a qualified welcome to the regional-list system which was to be used for future European Parliamentary elections.[4] But they suspected that the government was at best lukewarm about the Jenkins committee's report on proportional representation for Westminster. Jenkins reported in October 1998, recommending an alternative-vote system supplemented by a top-up list to deliver broad proportionality.

The government's record on freedom of information also caused reformers disquiet. It did appear in the legislative programme in 1999 – but only after a draft Bill which was criticised as a pale shadow of the radical White Paper *Your Right to Know*, published in December 1997. The legislation was finally passed in 2000 but not without continued criticism that the government had lost its nerve, or had become too comfortable with the secrecy traditionally associated with Whitehall.

By the time of the 2001 general election Labour could fairly claim to have implemented its manifesto commitments on constitutional reform (see Appendix A). Some of its reforms were more modest than reformers had hoped. For example, modernisation of the House of Commons had fallen short of its early promise and the regional chambers which were created to supervise regional government in England were no more than voluntary, non-statutory bodies. But the record of achievement against commitments was undeniable.

It was equally clear that much remained to be done. Lords reform had been begun but not completed and proportional representation for Westminster could not be ignored, even though Labour's relationship with the Liberal Democrats was now more tenuous than it had been in 1997. In its 2001 manifesto, Labour pledged broadly to implement the recommendations of the Wakeham commission on Lords reform. After the first phase of Lords reform, the government had referred the question of composition of the House to a Royal Commission chaired by Lord Wakeham. It reported in 2000, setting out a menu of options for the introduction of a minority of elected peers. On proportional representation meanwhile, the manifesto promised another review – this time of Jenkins and of the experience of the proportional representation systems which had been introduced for the devolved administrations and for the European Parliament.

Of the two, proportional representation was to present the government with fewer problems. A review was under way in government by the time of the 2005 general election, but it had received little attention and there was no move to a decision. By contrast, the spectacle of Lords reform was played out in public, to the government's evident exasperation. Faced with differences of view on its own benches as to the composition and powers of the Lords, the government sought to fashion a compromise which might secure enough support in both Houses. It failed. Its first attempt was the 2001 White Paper *Completing the Reform*, which proposed the removal of the remaining hereditary peers and the election of 20 per cent of the new House. Maximalists saw no reason to compromise: they continued to argue their case for a wholly elected House or for a wholly appointed one. And the remaining hereditary peers were unmoved: they argued that the 1999 deal allowed them to stay until Parliament approved a new, permanent basis for the second chamber and few were willing to concede that the government's proposals constituted that permanent solution. The next step on this journey was a series of votes in both Houses on the future composition of the Lords: of the seven options put to a vote in February 2003, none commanded a majority. It would have been hard to think of a worse outcome for reformers (or for Parliament as a whole, which was seen to have mishandled the voting). Subsequently, the government sought to make progress where it could, bringing forward proposals later in 2003 to remove the remaining hereditary peers and to strengthen the Appointments Commission which had been introduced in Labour's first term to oversee the creation of crossbench peers. The argument about the interpretation of the 1999 deal was reignited and Lord Strathclyde, Cranborne's successor as Conservative leader, pledged determined opposition to the proposals. A Bill to give them effect was prepared but was dropped shortly before its intended introduction in March 2004. No further progress was made before the 2005 general election.

The government suffered a setback of a different sort over its plans for regional devolution within England. Its commitment to an elected tier of regional government had always been qualified: it would proceed if there was demand for it and it would test the demand by a referendum. Ultimately it chose to put the issue to the vote in just one region, the North-East, which was thought to have a strong sense of its own identity. In the all-postal ballot in November 2004 the proposal was rejected by almost 80 per cent of voters, on a turnout of 47.7 per cent. The government's proposals had been vulnerable to the charge that they would have changed little: the new assembly would have modest powers and its opponents successfully branded it a white elephant. In the event, the rejection was so decisive that it became clear that regional assemblies would not be put to a vote again in the foreseeable future. Instead, the government began to focus its energies on the renewal of local neighbourhoods, partly through a regeneration of local democracy.

The reform agenda in the 2001 parliament included a surprise every bit as remarkable as operational independence for the Bank of England. In appointing Lord Falconer to the office of Lord Chancellor in a ministerial reshuffle in June 2003, No. 10 issued a press notice announcing a new departure in constitutional reform. The office of Lord Chancellor was to be abolished, a new Supreme Court was to be established and a Judicial Appointments Commission was to have responsibility for the appointment of the judiciary in England and Wales. The proposals were welcomed by many reformers but they attracted fierce criticism for the manner of their announcement and for the failure to prepare the way for them. Consultation papers duly followed the announcement but goodwill had already been lost, a point subsequently acknowledged by the Prime Minister when before the Liaison Committee. The passage of the Constitutional Reform Bill – which embraced all three proposals – was troubled. Exceptionally, the Lords referred it to a select committee, arguing that this was necessary if the measure was to attract the scrutiny it merited. Eventually, the Constitutional Reform Act was passed shortly before the 2005 election, much amended but securing the government's principal policy objectives.

In drafting its 2005 election manifesto Labour must have felt some sense of déjà vu when it came to its constitutional commitments. Its pledge on proportional representation – a review – echoed the wording of the 2001 manifesto. On Lords reform it placed a new emphasis on looking at the powers and the composition of the House in tandem; and it confirmed the Prime Minister's earlier commitment that there would be a free vote on the composition of the new House. But the manifesto was striking for three other themes. The first was the return of devolution. There were commitments to give the national assembly in Wales new powers; to review the powers of the London mayor and assembly; and to grant new powers to regional government in England. The second theme was a return to unfinished business from the March 1997 agreement with the Liberal Democrats, with a renewed commitment to a Commission on Human Rights.[5] And the third was a new emphasis on boosting democratic participation.

By July 2006 the government had passed legislation on all three topics. The Government of Wales Act provides a new settlement for Wales (wholly replacing the 1998 Act), which will transfer primary legislative powers to Wales in three stages. The Equality Act creates a new combined Commission for Equality and Human Rights, which brings together the Equal Opportunities Commission, the Commission for Racial Equality and the Disability Rights Commission. The Electoral Administration Act makes new provision for voter registration and tightens the regulation of political parties, in particular in declaring loans. Table 1.1 demonstrates that the pace of constitutional reform slowed after 1998, but it was clear from the start of Labour's third term that the government had yet to exhaust its constitutional agenda.

Making sense of it all

Before attempting a thematic analysis of the programme it is worth considering whether we are studying a programme at all. Does Labour's reform agenda constitute an integrated whole? The individual commitments arose from quite distinct origins – some old and some new. Devolution may have been unfinished business from the 1970s but it was also a political obligation for the party north of the border. Freedom of information was also a child of the 1970s, having first made its bow in a manifesto in 1974 and dutifully putting in an appearance in every subsequent manifesto until it finally secured the limelight in 1997. Labour's wholehearted conversion to the incorporation of the European Convention on Human Rights happened in 1993, when John Smith was leader, and its more equivocal conversion to proportional representation had been hastened by the Labour–Liberal Democrat 'project' since 1994 – distinct commitments arising from quite different origins.

And once in office Labour was hesitant about drawing together the distinct strands into a single narrative. Bagehot in the *Economist* was one of many to observe that the government did not start its reform programme with a White Paper explaining what it was seeking to do.[6] Lord Irvine of Lairg, Labour's first Lord Chancellor, could not see the point in doing so: the manifesto provided a clear prescription for Britain's ills and it was the government's job to make good its commitment to the electorate. The agenda was, he maintained, coherent but 'many elements of the package are not interdependent ... The strands do not spring from a single master plan, however much that concept might appeal to purists'.[7] What mattered, he stressed – in a New Labour nostrum – was what worked. It was not until Lord Falconer's appointment as Lord Chancellor in June 2003 that the tone of the government's public presentation changed. Falconer has done more to explain the programme's common themes – in public lectures and in parliamentary debate.

And so we have a reform agenda which sprang from different origins, served different purposes and, in the early days of the government, was rarely explained as a whole. But Irvine's emphasis on the manifesto is relevant: it was the single document by which he steered the reform agenda in the first couple of years. Chapter 5 shows how this was effected in Whitehall: Irvine and the Cabinet Office Constitution Secretariat co-ordinated action – and kept the policy owners up to the mark. During the government's second term, constitutional policy responsibilities were consolidated in one department and a formal programme was established to take forward the development and the delivery of the reforms. But even if the means of delivery has varied over the lifetime of the government, the consistency of its focus on the agenda set out in 1997 is remarkable (see Appendix A). Some new themes have been introduced in response to later events; for example, the government's interest in democratic participation was sharpened by the 2001 general election, in which turnout fell to just 59 per cent. But these are exceptions to the rule: the policies which have been pursued determinedly since 1997 are essentially those set out in the 1997 manifesto.

Table 1.1: Constitutional statutes under New Labour, 1997–2006

This table includes measures deemed to be of some constitutional significance. There is inevitably some room for argument about what should be included and what should not. This table takes in the frequent adjustments of electoral legislation (some substantive, some more minor) and changes to rules regarding eligibility for membership of the Commons. Northern Irish constitutional legislation – of which there was plenty in this period – is not in this table because the focus of this chapter is Great Britain rather than the United Kingdom. The table includes legislation passed before the 2006 summer recess.

	Statute	Policy objective
1997	Referendum (Scotland and Wales) Act 1997	To authorise pre-legislative referendums in Scotland and Wales
1998	Scotland Act 1998	To establish Scottish Parliament
	Government of Wales Act 1998	To establish Welsh Assembly
	Human Rights Act 1998	To incorporate ECHR into UK law
	European Communities (Amendment) Act 1998	To incorporate Treaty of Amsterdam of October 1997
	Regional Development Agencies Act 1998	To establish regional development agencies and to designate regional chambers
	Bank of England Act 1998	Independence for the Bank of England
	Greater London Authority Referendum Act 1998	To authorise referendum on Greater London Authority
	Data Protection Act 1998	To give effect to EC Data Protection Directive (95/46/EC)
	Registration of Political Parties Act 1998	Provision for legal recognition of political parties
1999	European Parliamentary Elections Act 1999	To change voting system to regional-list proportional representation
	Greater London Authority Act 1999	To establish Greater London Authority
	Access to Justice Act 1999	To establish Legal Service Commission and reform legal aid, rights of audience, family court reform
	House of Lords Act 1999	To remove all but 92 hereditary peers
2000	Disqualifications Act 2000	To allow members of the Irish Parliament to sit in the House of Commons and the devolved assemblies
	Local Government Act 2000	To provide for elected mayors and separate executives
	Freedom of Information Act 2000	To create new statutory right of access to information
	Political Parties, Elections and	To establish Electoral Commission and

	Referendums Act 2000	regulate elections and referendums
	Terrorism Act 2000	To amend and extend existing counter-terrorism legislation
	Representation of the People Act 2000	To introduce rolling voter registration and experiments in new voting methods to make voting easier
2001	Election Publications Act 2001	To postpone the operation of requirements introduced by Political Parties, Elections and Referendums Act 2000
	House of Commons (Removal of Clergy Disqualification) Act 2001	To remove the disqualification of members of clergy from membership of the House of Commons
	Elections Act 2001	To defer local government elections to coincide with general election on 5 May 2001
	Anti-Terrorism, Crime and Security Act 2001	Series of anti-terrorism measures
2002	European Communities (Amendment) Act 2002	To ratify the Treaty of Nice signed by UK government in February 2001
	Sex Discrimination (Election Candidates) Act 2002	To exclude from the Sex Discrimination Act 1975 certain matters relating to selection of candidates by political parties
2003	Regional Assemblies (Preparation) Act 2003	To authorise referendums on regional assemblies in English regions
	European Parliament (Representation) Act 2003	To reduce number of UK seats in European Parliament from 87 to 78, and enfranchise Gibraltar
	European Union (Accessions) Act 2003	To give effect in UK law to EU enlargement, increasing EU from 15 to 25 member states
	Courts Act 2003	To modernise criminal justice system through unified courts system
2004	European Parliamentary and Local Elections (Pilots) Act 2004	To enable experiments with more flexible methods of voting
	Scottish Parliament (Constituencies) Act 2004	To maintain Scottish Parliament at 129 members
	Civil Contingencies Act 2004	To provide for unified executive control in a state of emergency
2005	Constitutional Reform Act 2005	To abolish office of Lord Chancellor, and establish new Supreme Court and Judicial Appointments Commission
	Prevention of Terrorism Act 2005	To introduce control orders to restrict suspected terrorists who cannot be deported
	Inquiries Act 2005	Statutory framework for operation of government inquiries

2006	Equality Act 2006	To establish the Commission for Equality and Human Rights
	Electoral Administration Act 2006	To reform voter registration and tighten voter security
	Government of Wales Act 2006	To increase powers and reform structure of the Assembly and to end dual candidacy in constituencies and top-up list

And so we can speak of a consistent agenda, even if it had diverse origins and the individual components served quite distinct purposes. But when it comes to identifying the programme's underlying themes, we face renewed difficulty because the public presentation of Labour's plans did not always delineate those principles consistently. In 1998 Irvine seemed to address those who were seeking theoretical rigour, when he defined the government's purpose in a sentence: 'Our objective is to put in place an integrated programme of measures to decentralise power in the United Kingdom; and to enhance the rights of individuals within a more open society.'[8] Two of the recurring themes are clear here – decentralisation and the rights of the citizen. A third – openness – was especially prominent while Labour was in opposition, not least because it was used as a stick with which to beat the Major administration, which had been beset by ministerial scandals. But openness is perhaps best understood as a sub-set of citizens' rights. Two further themes might be added to Irvine's list. The first concerns democracy: it was there in 1997 in the manifesto commitments to introduce changes to voting systems and to tighten up electoral administration; and it remains there today with the new emphasis on democratic participation. The fourth concerns reform of the judiciary – the surprise which emerged from the June 2003 reshuffle. This is not in Irvine's summary, not least because he did not see the case for doing away with the Lord Chancellor and for curbing ministerial involvement in the appointment of the judiciary.

We will use these four themes for our analysis: decentralisation of power; strengthening of the rights of the citizen against the state; democratic reform and innovation; and rebalancing of the relationship between the executive and the judiciary. In each case we will consider what progress has been made towards that end and will assess whether the change is stable and whether the reform is irreversible. Any judgement on this final point must be tentative. In theory, there is nothing stopping Parliament from setting out tomorrow to reverse all of these changes. But in many cases it is now inconceivable that this would happen, and in some instances there are serious practical obstacles in the way of a retreat to the status quo ante.

Devolution

Since 1997 Great Britain has been reshaped. Scotland has its national parliament, Wales its national assembly and London its mayor and assembly. All three reforms were validated in popular referendums. And in the three major parties there is no appetite for rolling back the reforms.

The Westminster Parliament is becoming a federal legislature for the United Kingdom as a whole and a domestic legislature for England and, for the moment, for Northern Ireland.[9] Vernon Bogdanor has gone so far as to ask whether Westminster remains sovereign over the domestic affairs of Scotland and Wales. The technical answer to that question is clearly yes but Bogdanor notes that political authority has to be exercised if it is to remain legitimate. It is true that the Holyrood Parliament has frequently allowed Westminster to legislate on its behalf – but that procedure (by legislative consent motions) simply confirms that authority is now in Edinburgh and not London. The political culture of Edinburgh and Cardiff has been changed for good: each provides a distinct focus for national political life and each is now attracting a new generation of politicians who are choosing to make their careers there rather than in Westminster. Labour is the dominant political party in each of the three capitals but that has not prevented the emergence of distinctive domestic policies in Scotland and Wales. And the Labour leaders of those administrations have been at pains to stress that distinctiveness: Jack McConnell has gone out of his way to emphasise his Scottish identity over his Britishness and Rhodri Morgan has emphasised that on social policy there is 'clear red water' between Cardiff and London.[10]

But if these changes are irreversible, that does not mean that they are necessarily stable. It is a truism that devolution is a process rather than an event. Anybody who questioned the wisdom of this observation may finally have been persuaded by the events of the last two years: devolution of additional power to Cardiff, Edinburgh and London is either under way or under consideration.

The process of review is furthest advanced in Wales. It began with an all-party commission established in 2002 by Morgan, the First Minister, and chaired by Lord Richard to consider the powers and electoral system of the

Assembly. Devolution has had a more difficult journey in Wales than in Scotland: it only squeaked over the 50 per cent approval threshold in the 1997 referendum; turnout in Assembly elections has been disappointing; Labour's first candidate for the leadership in the Assembly – and his successor – both succumbed to misfortunes of one sort or another; the Welsh Labour Party is opposed to the electoral top-up system (whereby losers in a constituency battle can be reborn as victors on the top-up list); and the constitution and powers of the Assembly have been criticised as modest and/or unworkable. The Richard commission's report, delivered in March 2004, proposed major structural changes. It called for a new constitution for the Assembly, scrapping its unitary structure and effecting a formal separation between executive and assembly. Beyond that, it recommended that the Assembly should be given primary legislative powers; and that the number of members should rise from sixty to eighty, elected by single transferable vote (STV).

Richard was received with modified rapture in London. The government's response, published in June 2005, conceded the new constitution of the Assembly. It proposed a three-stage move to greater powers – proceeding by way of more framework legislation, to further grants of legislative authority by Order in Council and, finally, to primary powers (but only if approved by a referendum). And, finally, it rejected the move to STV, preferring to keep the existing additional member system (AMS) but barring candidates from standing both for individual constituencies and for the top-up list. The government's response has, in turn, been criticised for proceeding too cautiously on the extension of powers and for ignoring Richard's strictures on AMS. Lord Richard himself was particularly critical of the government's approach. The House of Lords resisted the ban on dual candidacy but ultimately it yielded to the Commons and the Government of Wales Act 2006 was passed.

The Scottish review has also been initiated by the devolved administration and it, too, is considering whether Westminster should surrender further powers. But the scope of the review is narrower and it is currently unclear what it will yield: the First Minister has suggested that the Holyrood Parliament might acquire control over firearms, drugs, casinos, abortion, broadcasting and immigration. And in truth, there is less to play for in Scotland. The 1998 devolution settlement was more radical than its Welsh counterpart: aside from a defined list of powers reserved to Westminster, the remainder was all devolved to Edinburgh. The result has been a stable, and increasingly self-confident, parliament and executive, which have, for example, followed quite distinct policies in university education and care for the elderly. Edinburgh and London have found a modus vivendi in their ministerial and official dealings without undue difficulty. But it is fair to add that the true test of the London–Edinburgh dynamic is yet to come: the relationship will come under greater pressure once Labour loses its dominant position in Westminster or Holyrood.

The review initiated by McConnell will not be considering reform of the Barnett formula, which determines changes to the financing of the Scottish executive. At present, the administration is funded wholly by a block grant from Whitehall; so far it has shown no interest in changing the formula or in making use of its own tax-raising powers. And given the benefit Scotland has derived from the increases in Exchequer spending sanctioned under New Labour, one can understand this reticence. But opposition parties in the Parliament are beginning to question Barnett, and if the balance of advantage for Scotland shifts, the issue may force itself onto the agenda. That would lend a new and challenging dimension to relations between London and Edinburgh. Arguments over the financing of provincial or state governments are commonplace in most federal states: it is perhaps their absence rather than their imminence in the UK which is notable.[11]

The review in London was initiated by the government and confirmed in its 2005 manifesto. The story in London has not been without its alarms for Labour – mostly over the election of Ken Livingstone as mayor in 2000, who had left the party amidst much acrimony, arguing that his election as Labour's candidate had been blocked. But as an exercise in the devolution of power London's story is remarkable. The government's proposed solution for London-wide government was bold: it wanted to introduce a single-person executive to be chosen not by an assembly, but by the votes of an electorate of more than seven million. The powers initially granted to the mayor were relatively modest and they remained subject to checks by Whitehall. But crucially the mayor's remit included transport, and Livingstone's flagship policy was the imposition of congestion charges for vehicles entering central London. Their introduction was watched nervously not just in London, but in cities across the country; its signal success and the mayor's role in London's 2012 Olympic bid have contributed much to the sense that the mayoral system is working well. The review was undertaken in that context and resulted in new powers for the mayor in respect of housing, planning, skills, culture and waste management.

These reviews – and the reforms in their wake – demonstrate that the devolution process is not static, but nor is it reversible. Within just nine years, the structures and political cultures of the country have been transformed. The UK is becoming a quasi-federal state. In theory sovereignty has been delegated by Westminster to Cardiff and Edinburgh. But in practice it would be exceptionally difficult to reclaim: with Scotland, at least, sovereignty has been shared, just as it is shared in all federal states. The distribution of powers has purposely been uneven, and so it will remain; but the dynamics of devolution, not least the demands from the new representatives in Cardiff and Edinburgh, will ensure that the term 'devolution settlement' remains misleading.

Citizens' rights

In his review of the first two years of the Human Rights Act, Lord Irvine proposed that Britain start to celebrate what the statute had achieved. It was not hard to understand why he had to make an official plea for the rejoicing to start. The Act, passed in 1998 and implemented from 2000, has attracted repeated criticisms in the media. It is variously portrayed as a cranks' charter, an offence to British common sense and (in the face of all the facts) an import from the European Union drafted by foreigners unfamiliar with the British way of life. And since Irvine's appeal, the government has found itself having to reconcile the Act's obligations with the threat posed by international terrorism. It had to derogate from Article 5 of the Convention and has been criticised for the balance it has struck between civil liberties and the protection of national security.[12]

But it is easy to see why Irvine feels that there is cause for celebration. The Act gave British citizens recourse to their rights under the European Convention on Human Rights in domestic courts. And it did so without challenging the doctrine of parliamentary sovereignty: judges are empowered to declare statutes incompatible with the Act, but not to strike those laws down. Once a declaration has been made Parliament may choose to use a bespoke fast-track procedure to decide what to do about the offending statute. Alternatively, it may choose simply to repeal the statute and replace it with something entirely different.[13] The careful balance between judicial review and parliamentary authority provoked much agonising when the Human Rights Bill was under discussion. Some suggested that the Act would open the door to judicial activism and they conjured up the spectacle of the courts filling up with cases taking spurious human rights points. The Bill was duly passed, public authorities and the judiciary were trained in what the legislation meant, and the statute book was audited to weed out provisions which would not survive the new dawn.

That dawn did not bring with it the collapse of the court system. Nor did it provoke aggressive activism by a newly emboldened judiciary. All parties became accustomed to their new roles – from the minister advising Parliament that a new Bill was compatible with the Act through to a judge declaring that a statute was in conflict with rights granted under the convention. In practice, the judiciary has made modest uses of its new powers. In the first five years, judges have used their power to reinterpret statutes to make them compliant in just ten cases and they have made seventeen declarations of incompatibility.[14]

What are we to make of this? The Human Rights Act does not (yet) have strong institutional champions; by contrast, devolution is reinforced by pressure from the elected representatives in Cardiff and Edinburgh. The Act remains politically controversial and at the 2005 general election the Conservatives spoke of the need to review it. Subsequently, the party has returned to the earlier debate about the merits of a distinctively British Bill of Rights. But it would be difficult for any future government to repeal the Act: unless Britain were to withdraw from the European Convention itself, repeal would mean that British citizens would again have to travel to Strasbourg to secure their rights. Amendment remains possible, but the government's own review of the perceived tension between the Act and counter-terrorism policy found no case for legislative action, not least because domestic legislation cannot alter the convention or the government's obligations in international law to give effect to it.[15]

The most likely outcome is that the Act will remain and that government and judiciary will continue to explore its potential. Over time, we can expect that the judiciary will make greater use of the broad principles expressed in the convention. The British judicial culture may be more conservative and legalist than other common-law traditions, but the increasingly bold and innovative use made by Canadian judges of that country's Charter of Rights and Freedoms demonstrates that judicial cultures change – and that judges learn from the innovations made in other jurisdictions. There is no necessary reason why the judicial reforms initiated in 2003 should influence the development of human rights jurisprudence. But they may well encourage a new self-confidence on the part of the judiciary and a greater willingness to exert its authority.

By 2007 the Human Rights Act will have a new champion: the government is creating a Commission for Equality and Human Rights

(CEHR). Aside from bringing together the existing anti-discrimination commissions, the new body will have an advocacy role for human rights. To date this role has been taken on by the Joint Committee on Human Rights – authoritative but little known beyond Parliament – and by the government itself, where the role has sat alongside the executive's own obligations to observe the Act. The commission will have greater freedom of manoeuvre. Whether it can make the British love the Human Rights Act is another question. But it is safe to conclude that the Act is here to stay, even if currently we can only guess at its long-term potential.

An even more provisional judgement has to be offered on the government's freedom of information legislation. After its circuitous route to the statute books in 2000, the Act was not implemented in full until January 2005. And so there are two reasons to be cautious in our judgement. First, it is simply too early to say what impact it will have: at the time of writing the Information Commissioner has yet to make many substantive rulings on appeals and only a handful of cases have made their way beyond the commissioner to the Information Tribunal. And second, the forces unleashed by access legislation tend to work against it, rather than reinforce it. In Australia and Ireland, to take just two examples, governments reacted to their early discomfort with freedom of information by increasing access charges to curb demand.

All that can be said at this stage is that the rights conferred by the 2000 Act are comparable to those in many access statutes passed in other jurisdictions in the last 10–15 years. The fee regime in Britain is relatively liberal and access to the commissioner – the independent adjudicator – is theoretically straight-forward, even if the commissioner's office found it difficult to cope with the early demand. More than 38,000 requests were made of central government within the first year, a figure well within initial estimates; and the quarterly breakdown of applications shows a sharp decline after the early surge in demand in January 2005.[16]

The first judgements on the efficacy of the legislation were made by media commentators before the end of February 2005 – as the early requests were being processed. Some delayed their judgement a few weeks longer, declaring the Act a failure when the government refused to give access to the Attorney General's advice on the legality of the war in Iraq. But these are no more than the early skirmishes that have accompanied the introduction of access legislation in all jurisdictions. We will have to wait years, not months, before we can take a view on the efficacy – or durability – of Britons' right to know.

Democracy

Reformers' sternest criticisms of the government's record have been reserved for its changes to Britain's electoral and parliamentary systems. New Labour's reforms, it is alleged, have been faltering and self-serving, and critics fear that the partial reforms which have been achieved will ossify into permanence, because it is now too difficult, and too expensive of political capital, to do more.

But before we consider the to-do tray, it is worth examining what has already been achieved. On three fronts – referendums, proportional representation and electoral regulation – the pace and scale of change have been extraordinary.

Britain's first national referendum was the 1975 vote on whether or not to remain part of the European Community. The exercise was a device to manage the tension within the Wilson government over Europe: Cabinet ministers were free to campaign as their conscience dictated, the country voted and party unity was maintained. But Britain's experiments with the referendum remained tentative: there had been a border poll in Northern Ireland in 1973 and the Scots and Welsh voted on devolution in 1979. Since 1997, however, the British constitution has become more accustomed to direct democracy. There have been votes on devolution to Scotland, Wales, London and North-East England; the government has committed itself to a referendum before entering the euro; and preparations for a vote on the European Constitutional Treaty were under way before it succumbed to rejection by voters in France and the Netherlands.[17] And Britain took a step closer to popular sovereignty when citizens in England were given the right to initiate referendums on whether their community should have a directly elected mayor.

New constitutional conventions emerge mysteriously in Britain: a new practice becomes established, and it may (or may not) be blessed with acceptance in a government statement or in parliamentary standing orders. As yet, the role of the referendum is a convention waiting to be born. But Britain is close to accepting the notion that a referendum should (must?) be used if Westminster is to yield its authority, either to its own nations and regions, or to the European Union. It might be objected that this is a deduction from a miscellany of recent votes, each motivated by distinct political calculations. But that is not the point. Constitutional conventions have rarely emerged from theoretical textbooks: they are commonly a by-product of party politics.

The referendum is now established in British political life and any attempt at significant constitutional change in future will prompt calls for a referendum.

If this constitutes rapid change, the same must be said for the progress made by proportional representation. However much its advocates protest at the government's inaction on reform for Westminster, they have much to cheer elsewhere. Proportional representation has become established as the appropriate mechanism for electing all new tiers of government: Wales and Scotland use AMS; Londoners elect their mayor and assembly by supplementary vote; and the elections to the Assembly in Northern Ireland have been by STV. And the momentum has not yet ceased. The Scottish Parliament has approved the introduction of STV for local government north of the border. And supporters of the Richard commission still hope that Wales will eventually adopt STV for its Assembly elections.

Scotland and Wales have both experienced a new pluralism in the management of their national affairs. Both have now had experience of coalitions and the experience has not been destabilising. A return to majoritarian politics and to a first-past-the-post electoral system in Scotland and Wales is surely unthinkable. Rather, the debate now is about which form of proportional system is to be preferred.

The third reform of note concerns the regulation of elections and political parties. This had its origins in the opposition politics of the 1990s, when Labour charged that the Major administration was tainted by sleaze. Labour's 1997 manifesto spoke of the need to clean up British politics and it backed this rhetoric with commitments on the control of party funding. These were duly made good within a new framework for the oversight of party politics. Political parties were subject to registration for the first time (a necessary preliminary to list-system proportional representation for the European Parliament); and the Electoral Commission was established with oversight of the new funding arrangements. It was to be responsible for the running of referendums and was to provide an independent source of expertise on the conduct of elections. The commission has had a tough start: not only has the electoral landscape been changing under its feet, but the issues thrown up by the reforms have led to some bruising arguments with government, notably over the choice of regions in which all-postal ballots were to be used in the 2004 European elections. And the coming years will be no less challenging: the commission may well acquire additional responsibilities for the regulation of political party finances and at some point it will be asked to run its first national referendum – a daunting prospect.

Are the new arrangements for electoral regulation stable? The Committee on Standards in Public Life instituted a review in November 2005 of the Electoral Commission's mandate and governance. The distribution of administrative responsibilities between local electoral officers, national government and the commission has evolved piecemeal and the system is now being put under increased pressure as government introduces new – and novel – forms of election. Local autonomy in electoral administration is much prized, but some have begun to call for a national elections agency with responsibilities akin to the Australian Electoral Commission. Add to this the renewed interest in additional state funding of political parties and one can see the case for a more thorough overhaul of the administration and regulation of electoral matters. But we should expect independent oversight to remain and the regime governing party donations to tighten rather than loosen.

During Labour's first term it seemed possible that the two most intractable items on its constitutional agenda might both be addressed in one 'Big Bang' referendum. In talks with the Liberal Democrat leader, Paddy Ashdown, Tony Blair toyed with the idea of a vote on a new composition for the House of Lords and on a new voting system for Westminster.[18] Nobody now suggests this as a way forward.

Reformers were discouraged by the phrasing of Labour's 2005 manifesto on the voting system: it echoed the text in 2001 and little had appeared to happen in the intervening four years. If anything, the political dynamic had worked against change: the Liberal Democrats had moved further from Labour under the leadership of Charles Kennedy and any talk of a 'project' between the two parties had ceased.

By contrast, the 2005 manifesto showed evidence of new thinking on Lords reform: Labour wanted to unlock the problem by broadening its scope. By considering the powers of the Lords alongside its composition there may be some prospect of securing a majority for proposals which simultaneously narrow the Upper House's powers and make it more legitimate. But the way ahead remains difficult: the government has said it will offer a free vote on the composition of the Lords and so a majority may prove elusive in the Commons, let alone the Lords. And the Liberal Democrats have indicated that they will not sign up to a codification of the powers of the Lords. More than that, they have questioned the Salisbury convention, by which the Lords accept that a government Bill announced in its manifesto will not be frustrated. Cross-party consensus on Lords reform has always been elusive but the government continues to search for agreement. The Joint Committee on

Conventions was established in May 2006 to consider the relationship between Lords and Commons, but not the composition of a reformed House of Lords.

Lords reform and proportional representation have long seemed the most contentious items in the government's constitutional in-tray. But they have now been joined by a third dossier which looks every bit as challenging as the other two. And if much of Labour's reform agenda is peculiarly British, this new arrival is an international phenomenon. All political parties were shocked by the steepness in decline in voting at the 2001 general election and they could draw little comfort from the recovery of less than three percentage points at the 2005 poll. The evidence is now clear that the problem is most pronounced among ethnic minorities and the young – and there are fears that if the voting habit is not acquired when young then it will not be learned later. Add to this declining party rolls and it is not hard to see why Britain is seen to be one case among many of democratic disengagement.

In the 2001 parliament, the government's responses included experiments with new forms of voting. All-postal ballots proved to be more successful than electronic voting in boosting turnout, but critics alleged that the postal ballot was more vulnerable to fraud. The run-up to the 2005 general election was accompanied by speculation that the availability of on-demand postal voting was exposing the ballot to new levels of fraud. The fears were not substantiated but in matters of electoral security, the suspicion of fraud is almost as damaging as its discovery. In its Electoral Administration Act 2006 the government included new provisions to safeguard the ballot – however it may be cast. The same Act empowers local electoral officers to promote participation and the government has committed dedicated funding to this task.

But it is now clear that the government is broadening its policy response to democratic disengagement. Citizenship education is to be extended – for schoolchildren and for new citizens – and for the first time it is to include a component on democratic participation. And Whitehall departments are to pilot new approaches to involving citizens in policy-making, building on a large-scale exercise in the National Health Service.

Nobody suggests that these initiatives will be sufficient by themselves. But they are indicative of a new direction in constitutional reform, one whose ultimate trajectory is particularly difficult to predict. Britain is not following the course alone: across the Western world governments are now launching similar exercises in the hope of turning back democratic disengagement. The results in Britain are uncertain – but they will be keenly watched at home and abroad.

Judicial reforms

Our discussion of the government's judicial reforms will be briefer than our examination of the other strands, because they are more recent and they are contained in a single statute, the Constitutional Reform Act 2005. But that does not mean that they are any less momentous.

For all the defeats it suffered during the passage of the legislation through the House of Lords, the government finally emerged with a statute which reflected the broad lines of the policy it had first set out two years before. We will consider the three limbs of the policy in turn.

Some time in 2009 we may expect the UK to have a new Supreme Court. The precise timing of the court's creation will turn on the provision of suitable accommodation – surely a first in constitutional history – but we may safely assume that this hurdle will be cleared. The court will take on the jurisdiction of the Appellate Committee of the House of Lords and it will acquire the Judicial Committee of the Privy Council's role in respect of devolution disputes within the UK. Judges who are Law Lords at the time of the court's creation will automatically become the first Supreme Court Justices and they will cease to participate in the Lords until their retirement from the court. The symbolic link between judiciary and legislature will have been broken.

The popularity of the office of Lord Chancellor had not been obvious in the press until the government threatened it with abolition. This then prompted a wave of nostalgia for the passing of an office which some imaginative sub-editors dated to the year 600AD. The less imaginative mounted a defence of the office, which combines the roles of minister of justice, most senior judge and Speaker of the House of Lords. It was argued that the independence of the judiciary could best be preserved by having one of their number in the Cabinet, speaking for them. Others maintained, more modestly, that the office should remain but that the Lord Chancellor should no longer straddle all three branches of government. The defenders of the post claimed a number of victories in Parliament, but the government secured its principal policy objectives. The office of Lord Chancellor is to remain but stripped of many of its former responsibilities. The office holder will no longer be a judge and, as of July 2006, he has ceased to be Speaker of the House of Lords: peers have elected one of their number to the new office of Lord Speaker. In making future appointments to the role of Lord Chancellor, Prime Ministers will be required by statute to have regard to the advantages of appointing a member of the Lords and a senior lawyer, but neither is an absolute requirement.

The Lord Chancellor will remain involved in the appointment of the judiciary, but his role will be much reduced. A new Judicial Appointments Commission is to take on responsibility for the appointment of the senior judiciary in England and Wales. The commission, which will be independent of government and will have a lay majority, will put one name forward for the Lord Chancellor to recommend to the Queen. He may – once and once only – ask the commission to reconsider its nomination, but he cannot block its nominee. In practice, the commission will be in a position to shape the future composition of the judiciary. A separate commission will be summoned into existence to handle appointments to the Supreme Court as and when they arise.

The new arrangements are being implemented progressively, the Appointments Commission having come into being in April 2006. Taken together, will the new institutional arrangements describe a new relationship between the judiciary and the executive? If that question is understood to mean 'will these statutory arrangements persist for the foreseeable future', then the answer must surely be 'yes'. None of the participants has the appetite to renew hostilities: the parliamentary battles over the Bill were peculiarly bruising and they put into play the role of the judiciary in a way which many found disturbing. But, as Kate Malleson points out in Chapter 6, we can also expect institutional pressures to reinforce the reforms. Some of the judiciary, including Law Lords, were critical of the government's proposals, but now that the changes are enshrined in statute the balance of advantage has shifted. The judiciary has emerged with new statutory protection for its independence and with a public concordat setting out the terms of its relationship with the government. It is now to be led in England and Wales not by the Lord Chancellor but by one of its own, the Lord Chief Justice, who has been given the administrative support needed to make a success of the new role. And although it is in a minority on the Appointments Commission, it has more influence than ever before over the future composition of the bench.

And so we may expect the statutory reforms to endure. But we can expect the judiciary's relationship with the other branches of government to change. The conjunction of the Human Rights Act with the new Supreme Court and the judicial concordat may nurture a new self-confidence in the judiciary. One symbol of this will be the evolution of the Supreme Court itself, which we may expect to take fewer private law cases than the Law Lords and to focus harder on issues of constitutional importance. Those are just the issues which will direct attention back to the judiciary's authority with regard to the executive and Parliament. Separate strands of the constitutional reform agenda, conceived for distinct purposes, may well serve to reinforce one another and to bring further change.

Britain changed for good?

Did 1997 witness the dawn of a new constitutional settlement for Britain? In a country without a codified constitution, where the barrier to further change is low, it is impossible to answer this question definitively. But this survey suggests two conclusions which point us in rather different directions. First, we have experienced profound change, every bit as significant as Anthony Barnett's portentous assessment. And second, we have not (yet) witnessed a new settlement. This is not simply because some parts of the agenda set out in 1997 have yet to be completed – although that observation is fair. But it is in the very nature of radical, multi-dimensional constitutional reform that it creates a dynamic which encourages further change. Devolution to Scotland and Wales continues to raise questions about how to manage English business in what is now a quasi-federal parliament. The rejection of devolution in the North-East raises questions about the democratic accountability of regional government across England. These challenges and tensions are probably inescapable and some will, in time, spark new substantive proposals for reform.

But we have also seen that the reform agenda has expanded to take in issues which had not been foreseen in 1997 – most notably democratic participation. And as the programme has matured priorities have changed. Nine years on there is, inevitably, a new emphasis on implementation: it is one thing to establish new institutions and create new rights, but it is quite another to foster a new relationship between state and citizen. Lord Irvine's vision of empowered citizens living in an open, decentralised society cannot be realised by statutory draughtsmen and policy makers in Whitehall. Citizens have to understand and learn to use their rights. Seen in this light, it is easier to understand the government's new emphasis on democratic participation, on citizenship education, on the successful implementation of Freedom of Information and on the advocacy role of the CEHR. And it is easier to see why Lord Falconer has been receptive to calls for a single narrative to connect and explain the individual strands of the reform programme.

We should continue to expect the reform programme to move on to fresh territory, whether that is in response to new political priorities or to resolve tensions thrown up by the earlier reforms. One possibility must be that the role of Parliament itself will come under scrutiny. We have described profound changes to the executive and the judiciary but have said little about the third – and sovereign – branch of government. After its modest start in Labour's first term, the pace of reform in the Commons did pick up in the second, with changes to hours and to the timetabling of legislation. But few would suggest that the changes were momentous. The government's current proposals for the Lords might lead to more profound changes in the role of the Upper House in tandem with the reform of its composition. And there is some suggestion that current concerns over democratic disengagement will lead to a broader examination of the role of Parliament.

There is no suggestion that the government's future plans include the codification of the reforms in a new and comprehensive settlement. The exercise would be daunting in its complexity and it would, presumably, require extensive consultation, education and ultimate endorsement in a referendum. Given the investment in parliamentary time and political capital that has already been made, it is difficult to foresee this outcome in the short term.

But codification is already happening – by stages. Britain's entry into the European Community introduced it to a form of superior law which could not be struck down by Parliament. The Human Rights Act took the process a stage further, giving the judiciary a new and powerful lens through which to view British law. And increasingly the obligations of the state and the rights of the individual are being shaped by international treaties and convention. Parliament could, of course, renounce such treaties and repeal the Human Rights Act but over time those options become less realistic and more costly. We can continue to expect the constitutional reform agenda to move; the progressive codification of the law, allied to the institutional pressures created by the earlier reforms, will ensure that the direction of travel will be forwards and not back.

Was Anthony Barnett right to claim that 1997 had changed Britain for good, institutionally and emotionally? Judgements on the country's emotional trajectory are best left to others. But there can be no doubt that the institutions of the state have been transformed by the reforms of the last nine years.

Part II

Origins

2

Labour's conversion to constitutional reform

Peter Riddell

Constitutional reform has an ambivalent place in the history of the Blair government. The changes to the way Britain is governed are unquestionably among the main legislative landmarks since 1997, and are likely to be among the most significant, and lasting, legacies of the Blair years. Yet the Labour Party, and in particular Tony Blair himself, have never fully embraced constitutional reform and a pluralist view of politics. At times, it has seemed that constitutional reform has been additional to, and separate from, the main New Labour programme. This chapter will examine the roots and consequences of these ambiguities. The explanation lies back in the experiences of opposition from 1979 until 1997, which led to the creation of the reform package in the late 1980s and early 1990s under the leaderships of Neil Kinnock and John Smith, before Blair was elected Labour leader in July 1994.

Labour and the constitution

Traditionally, the Labour Party has defended the constitutional status quo and taken a majoritarian view of politics. Labour has wanted to hold power, not share it. (Labour's changing views on democracy, and the divisions between advocates of liberal representative and of participatory/pluralist concepts, are discussed by Mark Bevir in Chapter 3). The interest in proportional representation expressed by Labour's founding fathers before the First World War quickly disappeared when the party eclipsed the Liberals. Then, Labour leaders, and particularly its intellectuals, championed the first-past-the-post (FPTP) electoral system as the only way to obtain a sufficient Commons majority to push through a fully fledged socialist programme. There was, for example, little tolerance of dissent when Labour won power in 1945: Herbert Morrison as leader of the Commons even dispensed with private members' Bills for two parliamentary sessions. Labour was also traditionally centralist, on the grounds that only a strong government could remove regional and local inequalities. That tension explained much of the opposition to devolution during the 1970s from both older Labour members and younger socialist radicals such as Robin Cook and Neil Kinnock. Willie Ross, Scottish Secretary during the Wilson years, was only reluctantly persuaded to agree to limited devolution plans in order to counter the then serious electoral challenge of the Scottish Nationalists. The legislation for Scottish and Welsh devolution had a tortuous path through the Commons in the late 1970s: suffering defeats, having to be reintroduced and, always, facing vocal opposition from a minority of Labour MPs, not only from England but also from some in Scotland and Wales, for example Cook and Kinnock. The fate of the legislation became tied up with the future of the Callaghan government itself. In the referendums of March 1979, the Scottish proposals failed to reach the statutory threshold (not just a majority of those voting but also 40 per cent of the Scottish electorate) and the Welsh plan was defeated by four to one. This was not just because of the inadequacies of the proposals and the scale of opposition to them, but also because the government had become very unpopular generally by then after the worsening economic situation, strikes and disruption of the 'winter of discontent'. Labour looked doomed and the devolution referendums were seen as a way of protesting against the government and of hastening its demise. This is what happened after the defeat of the proposals, when the Scottish and Welsh Nationalists went into outright opposition to the Callaghan government, triggering the successful Conservative no-confidence motion in the Commons at the end of March 1979. Not only did this usher in what turned out to be eighteen years of Conservative government, but it also prompted a lengthy rethinking of devolution over the subsequent decade.

The only major constitutional issue which Labour consistently pressed from the 1940s until the 1970s was reform of the House of Lords: first, through the reduction in the length of its delaying powers from two parliamentary sessions to one in the 1949 Parliament Act; and, second, through the ultimately abortive talks in the 1968–9 period and in the late 1970s aimed at long-term reform of the second chamber. These were intended to assert the primacy of the elected chamber and limit the powers of the Lords – and were one of the main reasons why the talks failed. Hostility to the Lords, particularly on the then strengthening left, fuelled demands for unicameralism, and a motion calling for abolition of the Lords was passed by a majority of six million votes to 91,000 at the 1977 Labour conference. While James Callaghan ensured that the pledge did not appear in the 1979 manifesto, much to the fury of the left, it did feature in the 1983 'longest suicide note in history' manifesto. Labour leaders and MPs, like Conservatives, did, of course, care passionately about the major constitutional change of the past half-century, Britain's membership of the European Community (later Union). This had profound consequences for ideas of sovereignty and the role of judges. But Europe, like Northern Ireland, was generally considered separately from the main constitutional agenda and will not be discussed in this chapter. Relations with the EC/EU were in the background to the debates noted below and seldom impinged directly upon them.

Reform prospects during the Thatcher years

At this period, in the late 1970s and early 1980s, more Conservative than Labour MPs appeared to be interested in constitutional issues, though this interest was never shared by Margaret Thatcher, whose radical instincts were mainly focused on economic and industrial policy and on the structure of the public sector. Tory support for constitutional reform was partly in reaction to the economic and political crisis of the mid-1970s, which led to a fevered debate about whether Britain was governable any longer. Most famous of all was the warning in 1976 by Lord Hailsham, the doyen of the Conservative legal establishment, about 'elective dictatorship'. The Tory historian Lord Blake had chaired a Hansard Society Commission in 1975–6, which called for a change in the way of electing MPs to the House of Commons along the lines of an additional-member system used in what was then West Germany. The late 1970s and early 1980s were to prove to be the peak period of Tory support for electoral reform, organised in Conservative Action for Electoral Reform, and attracting the backing of the likes of Douglas Hurd, Chris Patten and Michael Ancram.

The contrast between Conservative and Labour attitudes was highlighted by the debate over incorporation of the European Convention on Human Rights (ECHR) into British law. This campaign, which developed in the early and mid-1980s, was led in Parliament by Conservative, rather than Labour, lawyers. Notable among them were the Euro-sceptic Sir Derek Walker-Smith, later Lord Broxbourne, and Sir Edward Gardner, neither liberal figures in any sense. They were backed by Sir Geoffrey Rippon, later Lord Rippon of Hexham, a former Conservative Cabinet minister; by Leon Brittan, later Lord Brittan of Spennithorne, then a just ex-Cabinet minister; and by Hailsham, at the end of his long days as Lord Chancellor. In the key Commons vote, on 6 February 1987, the Gardner Bill failed by just six votes to get the hundred MPs necessary for a closure motion to force a second reading vote. The Bill was backed by fifty-eight Conservative MPs and eighteen from the SDP/Liberal Alliance, but just sixteen from the Labour benches, and two others. The Conservative Cabinet was divided, with Thatcher opposed, so Tory MPs were encouraged not to back the bill. Sir Patrick Mayhew, later Lord Mayhew of Twysden, the Solicitor General, opposed the Bill because of his fear that, if passed, judges would be thrust into the arena of political controversy.

The Labour view – as expressed by Nick Brown, its legal affairs spokesman, and after 1997 chief whip and then Minister of Agriculture – was hostile to the Bill on the grounds that the judiciary was predominantly drawn from a narrow, atypical section of the population. Moreover, contentious things might be said which would undermine support for the judiciary. Allowing the courts to question legislation would also throw the law into a state of uncertainty. Other Labour MPs viewed the judges as instinctively conservative and far too sympathetic to the establishment. This reflected a long-established, and understandable, suspicion of the judiciary after a series of what were seen as anti-trade union rulings. There was little inkling of the change in the nature of the judiciary and its attitudes, which resulted a decade and a half later in attacks from the *Daily Mail*, as well as populist Labour Home Secretaries such as David Blunkett, on senior judges for being 'too liberal' rather than 'too conservative'.

Resistance to involving the judiciary in 'political' matters, via incorporation of the Human Rights Act or a domestic Bill of Rights, was both broad and deep on the Labour side, with the exception of a few, mainly younger, lawyers. The mainstream view had been expressed by a leading left-wing academic, Professor J. G. Griffith of the London School of Economics. He argued at the time of the second reading debate that a Bill of Rights is 'by its nature anti-democratic and authoritarian'. In his view, 'law is politics carried out by other means and does not recognise the existence of extra-legal, so-called fundamental, inalienable, or natural rights'. So judges should not be asked to determine what is politically necessary. We may wish, he said, that Parliament did a better job, but 'that does not remotely justify transferring their responsibilities to the judges'.[1]

In retrospect, 1987 appears as a turning point in the debate on constitutional reform. Conservative interest in reform, already on the retreat in face of the Thatcher juggernaut, then rapidly dwindled to a few Tory peers and lawyers, and a small group of mainly pro-European supporters of electoral reform. But they were increasingly isolated voices. Mayhew's doubts about incorporation became the majority view of the Conservative Party in the debates over what became the Human Rights Act of 1999. But the balance started to shift. Labour began to move away from its simple majoritarian view towards a greater interest in creating checks and balances on a strong executive. This movement was never universal and was full of doubts and ambiguities. But it did occur, and can be dated from 1987, and particularly from the third Thatcher victory in the general election of that June.

The only consistent position was held by the SDP/Liberal Alliance. The Liberals had long advocated various measures of constitutional reform, notably proportional representation for the Commons. A key part was played by individual Liberals, especially Richard Holme, later a close adviser to both David Steel and Paddy Ashdown, and, as Lord Holme of Cheltenham, chairman of the Constitution Committee of the Lords. He founded and ran a variety of pressure groups on constitutional issues from the late 1970s onwards, both on electoral reform and then on incorporation of the European Convention, the latter with Lord Scarman. This culminated in the creation of the Constitutional Reform Centre in 1985 and Charter 88 three years later. The formation of the Social Democratic Party as a breakaway from Labour in 1981 also strengthened the reform campaign. This was partly through the leadership of Roy Jenkins, but more because of the activities of leading lawyers such as Anthony Lester, formerly a special adviser to Jenkins, and Robert Maclennan, an international and constitutional lawyer and MP. While working for Jenkins, Lester had drafted a Home Office discussion paper in favour of making the convention part of British law, which was published in June 1976. After the death of the Gardner Bill in 1987, they kept alive the flame of a home-grown Human Rights Act. Although constitutional reform was not a major factor in the 1981 break from Labour, these issues played a prominent part in the SDP and Alliance programmes. In the short term, the departure from Labour of Lester and Maclennan, as well as the active role of the lawyer William Goodhart in the SDP (all later life peers), deprived Labour of key advocates of constitutional reform. In the long term, however, many of the constitutional proposals in the SDP and Liberal manifestos of 1983 and 1987 surfaced in Labour's rethinking of the early 1990s.

At the same time, the non-party Charter 88 campaign in favour of constitutional reform was launched after the 1987 election by a group of 348 mainly left-wing intellectuals and activists. Modelled somewhat pretentiously on Charter 77, the informal grouping of dissidents and human rights activists in Czechoslovakia who campaigned for civil rights, Charter 88 sought to mobilise support for a declaration of a series of freedoms. These included a Bill of Rights; subjecting executive powers and prerogatives to parliamentary scrutiny; a statutory right to freedom of information; a fair electoral system based on proportional representation; a democratic, non-hereditary second chamber; ensuring the independence of a reformed judiciary; providing legal remedies for all abuses of power by the state; guaranteeing an equitable distribution of power between the nations of the United Kingdom and between local, regional and central government; and drawing up a written constitution. The main impact of Charter 88, and similar bodies, has been to make the broader constitutional reform agenda part of the common core of beliefs on the progressive left. Initially, however, many in the Labour leadership, including Neil Kinnock, were wary of, even hostile to, Charter 88, regarding it not unfairly as largely a middle-class elitist group. However, over the following years, Charter 88 provided a link between long-standing campaigners for constitutional rights in the Liberal Party and the SDP with sympathisers in Labour. These came increasingly not from the old right, who were seldom interested in these issues, but from the younger 'new' left around Kinnock, in groups such as the Labour Coordinating Committee, which by the late 1980s had abandoned its flirtation with the hard left. Their joint involvement in Charter 88 paved the way for the co-operation in the mid-1990s between New Labour and the Liberal Democrats which led to the Cook–Maclennan agreement of March 1997.

Opinion was also beginning to shift within the Labour Party, at first in a piecemeal way. There were both general and specific causes. The general one was a reaction to the long period of one-party rule under the Conservatives and to what were seen as the authoritarian and centralist tendencies of Thatcher herself. This was in many ways a mirror image of the Conservatives' interest in constitutional reform in the late 1970s in reaction to the crisis of confidence in Britain's governability. In particular, Thatcher was accused of stretching and abusing the familiar constitutional conventions, notably during the Cabinet arguments over the future of the Westland helicopter company during late 1985 and early 1986 when Michael Heseltine's resignation over her style of decision-making briefly threatened her hold on the premiership.

She was also accused of 'politicising' the civil service, while the abolition of the Greater London Council and the metropolitan counties was seen both as an act of vindictiveness against the Labour left (though little mourned in practice) and as a demonstration of the lack of formal restraints under the British constitution. American observers, with their historical memories of the 1860s, were understandably puzzled about how a central government and legislature could simply abolish duly elected local authorities (in each case larger than some US states). So as Tony Wright, a political scientist who became a Labour MP, later remarked:

> In a sense it is Mrs Thatcher who perhaps has the best claim to be regarded as the real architect of constitutional reform in Britain. She provided an object lesson in the nature of power in Britain's 'flexible' constitution, and, at the same time, a crash course of constitutional education for the Labour Party.[2]

Devolution

If the long period of Thatcherite dominance inspired a general rethinking about constitutional reform on the Labour side, the main pledges each had specific and distinct roots. The key role here was played by Scotland as the vanguard of the whole constitutional reform programme. Not only had the Thatcherite revolution never taken hold in Scotland – as successive Scottish Secretaries such as George Younger and Malcolm Rifkind sought to soften its edges north of the border – but the Tories' electoral dominance began to weaken there first. In the 1987 general election, when the Tories were still gaining seats in London, and more or less holding their own in England as a whole, the party lost half its seats in Scotland, falling to just ten out of seventy-two. By contrast, Labour gained nine MPs in Scotland in the 1987 election, accounting for nearly half their national gains of twenty seats. This had a double significance. First, Scotland provided the crucial ballast for Labour during its low point during the 1980s, accounting for a fifth or more of the party's MPs, twice its proportionate share in Britain as a whole. This gave Scottish MPs, such as John Smith, Donald Dewar, Robin Cook and, later, Gordon Brown and George Robertson, a powerful say within the party nationally. What they wanted they could usually get. (The same was true in Wales, though to a lesser extent, partly because the Labour Party there was deeply split, and with fewer high-quality MPs.) Second, the combination of big Conservative majorities at Westminster and the erosion of its electoral position north of the border created growing political tensions. Talk by the Scottish Nationalists of being ruled as a colony from London by Tory viceroys struck a chord, especially when the highly unpopular poll tax – introduced earlier in Scotland than the rest of Britain – was imposed by the votes of English MPs. The measure was rejected by all the opposition MPs from Scotland, the vast majority of the total.

The combination of the 1987 election result and the poll tax provided the spur to revive discussion of devolution in the Scottish political elite. The first manifestation was the publication in June 1988 of *The Claim of Right for Scotland*, an assertion of the right of the Scottish people to their own sovereignty. This bottom-up statement of sovereignty clashed with the notion of parliamentary sovereignty exercised by the Westminster Parliament. The eventual Scotland Act of 1999 reaffirmed that Westminster was sovereign in that it granted the powers of devolution to the new Scottish Parliament and, by implication, it could revoke them. The Scottish Nationalists have never accepted this view, but Labour and Liberal Democrat supporters of devolution, often signatories of *The Claim of Right*, have generally not taken up this point, largely to avoid giving ammunition to the nationalists.

The political result of *The Claim of Right* was the establishment in March 1989 of the Scottish Constitutional Convention to draw up plans for devolution. In decisions which set the pattern for the subsequent decade and a half of Scottish politics, the Conservative Party declined to take part, thereby pushing themselves to the margins, from which they have been only partially rescued by the proportional representation system of election for the Scottish Parliament, which they opposed. The Scottish Nationalists attended the first meeting, but then pulled out, underlining their uncertain position in any devolution settlement. The Labour Party in Scotland was initially wary but, under Dewar's lead, decided to take part, along with the Liberal Democrats, church leaders, academics, and people from the media, educational and voluntary worlds. The resulting scheme differed in a number of ways from the devolution proposals of the Callaghan government which failed to be approved in the 1979 referendum. The changes affected the definition and demarcation of devolved and reserved powers; the commitment to a system of proportional representation (to avoid single-party Labour dominance, vital to secure wider support); and the proposals for a funding system which would permit limited tax-varying powers (of up to three pence in the pound in the basic rate of income tax). The convention's plan was published in November

1990 and it was accepted, and advocated at the 1992 general election, by the parties involved. This created no problems for the Liberal Democrats, but many English Labour MPs felt they had been bounced by the powerful Scottish lobby at the top of the party, and acquiesced in, rather than enthused about, the plan. This underlines its key element: that it was a plan for Scotland devised by Scots with no English input, even though it had far-reaching implications for the constitutional structure of the UK.

Wales was always the junior partner in these discussions. This reflected not only political and personal divisions within Wales and the Welsh Labour Party, but also greater doubts about the merits of devolution, after the emphatic rejection of the Callaghan government's plan in the March 1979 referendum. There was no equivalent of the Scottish Constitutional Convention. The always tribal and inward-looking Welsh Labour Party resisted calls for such a cross-party body since it wanted to retain exclusive control of policy-making and did not want to give any influence to, or potentially share credit with, other parties. This was despite the creation, or rather revival, of the Campaign for a Welsh Assembly in November 1988 with backing from Plaid Cymru and the Liberal Democrats, as well as Labour. The resulting Labour plan was for largely executive devolution to an assembly without tax-varying powers and still dependent on Westminster for primary legislation. But, as with Scotland, this was largely a matter of the Welsh talking to the Welsh, with an eye over their shoulder to what was happening in Scotland, rather than a nationwide discussion also involving the English.

While there had been lengthy debates about regional government in England, going back to the Kilbrandon commission in the early 1970s, the debate about what to do there lagged behind Scotland and Wales. The initial impetus was as much economic as constitutional. This partly reflected an awareness of the differing levels of regional identity within England. The drive came from local councillors, notably in the north-east and northern regions, who were concerned about being left behind by the Scots. Their primary objective was to ensure democratic control over regional economic planning and transport, at first via indirectly elected regional chambers of local authority representatives, and only later, and on a piecemeal basis, via directly elected regional assemblies where there was evidence of popular support for them. The development of policy for England not only started later but also changed after the 1992 election, with proposals for a gradual, phased system of regional devolution depending on the level of popular support in particular areas.

Judicial activism and human rights

Quite separately, a debate developed among lawyers and academics about the balance between the legislature and the executive, and the judiciary. The growth of judicial activism and, in particular, of judicial review, from the 1970s through to the 1990s, led to conflicts between politicians and judges. The senior judiciary was increasingly ruling on the decisions of ministers and government departments, notably in immigration and social security cases.[3] These decisions, especially on judicial review cases, provoked an angry response from leading Conservative politicians, who complained about the encroachments of the judiciary into what had previously been regarded as the politician's terrain. This was against the background of a long period of government by one political party, which created a sense that only the judges could act as a check on arbitrary actions by the executive. For instance, in 1993 Lord Bingham of Cornhill, then Master of the Rolls, said that 'the courts have reacted to the increase in powers claimed by the government by becoming more active themselves', adding, controversially, that this had become more important at a time of one-party government. This view was reflected both in a more assertive judicial interpretation of statutes, leading to successful challenges to ministers' decisions, and in a generally more outspoken view of the judicial role in relation to Parliament. There was a growing discussion about the role of the judges in filling gaps in the law, such as over privacy, if Parliament failed to act. However, some judges went further and sought to qualify the doctrine of absolute parliamentary sovereignty on the grounds of the increasing power delegated to ministers, largely outside adequate parliamentary scrutiny. This was linked to suggestions about 'a higher-order law', above both Parliament and the courts (as discussed in Chapter 6).

This debate tied in with the growing demands for incorporation of the ECHR and for a domestic Bill of Rights. As noted above, this campaign was mainly led by lawyers, even in Parliament. Political support spread only slowly, fostered by groups such as Charter 88 and Liberty. There was a sense that this was primarily a lawyers' demand, rather than a more broadly based campaign. As with Scottish devolution, a specific group, albeit a very significant one, had successfully pushed forward its own agenda. Nevertheless, a commitment to a charter of rights and a Bill of Rights was included in Labour's 1992 manifesto. At this stage, before the 1987 election, Labour leaders stressed a domestic Bill of Rights, or more vaguely a charter of rights, without mentioning incorporation of the ECHR. It was only after 1992 that incorporation became the primary objective for Labour and the party's official policy. This reflected both the cumulative impact of the lobbying campaign and the growing support among younger Labour MPs, and, more specifically, the backing of John Smith and of Derry Irvine, later Lord Irvine of Lairg. Irvine, a strong supporter of incorporation, was a crucial link between the Smith and Blair eras. He had been both a close friend of the former and the pupil master, or mentor and supervisor, of the latter as an apprentice barrister. Smith first appointed him to the role of Shadow Lord Chancellor, a post he retained under Blair, before becoming Lord Chancellor in 1997.

Another proposal which gained support in this period was for a Freedom of Information Act. Support for such an act, based on experience in the USA and in Commonwealth countries, had featured in Labour manifestos from 1974 onwards, and was regularly the subject of private members' Bills from backbenchers. One such Bill died when the Callaghan government fell in 1979, though ministers were lukewarm about a statutory right of access, as opposed to a code of practice. Margaret Thatcher, as ever a traditionalist on matters of accountability to Parliament, was even less enthusiastic. So further backbench Bills to provide a general right to officially held information all failed because of a lack of government backing, though some private members' Bills did succeed and establish, for example, patients' rights to their own medical records. Moreover, the all-encompassing scope of the 1911 Official Secrets Act was replaced by a more limited, though still restrictive, Act in 1989. Labour formally pledged itself in 1992 to introduce an Act which 'will open up government to the people', with 'tightly drawn' exemptions. The Major government later made more official information available under the 'open government' mantra, but this was under an administrative code and ministers stopped short of a fully fledged Act.

Labour's commitment to reform

These various strands came together as part of Labour's policy review, in the document *Meet the Challenge: Make the Change*, published in May 1989 and approved at the party conference that autumn. They included the main proposals listed above on devolution, a less precise decentralisation within England, a charter of rights and the creation of an elected second chamber. So from then onwards, Labour was formally committed to a wide-ranging con-stitutional reform programme. Yet the party was still deeply divided, as it was to remain, on the central question of how far to share power at Westminster. There was, and remains, a sense that it was all very well to adopt a more pluralist framework away from London, but not within the Palace of Westminster. A working party was established on electoral reform under the chairmanship of Professor Raymond Plant (later Lord Plant of Highfield), a leading political scientist.[4] The initial intention was to look at the methods of electing the various devolved bodies which the party was suggesting. But the remit of the Electoral Systems Working Party was widened to include the House of Commons by a vote at the 1990 party conference, against the wishes of the party's national executive, although it was agreed that any proposals on the Commons would not appear until after the coming general election. An additional-member system was duly recommended for the Scottish Parliament. By this stage John Smith had taken over from Neil Kinnock as Labour leader after the party's fourth consecutive election defeat in July 1992. Smith was alarmed when told by Plant that a straw poll of the members of the working party showed that a majority was not only opposed to the FPTP system but favoured an additional-member system for the House of Commons. After a good deal of manoeuvring before the final meeting, the compromise emerged of the supplementary vote, allowing the expression of first and second preferences (in the event only used for the election of the mayor of London). Smith was not convinced about the merits of any system of proportional representation, and tried to defuse the issue by promising that a decision on electoral systems would be put to voters in a referendum.

Under the title of *A Modern Democracy* Labour's 1992 manifesto said: 'Central to Labour's purpose in government is our commitment to radical constitutional reform.'[5] There were commitments to

- a charter of rights, 'backed up by a complementary and democratically enforced bill of rights';
- a Freedom of Information Act with 'tightly drawn' exceptions;
- a Scottish Parliament elected under the additional-member system;
- 'in the lifetime of a full parliament', an elected Welsh Assembly with 'powers and functions which reflect the existing administrative structure';
- a regional tier of government in England to take over many powers hitherto exercised nationally, such as regional economic planning and transport. This would later form the basis for elected regional government;
- a new, elected Greater London Authority;
- fixed parliamentary terms;

- improvements to the procedures of the House of Commons, with strengthened scrutiny of European legislation and an end to 'ministerial misuse of the Royal Prerogative'.

The manifesto went on to state that the reforms 'will include those leading to the replacement of the House of Lords with a new elected second chamber which will have the power to delay, for the lifetime of a parliament, changes to designated legislation reducing individual or constitutional rights'. And it promised that a Labour government would encourage a debate on the future of the electoral system.

Constitutional issues were not prominent in the election campaign until the final few days, when opinion polls suggested that the result could be close and there was speculation about a hung Parliament. A week before polling day, which had been designated by Charter 88 as Democracy Day, Kinnock hardened up his party's attitude to proportional representation and hinted at a more broadly based approach to government, implicitly involving the Liberal Democrats. He referred to the establishment of the Plant working party, but went further in inviting the Liberal Democrats to join it. At the time, Kinnock's decision to highlight PR rebounded on Labour, and particularly on the Liberal Democrats, by providing an opportunity for the Conservatives. As David Butler and Dennis Kavanagh concluded in their study of the 1992 election, the Kinnock intervention 'deeply worried the Liberal Democrats who realised that anti-Labour voters, seeing Labour and the Liberal Democrats getting closer together, might recoil into the arms of the Conservatives'.[6] Moreover, raising constitutional issues provided an opening for John Major to make his most passionate and effective attack of the whole election campaign on the theme of 'the United Kingdom is in danger'. This helped to rally Tory supporters. Constitutional reform was not a decisive issue in the election, even in Scotland, where the Conservatives regained one seat after their rout of five years earlier. While there was no evidence that Labour, or the Liberal Democrats, had been helped by their strong commitment to constitutional change, the re-election of the Conservatives for the fourth successive time appeared to many on the left to strengthen the argument for reform and for new constitutional checks and balances.

John Smith, who took over from Kinnock as Labour leader in July 1992, had an even greater commitment to constitutional reform, for three inter-connected reasons. First, he was a Scot, and had been involved in the debates north of the border. Second, he had been the main minister in the Commons taking through the abortive devolution legislation in the late 1970s. Third, he was a lawyer. Even if he was not the main author of Labour's constitutional proposals, he gave them a central political place. Just two weeks after Labour's defeat in 1992, and before he was elected leader, he reaffirmed his commitment to bring the proposals for a Scottish Parliament to 'active fulfilment. For me, in a personal sense, it is very much unfinished business.'[7] In his fullest statement on constitutional reform, delivered to Charter 88 on 1 March 1993, he attacked the 'relentless centralisation' of Conservative governments.[8] He repeated the main Labour proposals and promised devolution not only for Scotland and Wales but also for the English regions. He confirmed the existing pledges to incorporate the ECHR into British law, to a Human Rights Commission and Justice Ministry, to a Freedom of Information Act, to an annual pre-Budget report and to new rights for consumers. Virtually all these proposals had appeared in Labour's 1992 manifesto. What was novel, and significant, was the emphasis put on them as part of a coherent package by Smith. He explained how he had come to realise the importance of constitutional reform:

> It used to be said that the subject of constitutional reform was of interest to no one but the so-called chattering classes. Critics considered it a distraction from the bread-and-butter issues that matter most to voters. But in this atmosphere of decline and gloom it is abundantly clear that people across the nation do care deeply about the way they are governed, and they feel angry and frustrated with a system that isn't working. So our crumbling constitution can no longer be dismissed as a side-show. It is at the heart of what is wrong with our country. People care, and they want change. Indeed, the more we scrutinize the way in which we are governed and the lack of legal rights at our disposal, the more clear it becomes that our present democratic process is both anachronistic and inadequate.

This approach was brought out in the report of a Labour Party policy commission, *A New Agenda for Democracy: Labour's Proposals for Constitutional Reform*. This document was the high point of Labour's constitutional ambitions and of its commitment to pluralism and to an explicit system of checks and balances:

> Our aim is to create a revitalised democracy which protects the fundamental rights of the citizen from the abuse of power, which proposes the substantial

devolution of central government authority, and which insists that the legitimacy of government rests on its being both open and accountable to the people it serves.

There were references to a diversity of political institutions with their independence guaranteed. Many of the commitments in the 1992 manifesto were repeated. However, it was only in this 1993 document that incorporation of the ECHR was formally adopted as party policy. But this was presented as just a first step. The convention was described as 'inadequate and outdated' and so there would be an all-party commission to draft a domestic Bill of Rights and to consider a more permanent form of entrenchment. But in practice this turned out to be a first step towards the downgrading – first by Blair and then by Jack Straw – of the commitment to a domestic Bill of Rights. Incorporation of the ECHR came to be the primary objective. The official secrets legislation was to be reformed with proper scrutiny of the security services. The Royal Prerogative was also to be reformed with ratification by Parliament both of treaties and of the declaration of war. When the paper was presented to the Labour conference in autumn 1993 by Blair, then the shadow Home Secretary, he was enthusiastic:

> Today we pledge ourselves to a task as great as any undertaken by any Labour government in the past, as far-reaching in its effects as the Reform Acts of the last century, as important in its impact on the lives of the people of this country as universal suffrage. We cannot renew our country, its community or its citizenship unless we first renew its democracy. Our purpose today is not a change in the management of our system, it is to change the system itself.[9]

So it is wrong to say that Blair had no involvement in the creation of Labour's constitutional reform programme. He did, even if it was a secondary one. Indeed, his largely unappreciated role before 1994 – and his high-flown language in his autumn 1993 conference speech – makes his subsequent detachment from the constitutional reform programme all the more significant.

Blair as leader

When Tony Blair took over as Labour leader in July 1994, two months after John Smith's death, the main outlines of the constitutional package had already been decided. But in the nearly three years before the 1997 election, he introduced some important modifications. These reflected both his doubts about some aspects of constitutional reform and his desire to ensure that such changes did not create electoral and political opposition which would obstruct the rest of the New Labour programme. He appointed Jack Straw as Shadow Home Secretary, then responsible for these issues, and replaced Graham Allen, an out-and-out enthusiast for reform, as constitutional spokesman by Kim Howells, who was much cooler towards devolution. Straw was also less passionate about constitutional reform, and he was determined that the interests of England should be taken into account; he did not want the whole policy to be determined solely by the Scots. Within six months of Blair taking over, Allen, by now a Labour whip, expressed his worries in a pamphlet in January 1995 intended as a homage to Smith and entitled *Reinventing Democracy: Labour's Mission for the New Century*. He wrote of his fear that 'without the personal impetus supplied by John Smith, both the witting and unthinking centralists will halt the process of policy development on democracy, or even quietly inter existing commitments'.[10]

Blair surprised and shocked the Scottish and Welsh Labour Parties by announcing in June 1996, without any prior warning, that referendums would be held there in advance of introducing detailed legislation, rather than afterwards, as happened with the defeated 1978–9 proposals.[11] Moreover, in Scotland, there would be a second question on the tax-varying powers. In Wales, Blair insisted that the electoral arrangements should be rethought. This was largely because of his fears that any plan which seemed likely to guarantee the Labour Party domination for the foreseeable future would be rejected by Welsh voters. So the Welsh devolution proposals were modified from FPTP to the additional-member variant of proportional representation, as in Scotland. At the time, these pledges were seen as undermining the campaign for devolution, leading to strains (never entirely healed) between Blair and the Scottish and Welsh Labour Parties. Some Scottish and Welsh Labour MPs, as well as Liberal Democrats and nationalists, suspected that Blair and some English members of the shadow Cabinet were unenthusiastic about devolution. As discussed below, Blair's motives were matters more of tactics than principle.

In retrospect, the holding of referendums looks a shrewd move, not only in facilitating the passage of the necessary legislation and avoiding all the problems that were so divisive and time consuming in the 1974–9 parliament, but also in entrenching the changes. The approval of the devolution plans in the September 1997 referendums, even by a wafer-thin margin in Wales, has had the effect of making it politically, if not legally, impossible to abolish them without holding further referendums. No future Conservative government could use its Commons majority to do away with the Scottish Parliament and Welsh Assembly – as the Greater London Council and the metropolitan authorities were abolished in the mid-1980s – without provoking a nationalist backlash which might lead to the break-up of the UK. This may not have been Blair's reason in 1996, but it has been the result.

After 1994, the original convention plan in Scotland was also modified to remove references to the powers to 'initiate some form of public ownership'. The financing scheme was also amended to retain the block grant from Whitehall, rather than allowing Scotland to retain a proportion of taxes paid in Scotland.

When Blair became leader, Labour was committed to a far-reaching reform of the House of Lords. Attacking the 'unelected' Lords was a popular and effective way for any Labour leader to rally his own side. The Labour policy statement in 1989, the 1992 manifesto and the 1993 comprehensive package all contained a specific commitment to an elected second chamber. The 1992 manifesto, it should be remembered, also proposed strengthening the powers of the Lords: 'A new elected chamber will have the power to delay, for the lifetime of a parliament, changes to designated legislation reducing individual or constitutional rights.' Moreover, even after becoming leader, Blair talked in his 1995 conference speech about 'replacing the House of Lords with an elected second chamber'.[12] But then the proposal began to be watered down. This was because of Blair's general caution about constitutional reform: he was concerned to avoid legislative commitments which would take up a lot of parliamentary time and which could create obstacles to other – to him more important – parts of his domestic programme. The priority shifted to removing the hereditary peers from the second chamber. The explicit pledge on a directly elected second chamber was dropped, as was the earlier reference to a specific constitutional role for that chamber. Instead, the 1997 manifesto referred to the need for reform of the Lords as

> an initial, self-contained reform, not dependent on further reform in the future; the right of hereditary peers to sit and vote in the House of Lords will be ended by statute. This will be the first stage in the process of reform to make the House of Lords more democratic and representative. The legislative powers of the House of Lords will remain unaltered.[13]

In other areas, John Smith's commitment to a referendum on the voting system for the Commons was repeated, and combined with a promise to move quickly to appoint an independent commission to recommend a proportional alternative to the FPTP system (what became the Jenkins commission). But references to the Royal Prerogative were dropped, as was talk of a home-grown Bill of Rights. Instead, there was the more limited, though still far-reaching, pledge to incorporate the ECHR into British law.

Blair was worried right up to polling day in May 1997 about whether Labour would gain an overall majority, and how large it would be. Together with his attempt to depict New Labour as a broad-based 'big tent' party, he was keen to explore closer relations with the Liberal Democrats, partly as insurance. These have been exhaustively documented by Paddy Ashdown, now Lord Ashdown of Norton-sub-Hamdon, in his two volumes of diaries. In a passage discussing a meeting between leaders of the two parties in May 1995 Ashdown makes clear how important discussions on constitutional reform were to co-operation between the parties.[14] This was partly because they were not far apart on the main issues by that stage. This led to the creation in October 1996 of the Joint Consultative Committee on Constitutional Reform, chaired by Robin Cook for Labour and Robert Maclennan for the Liberal Democrats. Its remit was to explore common ground on a legislative programme and to see how it might be implemented. Negotiations were not always easy, particularly over the nature of the pledge on electoral reform and the use of proportional representation for elections to the European Parliament. But the resulting document laid out a clear blueprint for much of what happened, especially in Labour's first term.[15] As important was the existence of the committee itself in creating closer personal links between leading members of the two parties, which made a difference after 1997, not only in passing the legislation but also in setting up the Scottish coalition.

The prime motive for these changes was, first, to remove impediments to New Labour's victory in the 1997 general election, and, second, to prevent arguments over constitutional reform from undermining the rest of the legislative programme. Blair was particularly worried that if Labour had only a small majority in the Commons, the Conservatives might use their inbuilt majority in the Lords to obstruct not just the constitutional programme but other legislation as well. Hence, also, the desire to bind in the Liberal Democrats via the Cook–Maclennan agreement. Blair also explained these changes, notably the devolution referendums, as a means of ensuring that his whole first term was not dominated by constitutional reform: 'the tail wagging the dog', as he put it, in markedly different language from his 1993 conference speech.[16] Blair's fears proved to be unfounded. The anti-Tory tide was so great, and the subsequent Labour victory so large, that the constitutional law programme passed into law remarkably easily, with only token parliamentary opposition.

Blair's caution almost certainly eased the path towards devolution. Without the referendum pledge, and the decision to hold the ballots before the detailed legislation on devolution was presented early in the life of the parliament, Blair helped to minimise opposition. If the reforms had been delayed, the proposals might have had rougher passages and the tiny majority in Wales in September 1997 could easily have been turned into defeat. Any delay might have created doubts about approval of the more controversial proposal (the second question in the Scottish referendum) on the tax-raising powers. Blair can also be credited with pushing forward the idea of an elected mayor for London and the proposal for a directly elected strategic authority for the city. This was part of his broader enthusiasm for elected mayors, against the opposition and scepticism of many Labour leaders in local government and of John Prescott, his deputy – and, for much of the post-1997 period, responsible for relations with local councils.

Nonetheless, Blair and advisers such as Philip Gould took the view that constitutional issues were of little interest to voters when compared with prices, jobs, the NHS and so on. Constitutional questions were treated as matters for academics and lawyers, 'the chattering classes' in John Smith's phrase, but not those seriously concerned with power, or with meeting the needs of ordinary people. In this respect, the New Labour electoral strategists shared the indifference towards constitutional interests of an older Labour generation. The ambivalence of the leadership towards constitutional reform was well caught by Peter Mandelson and Roger Liddle in their 1996 book *The Blair Revolution*, which was intended as a semi-authorised guide to what New Labour would do in office. After making the case for constitutional change as part of a wider programme of national renewal, the authors wrote that groups such as Charter 88 – important to building a consensus 'between and outside of political parties' – must 'appreciate that political reform is not Labour's sole concern. Labour's economic and social reforms will require parliamentary time, and to expect constitutional changes to take their place in the queue of priorities is not to renege on commitments but to be practical about making progress.'[17]

Blair also recast the argument about constitutional change away from the language which he and Smith had used in 1993. It was presented as part of 'cleaning up politics', a response to the alleged 'sleaze' of the Major years, an all–embracing term used to cover everything from overcentralisation to bribing MPs, via sexual misconduct. Labour committed itself to restoring faith in politics, a pledge which came back to haunt Blair. Moreover, constitutional change was presented as part of a broader programme of 'modernisation', a slippery word that begged all manner of questions about the direction and content of constitutional change. Blair's major speech on constitutional reform – still his only lengthy statement on the subject as Labour leader or Prime Minister – was delivered in the John Smith Memorial Lecture on 7 February 1996. The lecture was suitably respectful in tone. But along with the grand-sounding promises to 'redraw the boundaries between what is done in the name of the people and the people themselves', there was also caution. 'This is a programme for government. We do not propose, as some suggest, a Great Reform Bill which would attempt all this change at once. The ambition and the extent of the programme will not be achieved in one Bill but over a period of time.'

The Labour Party's 1997 manifesto referred to creating a 'new politics'.[18] There were references to a 'modern' Lords and Commons. There was always an ambiguity about what this meant: were changes meant to make the Houses more 'effective' in the interests of the executive, or to strengthen the accountability of the executive to the legislature? When compared with the 1992 manifesto, or the 1993 policy document, it reads more cautiously – perhaps inevitably, as Labour leaders were, for the first time in more than twenty years, presenting a manifesto that they would almost certainly have to put into practice in office. Several of the earlier pledges – on the future composition and role of the Lords, on a home-grown Bill of Rights, on subjecting prerogative powers to parliamentary scrutiny – were either dropped or watered down. The manifesto was also cautious on regional government for England, promising a step-by-step approach, starting with regional chambers to coordinate economic issues, and then, 'in time', legislation to allow people, region by region, to decide in a referendum whether they wanted directly elected regional government. There were, however, new pledges to require the open declaration of donations to political parties, a ban on foreign funding and a promise of an inquiry by the Committee on Standards in Public Life into the issue of regulation and reform of funding (which led to the 2000 Act overhauling party funding and setting up the Electoral Commission). But the overall effect of the changes both in substance and presentation made between Blair's election as Labour leader in July 1994 and the general election of May 1997 was to weaken the commitment to create a more pluralist system of checks and balances, notably at Westminster.

Underlying this is the central question of whether Blair is, or has ever been, really a pluralist. This arose quite early in his premiership over relations with the Liberal Democrats. Lord Holme, a strong supporter of closer relations with Labour, raised the question at the Liberal Democrat conference in September 1999. He said: 'The challenge for Mr Blair and his colleagues is whether they sincerely believe in pluralism, or do you want to create a New Labour hegemony?'[19] This was not just about short-term relations between the two parties. It was about the type of political structure that Blair wanted: his attitude to electoral reform and changes which might strengthen the House of Lords. Despite his well-documented flirtations with Ashdown, Blair's record – notably his relations with the Liberal Democrats and his scepticism about electoral reform – has shown that he has always wanted to dominate rather than to share power. As he has acknowledged in many interviews during his premiership, he has believed in strong leadership to achieve change rather than negotiation. In this, he has spoken for most of the Labour leadership, who have disliked not only the Liberal Democrats but also changes to the voting system which would result in the politics of co-operation, and probably coalition governments. Blair's doubts about pluralism in practice have been shared by most, though not all, Labour leaders and MPs.[20] The one notable exception was Cook, a genuine pluralist, but he was often on his own, failing to attract the support of many Labour MPs for some of his proposed reforms of the Commons and particularly in the votes on the future of the Lords in February 2003, before his resignation from the Cabinet a few weeks later over the Iraq war.

Labour revisionists have recently asked what would have happened if Smith had lived. Diverting as such counter-factual questions are, the main motive of such speculation has, of course, been to criticise and denigrate Blair and his record. It is all very well to say that Labour would have won under Smith in 1997. That is almost certainly true in view of the self-destructive state of the Conservative Party by the time of Smith's death in May 1994. It is much harder to speculate on the size of his majority and how he would have coped with the uncertainties and contingencies of office. It is, however, reasonable to assume that constitutional reform would have had a more prominent place in any Smith programme, even though he was much more cautious than, say, Cook about electoral reform for the Commons, as shown by his exchanges with Lord Plant. There is a danger of taking too romantic a view of Smith's contribution, and some constitutional reformers have attached their hopes and dreams onto him. In reality, Smith was a tough, at times cynical, realist, who was conservative in many of his attitudes. For him, these changes were a matter of conviction, even passion. He would probably not have been content to leave their implementation to his close friends Donald Dewar and Derry Irvine, as Blair largely did. Smith had a sense of the centrality of constitutional reform which has not been shared by Blair. Gordon Brown, like Smith a proud Scot, has seen the constitutional debate as part of defining Britishness. While supporting devolution, Brown has wanted to combat any implication of Scottish separateness: that Scotland, and its politicians, are no longer part of Britain's main political debate (an understandable concern for an MP from a Scottish constituency wanting to become Prime Minister of the whole UK). Hence, Brown has stressed common Britain-wide values of fairness and equity, such as are embodied in the National Health Service.

The Blair paradox

This chapter shows that the constitutional reform programme enacted after 1997 has had a wide range of sources: some derived from specific sub-national or regional circumstances, as with Scottish devolution; others from the changing views of particular interest groups, notably with the growing demands of a new generation of senior judges and lawyers for the incorporation of the ECHR; and some, such as the Freedom of Information Act, because they had been around as party policy for a long time. But underlying all these specific pledges, and giving them political force, was the reaction on the centre-left to the long period of Conservative rule. Thatcherism, or, rather, Margaret Thatcher herself, was the inspiration for the revival of the constitutional debate in Britain.

However, the programme as it emerged after 1997 was different from the one set out in Labour (not yet New Labour) policy statements in 1989 and 1993. Several pledges were watered down or made more specific, the first stage to later changes, as in the case of the House of Lords. Tony Blair had been closely involved as shadow Home Secretary in preparing the wide-ranging 1993 policy statement on constitutional reform. But as party leader from July 1994 onwards, he was also the main person seeking to limit the commitments. Moreover, since becoming Prime Minister in 1997, he has appeared to have little interest in the constitutional reform agenda, which will undoubtedly be seen as one of his most lasting, and important, legacies. He hardly ever discusses constitutional reform in public and he never treats the programme as one of his priorities. On the rare occasions when Blair does discuss the issue, he talks about it in terms of cleaning up politics or, even more vaguely, modernisation, rather than in terms of constitutional checks and balances.

The explanation for this apparent paradox is partly that his priority has always been ensuring that New Labour is successful electorally. That is why Blair ensured before 1997 that the constitutional programme was tightly defined and limited. He neither wanted to undermine New Labour's chances of winning the general election in 1997, nor did he want constitutional Bills to unbalance his broader legislative programme. For Blair, constitutional reform has always come second, both to New Labour's electoral goals and to his governing priority of public service reform.

However, the paradox is not just a matter of New Labour strategy. Blair has also been sceptical about some of the basic assumptions of the reformers. While open minded about having a debate on electoral reform – if only as a political tactic to keep open doors to Paddy Ashdown and the Liberal Democrats – he has been consistently opposed to any abandonment of the FPTP system at Westminster, though relaxed, or uninterested, in the use of other electoral approaches for all the new devolved bodies. Similarly, his personal intervention in February 2003 expressing his hostility to an elected House of Lords helped produce the stalemate when MPs voted down all the options for changing the composition of the second chamber. At root, Blair has shown himself as much a majoritarian in his instincts as Thatcher. He has taken a managerial view of politics, rather than embracing open debate and dissenting views. As the Ashdown diaries record, he was taken aback by the Liberal Democrats' insistence in the negotiations on the formation of the coalition in Edinburgh after the first Scottish elections that there should be a different system of funding higher education. Ashdown records Blair as saying: 'You can't have Scotland doing something different from the rest of Britain.'[21] After being told the power to be different was one of the points of devolution, Blair is said to have laughed and commented: 'I am beginning to see the defects in all this devolution stuff.' And he was not alone. His reservations on this and many other constitutional issues were shared by most of his Cabinet. This experience of devolution, and differences between ministers and the senior judiciary over the Human Rights Act and the handling of terrorism cases, have done nothing to encourage Blair to take a more positive view of constitutional reform, or a greater interest in it. Constitutional reform will undoubtedly be one of the enduring legacies of the governments he has led – but it has been delivered in the face of the Prime Minister's own ambivalence.

3

Socialism and democracy

Mark Bevir

How can democratic theory help us to make sense of the constitutional reforms introduced under New Labour? We could compare the reforms with different concepts of democracy. Perhaps we might thereby judge how well the reforms do or do not fit with whichever concept of democracy we find most compelling. We could give the reforms marks out of ten. It is arguable, however, that the marks we gave would say more about our own visions of democracy than about the reforms. An alternative approach becomes possible once we allow that concepts of democracy are embedded in the traditions which inspire political practices. Particular traditions and concepts of democracy have inspired New Labour's reforms. Other traditions and concepts of democracy were rejected – or not even considered. We can understand the reforms better if we identify the historical traditions that have inspired them.

Particular traditions of democratic thought have inspired New Labour. A sceptic might remind us that politicians are rarely political theorists. It is true no doubt that Tony Blair and Donald Dewar did not spend much time reading Locke and Rousseau (although when Labour was in opposition Gordon Brown was said to spend part of the parliamentary summer recess studying weighty tomes of economic theory in the libraries of Boston). Nonetheless, even the most unreflective politician acquires conscious and tacit beliefs through processes of socialisation, and these beliefs include their perspective on democracy. The politicians, civil servants and advisers responsible for New Labour's constitutional reforms operated within tacit frameworks of democracy.

One way to make sense of New Labour's constitutional reforms is to show how they draw on concepts of democracy that are themselves characteristic of the traditions of thought and practice that have inspired New Labour. From this perspective, the reforms draw on a representative concept of democracy that has been characteristic of the liberal and Fabian traditions of socialism that have been dominant within the Labour Party for most of its history. Similarly, New Labour's other public sector reforms often draw on a concept of democracy associated with communitarianism and the new institutionalism, which are the two strands of social science upon which New Labour has drawn to respond to issues raised by the New Right. It might not surprise us to learn that New Labour has drawn on liberal and Fabian traditions of socialism and on communitarian and institutionalist forms of social science. It is well worth pointing out, however, that New Labour has thereby neglected participatory and pluralist alternatives.

Traditions of socialism

The Labour Party has been divided on democratic issues from the moment of its inception in 1900 as the Labour Representation Committee. The main division is between a liberal representative concept and a participatory and pluralist alternative. The liberal model seeks to protect citizens from the government and to make sure government pursues policies in the interests of its citizens. Sovereignty resides with the people, but it is exercised by a small number of representatives elected by the people. The executive branch of government is accountable to a legislative assembly composed of representatives. The legislative assembly is held accountable by the people through regular elections. Typically, a constitution limits state power and also secures civil rights. By contrast, the participatory and pluralist concept of democracy focuses more on self-rule and hence on emancipation. Citizens should have as much control as possible over their own daily lives. Sovereignty might be dispersed among the several institutions that shape those lives. In each institution, it might be exercised by the direct participation of the members. Participation should be extended from decision-making to the processes of implementation. Measures might be needed to ensure that all people have the resources that they need for effective participation.

The early socialist debates over representative and participatory concepts of democracy reflected different visions of the role of the state within a socialist society. The Fabians, and some Marxists, argued that the state had to take on new functions and play a more active role in civil society: the state had to take control of the unearned increment and use it for social purposes. The Fabians advocated an extension of liberal democracy, notably the right to vote, in order to ensure that this increasingly active state would remain trustworthy. In contrast, ethical socialists and syndicalists argued that civil society needed to be purged of the abuses they associated with competitive individualism and capitalism. They called for the democratisation of civil society. The ethical socialists wanted civil society to embody a democratic fellowship. And the syndicalists wanted to establish democracy within the associations that made up civil society. Hence one of the main debates among the early socialists concerned the relative roles to be played in a socialist society by a democratic state and by democratic associations within civil society. To simplify, we might say that the view that came to dominate the Labour Party fused ethical socialism with Fabian economics to emphasise the role of the state, but that this view was always challenged by socialists influenced by syndicalist themes in Marxism or by non-governmental themes in ethical socialism.

A particular view of democracy came to dominate the Labour Party during the first three decades of the twentieth century. At that time, the leading figures in the party – James Keir Hardie, Philip Snowden and James Ramsay MacDonald – condemned capitalism in much the same terms as had the ethical socialists. In their view, the competitive market brought out people's base instincts, not their moral ones; capitalism turned people into selfish and acquisitive beings. The leading Labour politicians turned to the Fabians for an economic analysis of capitalism that buttressed their moral views. They accepted a Fabian analysis of interest as analogous to land rent: just as the landlord gets an unearned payment from the value of land, so capitalists do from improvements in productive methods and advantages of location that owe nothing to their efforts or abilities. The leading Labour politicians also accepted the Fabian denunciation of the uncoordinated nature of the market: whereas capitalism relied on a haphazard and chaotic clash of individual interests, socialism would eliminate waste by organising economic life on a scientific basis.

The Labour Party's reliance on Fabian economics led it to emphasise various forms of state intervention at the expense of attempts to democratise civil society. For a start, the existence of an unearned increment present in all economies suggested that the state should be in charge of collecting this surplus and using it for the benefit of the community. The Labour Party's mock Budget of 1907 advocated taxation so as to collect unearned increments of wealth and then use them for communal benefit. Labour politicians advocated several measures to deal with the social surplus in the economy. To secure the surplus, they called for taxation, legislative restrictions on property, and eventually public ownership of the means of production. To deploy the surplus for communal benefit, they called mainly for increased state provision of social welfare. They also advocated various degrees of public ownership of the means of production in order to end the anarchic nature of capitalist production. However, this reliance on the state to correct social failings raised the fear of too powerful a state. Labour politicians allayed this fear by stressing the ethical nature of a truly democratic state. As Ramsay MacDonald explained, 'The democratic State is an organisation of the people, democratic government is self-government, democratic law is an expression of the will of the people who have to obey the law.'[1] Labour politicians defined democracy in terms taken from Fabians and ethical socialists. They equated it with representative institutions and the spirit of fellowship. They rarely showed enthusiasm for other forms of popular control.

The dominant outlook in the Labour Party drew on Fabian economics. Opposition to this outlook drew on syndicalist forms of Marxism and non-governmental forms of ethical socialism. The leading syndicalists – notably Tom Mann and James Connolly – were Marxists. They argued that the ills of capitalism could be overcome only through a transformation in industry. The state was to play no (or almost no) role. Their Marxist economics did not demand a greater role for the state. They could envisage a harmonious civil society in which capitalism had been replaced by a system based on worker-owned industrial units. They also argued that any leadership became a self-serving bureaucracy. Leaders had to be subject to strong democratic control. Even worker-owned industrial units would need to institutionalise popular control through a range of varied measures. The syndicalists and other Marxists thereby opposed the Labour Party's restricted view of democracy as little more than representative government. They proposed an extension of popular control through devices such as referendums and the initiative, whereby citizens can propose legislative measures that might then appear on a ballot.

Ethical socialists often expressed a romantic medievalism. They wanted a world of craftsmen united in guilds. These guilds would embody an ideal of fellowship. A. J. Penty developed such medievalism in his *The Restoration of the Gild System*, which inspired the other begetters of guild socialism, A. R. Orage and S. G. Hobson. The early guild socialists drew on themes from ethical socialism. They identified fellowship as the spirit of democracy. They wanted individuals to exercise full control over their own daily activities in a co-operative and decentralised society. They advocated transferring the control of industry from financiers to craftsman. Ethical socialists also believed that the cure for capitalism lay in this moral ideal of fellowship. They suggested that the political realm was irrelevant – perhaps even detrimental – to such fellowship. In their view, the moral economy did not require state intervention, and in any event state-owned industries might replicate the commercial ethic of private companies. Hence social democrats should focus not on parliamentary politics but on promoting an ideal of fellowship. The guild socialists did not define democracy as representative government. They defined it to include local control of institutions in civil society. And they wanted these institutions to be largely autonomous from the state.

By the end of the First World War, the Labour Party had accepted social democratic ideas that committed it to an extended role for the state. This commitment gained additional strength from the many liberals who found their way into the party as it became the leading alternative to the Conservatives. These liberals challenged the idea that the market constituted a harmonious, self-regulating system. They had begun to look to the state to put right the failings of the market. They agreed with the Fabians about the need for democracy to ensure that the state could be trusted to play this expanded role. While a liberal socialism thus reinforced the dominant Fabian tradition in its emphasis on a representative concept of democracy, other groups within the Labour Party continued to draw on themes from syndicalism and non-governmental socialism – they continued to challenge the party's statism and its restricted concept of democracy. During and after the First World War, for instance, pluralists such as G. D. H. Cole and Harold Laski fused guild socialism with syndicalism, and also aspects of Fabian thought, in an attempt to revitalise democratic voices in the party. Cole wrote: 'A representative system on a geographical basis is certainly not the last word of democracy.'[2] Elsewhere he fleshed out the alternative: a democratic society that provided 'the greatest possible opportunity for individual and collective self-expression to all its members' by means of 'the extension of positive self-government through all its parts'.[3]

New Labour and the constitution

Surely we should not be surprised that New Labour has followed the dominant liberal and Fabian traditions in the Party? We might even suggest that Tony Blair, Gordon Brown and Peter Mandelson – three of the main architects of New Labour – are respectively exemplars of the ethical socialist, Fabian or social democratic and liberal traditions in the Party. Blair emphasises the value of community, relates community to his Christian faith, and places a heavy emphasis on moral exhortation. Brown appears more concerned to relate New Labour's ideas and policies to values such as equality. Mandelson is (or was) the most committed to the liberal themes of choice and the market.

It is perhaps because New Labour has followed the dominant liberal and Fabian traditions in the party that it has remained tied to a representative concept of democracy. Its major constitutional reforms exhibit little interest in extending participation beyond legislative assemblies. There is little concern to advance democratic pluralism within the associations that make up civil society. Nobody should underestimate the extent of New Labour's constitutional reforms, nor, as we shall see, New Labour's general impact on the public sector. The reforms will probably come to be seen as a decisive moment in British political history. Yet their extent and drama does not alter the fact that they concentrate pretty much exclusively on representative assemblies, elections and civil rights.

New Labour's reliance upon a liberal, representative concept of democracy was clear from the start. The Labour Party began informal talks about constitutional reform with the Liberal Democrats in the mid-1990s while still in opposition. The talks led to an agreement to work together after the election. This agreement reflected the Labour Party's growing willingness to pursue a liberal vision of multi-level territorial governments, electoral experiments and civil rights, to the exclusion of alternative socialist concepts of democracy. The agreement covered, among other things, reform of the House of Lords, devolution in Wales and Scotland, a referendum on proportional representation, and incorporation of the European Convention on Human Rights (ECHR) into domestic law.

Representative assemblies, elections and civil rights have remained the main planks of New Labour's constitutional innovations. In its first term in government, New Labour held a succession of referendums on the creation of national and regional assemblies. The referendums led to the creation of a national parliament for Scotland, a national assembly for Wales, and a mayor and assembly for London.[4] (Regional devolution in England proved more awkward: eventually, in New Labour's second term in government, a referendum was held in the North-East alone, but with the proposal being rejected by over three-quarters of those who voted, the government was quick to put the issue to one side.) The national and regional assemblies that were created have widely different powers. The Holyrood Parliament has the most extensive authority, including primary legislative powers. It also has limited powers to raise taxes, although it has not yet done so, preferring to rely on the block grant from the centre. In sharp contrast, London's mayor has few powers – the most notable are over public transport – and even those remain subject to checks and controls by Whitehall. As well as creating national and regional assemblies, New Labour moved to reform Westminster. Change in the House of Lords proved difficult, but, while it is currently stalled, the days of hereditary peers do appear, at long last, to be numbered. Modernisation of the House of Commons has been desultory.

If the Liberal Democrats hoped the reform of Westminster would include serious moves towards proportional representation, they were to be disappointed. True, a regional-list system is now in place for elections to the European Parliament. But the agreement on a referendum on proportional representation seemed to have become little more than a pious hope until it was restated in the 2005 manifesto. Even now, it would be foolhardy to bet on the referendum actually taking place. A party that has just won three successive elections has little reason to alter the rules of the game.

The final plank of New Labour's major constitutional reforms has been a series of legal reforms to promote civil rights. The ECHR has been made part of domestic law. British citizens can claim their convention rights in British courts instead of going to Strasbourg. And judges can declare parliamentary statutes incompatible with the law. The government has passed legislation to create the Commission for Equality and Human Rights (CEHR). Optimists argue that it will have a human rights advocacy role and that it will take on the promotion of anti-discrimination rights that are coming out of European legislation. Pessimists counter that because the CEHR also replaces the three existing equality commissions – those for Racial Equality, Equal Opportunities and Disability Rights – it remains to be seen what, if any, difference it will make. Some pessimists complain of tensions between the different responsibilities of the CEHR.

New Labour has also introduced legal measures designed to promote greater access to official information. The Freedom of Information Act 2000 replaced an earlier code of practice, although it was not fully implemented until 2005. Critics suggest that even then it failed what they see as its first test: the government refused access to the advice it had received from the Attorney General on the legality of the Iraq war. The Department of Constitutional

Affairs runs a clearing house for requests for information. It advises other parts of Whitehall on awkward cases. Critics suggest it blocks the release of sensitive information.

But New Labour began with a measure that does not belong in any of these three categories (representative assemblies, elections and civil rights). No sooner was Blair's first government formed than Brown announced that the Bank of England would have operational independence in the setting of interest rates. The Bank of England Act 1998 established the Monetary Policy Committee, chaired by the Bank's governor, with a remit to maintain price stability and, within that context, to support the government's economic policy. The committee has responsibility for setting interest rates to meet a target for inflation, which the government set at two and a half per cent. If inflation diverges from the target by more than one percentage point, the Bank's governor has to explain the discrepancy in an open letter to the Chancellor. Significantly, the committee's eight members are unelected appointees. They consist of a roughly equal mix of Bank officials and economic experts appointed by the government but confirmed only after hearings in front of the Treasury Select Committee.

It is hard to conceive of the Bank of England Act as an extension of democracy. New Labour appears, rather, to have been acting on empirical theories developed within the social sciences. New Labour acted in part on a longstanding argument of left-wing social scientists: Labour governments inevitably fail because the City reacts to them in a way that leads to a run on the pound. New Labour also acted in part on more recent economic theories that presented macro-economic stability and low inflation as necessary contexts for supply-side regeneration. We might get an even better understanding of the conceptual underpinnings of New Labour's reforms, then, if we consider traditions of social science.

Traditions of social science

New Labour's major constitutional reforms reveal a debt to the liberal and Fabian traditions of socialism with their representative concept of democracy. Nonetheless, we should not assume that New Labour has been unconcerned with the public sector and its relationship to civil society. On the contrary, it has made numerous attempts to reform state and society. It has promoted, in particular, joined-up government and social inclusion. How might democratic theory help us to make sense of these broader attempts to reform the British state? Once again we can relate reforms to concepts of democracy found in the traditions that have inspired New Labour. The relevant traditions are now those that arose out of the social sciences rather than political philosophy and socialist theory.

There is a clear intellectual history behind New Labour's use of social science to reform the state. For a start, the dominance within the Labour Party of a representative concept of democracy allowed authority to be ascribed to the kind of expertise social science purports to offer. The representative concept of democracy allowed the administration of government to be handed over to experts provided only that the experts were accountable to an elected assembly. In addition, the rise of theories of democracy that purported to be neutral, value-free and scientific allowed social scientists to claim to offer the relevant type of expertise. No doubt intellectuals will give advice to anyone willing to read their writings or listen to them talking. But the claim to be offering neutral scientific advice, independent of political values, is in a sense peculiarly associated with the rise of functionalist, elitist and institutionalist theories of democracy in the early part of the twentieth century. Finally, the elite of New Labour turned to these traditions of social science in an attempt to respond to issues highlighted by the New Right. They turned, in particular, to the new institutionalism to respond to issues of efficiency, and to communitarianism to respond to issues of legitimacy. Hence New Labour's public sector reforms embody the institutionalist idea that networks are more efficient than hierarchies and the communitarian one that dialogue and consensus can build legitimacy.

The new institutionalism gave New Labour an alternative to neo-liberal accounts of the perceived crisis of the state. Neo-liberals argued that the state was overloaded and excessively bureaucratic. The solutions were marketisation and new public management. New institutionalists proposed different solutions – networks and joined-up government. The institutionalists rejected the New Right's use of neo-classical economics and rational choice theory to analyse the state. They replaced analyses based on atomised individuals and market coordination with ones based on embedded individuals and networks. Often they did so to preserve approaches to social science that focus on rules and structures rather than the micro level of individual action. The new institutionalism attracted New Labour because it thereby offered an alternative to the ideas informing the New Right. New institutionalists typically implied that networks are the form of organisation best suited to our nature as social or embedded individuals. On the one hand, institutionalists use the concept of a 'network' to describe the inevitable nature of all organisations given that individuals are embedded in social contexts: hierarchies and markets are networks. The concepts of 'embeddedness' and 'network' suggest that action is always structured by social relationships. They give institutionalists a critique of rational choice theory. On the other hand, institutionalists typically suggest that networks are better suited to many tasks than are bureaucracies or markets. The concept of 'embeddedness' suggests that the state should rely on networks, not markets, trust, not competition, and diplomacy, not the new public management.

Institutionalists accept neo-liberal arguments about the inflexible and unresponsive nature of bureaucracy. But, instead of promoting markets, they appeal to networks as a flexible and responsive alternative. Institutionalists argue that economic efficiency and success derive from stable relationships characterised by participation, partnership and trust. Bureaucracies can provide a setting for trust and stability. But institutionalists often suggest that the time for bureaucracy has passed. Bureaucracies were appropriate for the routinised patterns of behaviour that dominated Fordist societies with their emphasis on mass production in large-scale factories. They are ill suited to delivering the innovation and entrepreneurship that states have to foster if they are to compete effectively in the new knowledge-driven global economy. The new economy requires flexibility, responsiveness and innovation. It requires networks.

Communitarianism reproduces the functionalist argument that social order depends on the creation of a consensus over the legitimacy of the political institutions governing it. Functionalists sometimes classified organisations as coercive, remunerative or normative, according to the main mechanisms by which they maintained social control and the corresponding functions they fulfilled for their members. Coercive organisations have to ensure compliance through force since the people within them tend to resist them. Remunerative organisations get individuals to conform to their norms by paying them to do so. Normative organisations manufacture conformity out of the feelings of obligation and commonality of their members, who join in order to pursue goals they believe to be morally worthwhile. Communitarians draw on this typology to suggest that democratic states are normative organisations. Democracies have to create appropriate feelings of obligation and commonality among their citizens if they are to maintain a stable social order.

Legitimacy is an issue of effective government. Indeed, communitarians worry that declining rates of participation undermine the quality and the legitimacy of elite decisions and political institutions. They hope that consulting actors beyond professional politicians and civil servants will make elite policies more acceptable to those whom they target. Communitarianism thus approaches participation from a top-down perspective. It is dominated by the imperative of preserving established elites and institutions from vulnerabilities associated with poor performance.

The idea of Tony Blair or Donald Dewar studying Amitai Etzioni or Robert Putnam might seem even less plausible than their reading Locke or Rousseau. Sceptics might argue also that the esoteric beliefs of social scientists are not ones politicians are likely to adopt through processes of socialisation. But the sceptics overstate the case. They underestimate the role ascribed to expertise in British politics, especially in the Fabian tradition. When Putnam visited Britain in April 2001, he was invited to give an address attended by Blair. Elaine Kamark, a special adviser to President Clinton, introduced Blair, and also Brown, to the ideas of Etzioni, who had himself served as a senior adviser to the White House. Besides, the main routes through which communitarian and institutionalist ideas reached New Labour were academic advisers and think tanks. So it was, for example, that the 1999 White Paper *Modernising Government* was formulated by institutionalists from the universities and from Demos.

New Labour and the public sector

Perhaps we should not be surprised that New Labour has drawn on the expertise offered by communitarians and institutionalists. Communitarianism and the new institutionalism are, after all, the main forms of social science that have sought to rebut the challenge of rational choice theory and so arguably the New Right. However, it is perhaps because New Labour has drawn on communitarianism and the new institutionalism that its public sector reforms remain tied to quests for legitimacy and efficiency. These reforms exhibit little interest in extending participation or pluralism save in so far as doing so serves functionalist ends.

New Labour has reformed the state and the public sector, including health and education, in ways that reflect an institutionalist faith in the benefits of networks and a communitarian one in civil society. It wants joined-up government and social inclusion. The search for joined-up government begins in Whitehall and Westminster. The Cabinet Office has housed a number of new units, such as the Social Exclusion Unit, the purpose of which is to tackle issues that cut across departmental boundaries. The Women's Unit and the Anti-Drugs Coordination Unit were established in 1997 to coordinate activity on their respective topics.[5] The Performance and Innovation Unit was established in October 1998 to drive up the quality of departmental work, not least on big projects that required collaboration across government. New Labour also pursues joined-up government by means of task forces, which are among the most distinctive features of its style of governance. During Blair's first hundred days alone, the government established more than forty task forces, advisory groups and policy reviews.

Beyond Whitehall, the government has introduced initiatives to create flexible frameworks for co-operation. The Invest to Save Budget (ISB) scheme provided extra funding to projects in which two or more public bodies collaborate to deliver more efficient services. Typical ISB projects included 'one-stop shops' that give users access to multiple services at one location. The Single Gateway scheme provides access at one location to services offered by the Benefits Agency, the Child Support Agency, the Employment Service and the benefits departments of local authorities. Sure Start and the Single Regeneration Budget are yet other examples of 'cross-cutting' initiatives that seek to transcend administrative boundaries. The government is moving further in this direction, creating Integrated Service Teams to explore ways of improving collaboration between service providers.

Networks have gone some way towards replacing the internal market in the National Health Service. The government has created a new statutory duty for NHS trusts to work in partnership with other NHS organisations. All the actors involved in the delivery of healthcare services – general practitioners, NHS trusts, and local authorities – are meant to collaborate to develop integrated systems of care based on health improvement programmes. These health improvement programmes specify standards for healthcare that have been agreed upon by all the relevant actors in consultation with one another. Joined-up government and negotiation, as well perhaps as markets and competitive contracts, are now the perceived means of promoting quality and efficiency within the NHS.

New Labour's advocacy of networks extends from joined-up government within the public sector to partnerships between public and private organisations. It actively encourages 'partnership networks' between local authorities and the private sector. Perhaps the most important links to the private sector arise from the government's resurrection and expansion of private finance initiatives (PFIs) or, as they are called now, public–private partnerships (PPPs). These schemes enable the private sector to invest in capital projects in the public sector and then to lease the new entities back to the state. Under the Conservatives, PFIs often maintained a clear division between public and private sector bodies: private companies planned, designed and constructed buildings or roads and then sold them to the public sector organisations that provided the relevant service. Under New Labour, however, PPPs have become a means of encouraging public and private organisations to form deeper partnerships. The partnerships involve collaboration at all stages of a joint venture. And the private sector brings management and expertise as well as finance. The overall scale of PPPs under New Labour is vast: during Tony Blair's first term in office, some 150 contracts were signed, covering four prisons, five hospitals, and 520 schools. Their total value was over £12 billion.

The government speaks of individuals relating to one another through trust, negotiation and agreement within networks. The contrast is with the competition and contracts that characterise markets. New Labour hopes that networks, especially those at the local level, will encompass frontline service providers and citizens. In the NHS, it set up the National Taskforce on Staff Involvement. The members of the task force included nurses, doctors and a hospital porter. More generally, New Labour modified the Citizen's Charter of earlier Conservative governments to establish Service First. The Service First charter programme encourages 'quality networks' composed of local groups, the members of which should come from all areas and levels of the public sector. 'Quality networks' are intended to contribute to the development and dissemination of principles of best practice, the sharing of troubleshooting skills and the building of new partnerships between appropriate organisations. The government thus aims to encourage public services to work together to ensure that services are effective and coordinated. This shift from the Citizen's Charter to Service First appears even more significant when we locate it alongside the introduction of public service agreements. These publish performance levels and demand measurable improvements from all central government departments and agencies. Each organisation specifies its general aims and objectives, the resources available to it, its performance targets and information about how it intends to increase its operational efficiency.

Citizens participate in this brave new world of networks not only as 'clients' but also through increased avenues for consultation and involvement in the planning and delivery of services. Service providers are now more or less required to consult and to involve users. The government recommends a wide array of methods for meeting this requirement – interviews, focus groups, citizen juries and citizen panels. Citizen juries consist of a small number of lay people who scrutinise specific proposals. They hear evidence from experts and interested parties over several days and then report their conclusions. Citizen panels consist of a larger representative sample of the population. They discuss specific proposals and also develop broader ideas about future services. The flagship citizen panel in Kirklees, West Yorkshire consists of a thousand local residents who three times a year receive surveys from the local authority and the local health authority. New Labour has even established an omnibus People's Panel made up of 5,000 members, representing a cross-section of the population, who are consulted about a range of issues, including transport, local democracy, new technology and care in the community.

The promotion of networks allows New Labour to embrace novel styles of service delivery. But it also fragments parts of the public sector and it leaves the state with fewer means of direct control. The government thus can appear Janus faced in its simultaneous promotion of local initiatives and its reassertion of central control through inspection and regulation. Alongside the creation of decentralised action zones for health and education, we have new organisations designed to impose the will of the centre. These organisations include the National Institute for Clinical Excellence (NICE), the Commission for Health Improvement, the Office for Standards in Education (Ofsted) and the hit-squads that take over failing schools. More generally, the remit of the Regulatory Impact Unit, formerly known as the Better Regulation Taskforce, has been extended from the private to the public sector. It has introduced a programme of public sector regulatory efficiency. This programme applies the principles that the government believes to constitute good regulation – transparency, accountability, targeting, consistency and proportionality – to domains such as healthcare, education, social services and the police. New Labour seeks to retain central control not only through inspection and regulation, but also, when deemed necessary, through direct intervention. The government developed schemes of 'earned autonomy' that distinguish 'green' and 'red' local authorities or agencies. 'Green' organisations are given increased powers and are even allowed to test new ways of delivering services. 'Red' organisations can be subject to government intervention to remedy their failings and they may even be taken over by the centre.

New Labour has adopted a regime of regulation to reassert the centre's control over public services and thereby attempt to guarantee standards of quality and efficiency. This new regime once again reveals the government's faith in networks. The regulators themselves are meant to operate through networks characterised by trust – or at least they are unless direct intervention is deemed necessary. In personal care, the government wants networks to counter a fragmented system in which regulation had been piecemeal and divided. New regional Commissions for Care Standards (CCSs) regulate care services in line with national standards developed by the government in consultation with relevant groups and individuals. The CCSs are independent of government. They consist of representatives from local government, health authorities, service providers and service users. The General Social Care Council regulates the training of social workers, helps to set standards of good conduct and recommends principles of best practice for all who work in social services.

A similar invocation of networks characterises New Labour's regime of regulation in the NHS. The government hopes to overcome problems of fragmentation and control – including unacceptable variations in the standards of health service – by building networks in which the deliverers of services can compare their performance and share principles of best practice. NICE regulates frontline healthcare. It aims to ensure high and consistent standards of clinical practice throughout the NHS. NICE draws on networks of health professionals, academics, economists and patients' representatives. The networks operate alongside NHS organisations at all levels, including local care providers, regional bodies and national groups such as the Department of Health. The National Framework for Assessing Performance monitors the quality of services against the criteria of improvement of health, fair access, effective delivery of appropriate care, efficiency, the experiences of patients and carers, and outcomes for health. Each of these criteria has detailed performance indicators: for example, fair access refers to the socio-economic and demographic characteristics of patients, the mean time from diagnosis to operation, and patients' evaluations of their experiences. National service frameworks specify national standards for specific types of service: for example, the Calman-Hine Cancer Service Framework defines the arrangements that are deemed appropriate to high quality and comprehensive cancer care. The Commission for Health Improvement provides independent scrutiny of healthcare providers such as NHS trusts. It monitors the implementation of the national service frameworks and the guidance provided by NICE. It has the power to investigate and to intervene when performance is deemed unsatisfactory.

What does it mean?

New Labour has made some dramatic reforms to the British constitution and to the public sector more generally. To exhibit New Labour's debt to a representative concept of democracy and communitarianism and the new institutionalism is not to deny the extent of the reforms. It is to draw attention to the limits of the reforms: they do not break out of the liberal and functionalist themes of so much of British socialism. It is also to draw attention to other possible reforms that were rejected or not even considered, reforms inspired by the participatory and pluralist strands within British socialism. Again, to locate New Labour's reforms within particular traditions is not to deny the extent of the reforms. They could well be New Labour's greatest legacy. They have already reshaped Britain, and they have opened the door to futures that the government probably neither intended nor would have wanted. Britain has been altered for good, and the processes of change are still very much playing themselves out. To locate New Labour's reforms within particular traditions is, however, to cast new light on familiar questions. How can we make sense of the content of the reforms? What prospects do they open up for Britain?

Let us look first at debates about the content of the reforms. One debate concerns the programmatic nature of the reforms. Many observers think that the reforms lack consistency. They claim that Lord Irvine of Lairg has admitted as much and that Lord Falconer has done his best to impose a retrospective consistency upon a hodge-podge of reforms. In their view, for instance, the schemes for territorial governments have diverse sources in the different demands of particular territories. Others – most notably the Constitution Unit at University College, London – imply that New Labour has in fact developed a fairly coherent constitutional agenda. They suggest that Irvine almost said as much and that Falconer then made it crystal clear. In their view, for instance, the schemes for territorial government appear as components of an admittedly vague plan for multi-level governance throughout the UK. To some extent the debate between these two views is a false one. Whether or not we find coherence depends above all on the level of abstraction at which we look for it. Equally, to recognise New Labour's debt to particular concepts of democracy is to cast new light on this debate. Even if New Labour did not set out with a consistent programme, the major constitutional reforms are loosely coherent in their shared debt to a liberal, representative concept of democracy. The wider reforms of the public sector are similarly loosely coherent in their shared debt to communitarian and new institutionalist thinking. And these two groups of reform loosely fit together in that a liberal, representative concept of democracy creates a space for the kind of expertise that the communitarians and new institutionalists offer.

A second debate about the content of the reforms concerns their compatibility with New Labour's style of government. Critics label New Labour control freaks and they point to tensions between the constitutional reforms and the desire of the centre to retain control. There is endless talk of a 'Blair presidency', with power supposedly concentrated within 10 Downing Street and the Cabinet Office. The idea of a Blair presidency of a Bonapartist order fuses several issues. It suggests that Tony Blair himself combines the charisma and ease of a rock star with remarkable tactical reach. It highlights the ways in which his government has tried to strengthen the control of the Prime Minister and his staff over policy and its presentation. And it suggests that Blair is the most powerful Prime Minister in living memory.

Few would deny that the changes at No. 10 and the Cabinet Office have had a centralising thrust. As soon as he was elected, Blair surrounded himself with a network of special advisers. The numbers of special advisers rose from eight under John Major to twenty-seven. Total staff employed at No. 10 rose from 107 under Major to 200 under Blair. At first, the new central institutions focused on improving communications, with Alastair Campbell heading the Strategic Communications Unit. Later the emphasis fell on policy advice. No. 10 does not shrink from attempts – often comically inept attempts – to influence outcomes in the national parliaments and in London's regional government. Nor does the government as a whole shrink from interfering in decentralised public services. However, the tension between the constitutional reforms and centralisation appears somewhat different once we recognise New Labour's debt to particular concepts of democracy. Consider the main constitutional reforms. The tension here is one between, on one hand, the multiple levels of government created by any programme of devolution and, on the other, a belief in the expertise offered by social science. Consider now the reforms of the public sector. The tension here is one between, on one hand, a clear-cut commitment to certain outcomes and, on the other, the expertise of the communitarians and the new institutionalists, according to which the outcomes are best achieved through increased citizen participation and a proliferation of networks. Neither tension is simply one of style. Both tensions reflect the limitations of the traditions on which New Labour has tacitly relied. What does government do when it follows the experts but does not get the predicted outcomes? It pulls on levers in an attempt to exert direct control over outcomes. But the levers are now rubber ones. The attempts to control fail.

A third debate about the content of the reforms concerns how radical they are. Tories and Whigs lament the radical nature of the reforms. They deride New Labour for undertaking an immoderate and wholesale onslaught upon the constitution. If there is need for reform – and they often suggest there is not – then they would have it be more gradual and more in accord with the grain of a constitution that has served so well to date. In contrast, other critics reprove New Labour for timidity. Typically they would have the government adopt a codified constitution. The contrast between these two sets of critics is again a false one. Their respective views clearly tell us more about their own political ideas than they do about how radical the reforms are. But to recognise New Labour's debt to particular concepts of democracy is, here too, to cast new light on a debate. The Tories and Whigs protest too much. No doubt the reforms unsettle the idea of the UK as a unitary state. But this idea was always something of a myth. Besides, the reforms clearly go with the grain of one of the most well-established traditions in British politics; they have their origins in the liberal, representative concept of democracy. This concept of democracy is, of course, perfectly compatible with a codified constitution. Hence the critics who advocate codification are perhaps not that far from New Labour. Is it a little too neat to say that they voice a radical liberalism that believes in abstract principles while New Labour enacts a Whiggish liberalism that looks more to guidelines drawn out from existing practices? Perhaps. Even so, New Labour and its radical critics clearly share underlying assumptions associated with a liberal, representative concept of democracy. The radical imagination would range further afield.

The radical imagination might look to various sources for inspiration, including New Labour itself, the European Union and perhaps civil society. Let us look now at the future trajectory of the reforms. Some observers suggest that the 2005 Labour Party manifesto broke new ground, or at least that it allowed for the enactment of some of the radical aspects of the old proposals. The manifesto suggested that new powers would be given to regional governments within England. It reiterated New Labour's belief in a review on the question of proportional representation. There was a clear commitment to a commission on human rights. And there was some discussion of increasing citizen participation. It is not necessary to deny the extent of these proposals to ask whether they differ significantly from what has gone before. The manifesto offers the same emphases drawn from a representative concept of democracy – devolved assemblies and powers for territorial regions, experiments with different electoral systems, and the legalisation of civic rights. The manifesto also shows a continuing sensitivity to the issues of efficiency and legitimacy as conceived by the new institutionalists and the communitarians. The low levels of turnout for the 2001 election might have added to such sensitivity, but they can scarcely be said to be its cause.

A second debate about the prospects for the reforms concerns the continuing impact of the EU. Britain's accession to the European Economic Community (as it then was) in 1972 left it subject to a higher law: changes in European law may bring about changes in Britain's constitution. Nonetheless, it is unlikely that the EU will be a source of changes that differ significantly from those made by New Labour. On the contrary, the impact of the EU has typically been through the legalisation and judicial review of various human rights. Nor is that all. The European Commission appears to subscribe to many of the communitarian and institutionalist ideas that lurk behind New Labour's reforms of the public sector. The commission released a White Paper on European Governance in 2001, which defines its goal as opening up policy-making to make it more inclusive and accountable, but inclusivity and accountability appear to be desirable because they will lead to more effective policies and lend them greater legitimacy. We might ask: what will happen if this inclusivity does not lead to the desired increase in effectiveness? Will the commission, like New Labour, find itself simultaneously devolving power and seeking to specify and control outcomes?

A third debate about the prospects for the reforms concerns their inner momentum. Once power has been devolved, it is hard to control not only outcomes but also processes. Perhaps the legislative assemblies and administrative bodies created by New Labour will take the reforms in directions the government neither intended nor would welcome. There have been some highly visible examples of their doing so. Londoners dared to elect Ken Livingstone. Rhodri Morgan eventually won through in Wales. There also have been other less well-publicised examples of New Labour losing control. It was arguably dissatisfaction in Wales itself that did most to instigate the Richard commission's proposals to move from the original devolution model (in which the national assembly fused executive and parliamentary aspects) to arrangements closer to the Westminster model – a recommendation the government has accepted. Again, the governments of Scotland and Wales have clearly defined their healthcare policies in contrast to those promoted by New Labour in England. The prospect of diverse public policies is one of the most exciting to emerge from New Labour's reforms. The new political authorities just might forge a pathway to participatory and pluralist alternatives to a representative concept of democracy filled out by the expertise of the social sciences. But if they are to do so, they will have to break with the dominant traditions in the Labour Party and indeed British politics.

What is the alternative?

New Labour's attempts to reform the British state embody a representative theory of democracy together with themes taken from communitarianism and the new institutionalism. The prospects for a radical alternative look bleak. Nonetheless, participatory and pluralist traditions within the Labour Party continue to inspire hope for an alternative. It is today a daunting task to retain faith in participatory and pluralist ideals – to distinguish them from liberal, representative ones and yet to meet the obvious objections to them. Tentative suggestions will no more establish clear water between participation and representation than they will reassure all those who worry that pluralism leads to elitism. Maybe we are dealing with fuzzy boundaries, not sharp dichotomies. Certainly participatory and pluralist themes find several echoes in New Labour's reforms, notably in devolution and in the advocacy of partnerships between the public sector and the voluntary and private sectors.

Participatory and pluralist democrats might rethink the representative concept of democracy that informs New Labour's constitutional reforms. They might attempt to extend democratic practices to various associations of producers, consumers and others. Whereas New Labour has adopted a programme of constitutional reform composed of devolution to national legislatures and doses of electoral reform, an alternative might establish new forums in which citizens can deliberate, formulate policies and connect with the state. Whereas New Labour typically relies on indirect representation within the institutions of the state, an alternative might promote ways in which citizens could participate directly in the process of policy-making and even policy implementation. Whereas New Labour promotes partnerships in which the state plays an active role, regulating and controlling outcomes, an alternative might hand over aspects of government to associations other than the state. Whereas New Labour's partnerships aim to deliver services more effectively with little concern for the inner workings of the organisations with which the state co-operates, an alternative might be committed to extending democratic principles to groups within civil society. This alternative would lead, for instance, to a greater concern for the democratic nature of the Labour Party itself.

Participatory and pluralist democrats might also rethink the institutionalist and communitarian measures with which New Labour has sought to reform the public sector. They might subdue expertise in favour of attempts to form and implement public policies in ways that encourage civic participation. This alternative too finds echoes in New Labour's reforms, notably the idea that networks should involve relevant stakeholders. But again there are important differences. New Labour appears to be wedded to a representative democracy in which public policy is implemented by a managerial elite, who are subject to direction and supervision by a political elite, who in turn are accountable to the popular will through elections. But an alternative might promote deliberation throughout the policy-making process, including the stage of implementation. New Labour seems to assume that administration can be a purely neutral or technical matter of implementing the will of the legislature. But an alternative might allow for the involvement of citizens throughout the processes by which administrative agencies actively interpret and define the will of the legislature.

New Labour has reformed the constitution in a way that remains tacitly inspired by a liberal, representative concept of democracy and a faith in the expertise offered by social science. Other socialists will continue to want citizens to promote greater pluralism and participation. They will want to rediscover a democratic utopianism.

4

Rights culture and constitutional reform

Joseph F. Fletcher

Themes of reform

Since taking office in 1997, Tony Blair's New Labour government has brought about a remarkable programme of constitutional innovations. These include devolution to Scotland, Wales and London, the introduction of new rights protection instruments including Human Rights and Freedom of Information Acts and the removal of most of the hereditary peers from the House of Lords. In Chapter 2, Peter Riddell details the varied roots of this agenda in longstanding Liberal calls for constitutional reform, the Charter 88 movement and Labour's own policy reviews and manifestos including its 1997 call for a 'new politics'.

The point of departure for this chapter is Andrew McDonald and Robert Hazell's suggestion that despite distinctive origins for individual reforms, there is nevertheless a discernible coherence to the constitutional innovations.[1] They suggest that this coherence is perhaps best captured in a statement made by Lord Irvine of Lairg when Lord Chancellor: 'Our objective is to put in place an integrated programme of measures to decentralise power in the United Kingdom; and to enhance the rights of individuals within a more open society.'[2] McDonald and Hazell identify four themes to the reforms. The first two, decentralisation and citizen rights, are clearly found in Irvine's statement, while the latter two, democratisation and judicial reform, are described as arising from subsequent political dynamics.

The focus of this chapter is on attitudes towards the four themes of reform identified by McDonald and Hazell. Attitudinal research of this kind, as Mark Bevir reminds us in Chapter 3, no doubt says less about the reforms than about the respondents to our surveys. But for just this reason, research of this kind is particularly useful in assessing the beliefs and values that inspire the reforms and thus form the basis for differences in attitudes towards them.

New Labour's agenda is broadly consistent with characterisations of a global process of constitutional renewal rooted in a new culture of human rights as described by Michael Ignatieff, Mark Tushnet, Ran Hirschl and others.[3] Building on their approach, I argue that an essential dimension of the constitutional reforms in Britain since 1997 is to be found in political culture – the underlying values, predispositions and beliefs that shape attitudes about the political sphere among political leaders and the public at large. This chapter documents the role played by basic values in supporting the recent developments in Britain.

Using data on the attitudes and values of the British public and a sample of their political leaders this chapter proceeds in two steps. The first considers views towards some of the key elements of the reforms pursued by New Labour since 1997. This section has two inter-related purposes. One is to ascertain the partisan basis of support for reforms among samples of politicians. The second is to consider the extent to which the constitutional reforms may be considered to be consistent with the views of the majority of Britons.

The chapter then moves on to examine the foundations in political culture of attitudes towards each theme of constitutional reform. This entails estimating the relationships between basic values and support for various reforms among the British public and their political leaders. Generally speaking, the results show that support for constitutional innovation is indeed rooted in a culture of rights, though not in an entirely uniform fashion. The coherence of the reform agenda lies not with a single belief or value but in the expression of an inter-related cluster of values. This approach enables us to appreciate the consistency among the reforms and to ask why this consistency is often not recognised. In this respect, McDonald and Hazell's thematic approach bears interesting fruit.

Data and principal lines of analysis

The data used here were gathered by William L. Miller, Annis May Timpson and Michael Lessoff in 1992, as part of the British Rights Survey (BRS).[4] What makes these data of particular value is that they consist of several elements essential to the present analysis. First, they contain measures of attitudes relating to virtually all the areas of reform pursued by the New Labour government since 1997. These include questions on support for devolution, a Bill of Rights, a freedom of information Act and reform of the House of Lords, plus questions on referendums and proportional representation relevant to the theme of democratic reform and even a few questions broadly with a bearing on the recent judicial reforms.[5] Considerable care was taken in the crafting of these questions to ensure that they were clearly understood by the public yet accurate in detail.[6] A second essential aspect of the BRS is that it contains a wide range of value questions which may be used to examine the influence of a rights culture on attitudes towards the reforms. And third, the BRS data consist of two matched surveys, one of the population at large and another of political leaders. The leader sample provides a picture of activist opinion within each of the main political parties as obtained through interviews with the leader or senior member for each of the three major political parties on virtually every local government council across Great Britain.[7] Accordingly, these data allow us to appreciate the partisan differences within the political class in the context of the views of ordinary Britons.

Finally, the timing of the BRS should be considered. While data more recent than 1992 would, of course, be desirable, little aside from piecemeal reports on selected reforms is available for secondary analysis. Nevertheless, from an analytic perspective the timing of the BRS is not an impediment at all. It is advantageous in that it provides us with a snapshot of attitudes and values among citizens and politicians just as Labour's policy of constitutional reform was beginning to coalesce after their defeat in 1992 and well before their electoral victory in May 1997. We therefore get to see the public's and the politicians' attitudes and values prior to the actual initiatives. In other words, the data provide us with a clear view of the political culture out of which the constitutional reforms emerged.

Views of constitutional reform

1: Attitudes towards decentralisation

The first theme of New Labour's reforms, as identified by McDonald and Hazell, is decentralisation. And since, as Peter Riddell comments in Chapter 2, Scotland was 'the vanguard of the whole constitutional reform programme', the place to start is with attitudes towards devolution for Scotland. The results from the BRS in this regard appear in the first panel of Table 4.1.

Table 4.1: Support for devolution among British political leaders and the British public

Devolution for Scotland

	Political leaders			Public
	Con	Lab	Lib Dem	
Support	27.3%	91.3%	96.0%	62.5%
If locals want it	12.6%	3.8%	3.2%	11.9%
Oppose	55.4%	4.4%	0.7%	18.0%
Don't know	4.7%	0.6%	0.0%	7.6%
(survey size)	(341)	(343)	(278)	(2,054)

Devolution for Wales

	Political leaders			Public
	Con	Lab	Lib Dem	
Support	25.0%	87.5%	91.4%	55.1%
If locals want it	11.8%	4.7%	5.8%	13.1%
Oppose	58.2%	7.3%	2.9%	23.0%
Don't know	5.0%	0.6%	0.0%	8.8%
(survey size)	(340)	(344)	(278)	(2,053)

Devolution for Northern Ireland

	Political leaders			Public
	Con	Lab	Lib Dem	
Support	30.5%	76.1%	88.8%	55.9%
If locals want it	15.5%	6.1%	5.8%	11.6%
Oppose	48.4%	14.3%	3.6%	22.4%
Don't know	5.6%	3.5%	1.8%	10.0%
(survey size)	(341)	(343)	(278)	(2,047)

Devolution for London

	Political leaders			Public
	Con	Lab	Lib Dem	
Support	9.0%	74.4%	78.1%	31.7%
If locals want it	4.3%	2.3%	4.0%	5.8%
Oppose	84.7%	22.1%	16.9%	55.4%
Don't know	2.0%	1.2%	1.1%	7.1%
(survey size)	(346)	(344)	(278)	(2,051)

Devolution for regions of England

| | Political leaders | | | Public |
	Con	Lab	Lib Dem	
Support	9.0%	78.7%	84.2%	31.4%
If locals want it	4.7%	4.7%	6.1%	6.8%
Oppose	85.2%	15.5%	9.0%	55.2%
Don't know	1.2%	1.2%	0.7%	6.6%
(survey size)	(344)	(343)	(279)	(2,056)

Immediately apparent in the first panel is the sharp partisan divide between the Conservatives and the other two parties over support for powers of self-government in Scotland. The Conservatives are perhaps more divided in their own views than are the other two parties, but the clear weight of the opinion among Conservatives is against devolution. By contrast, the near unanimity among Labour and the Liberal Democrats is particularly striking. Nevertheless, the Liberal Democrats score slightly higher in their support for self-government for Scotland, but given the overwhelming support exhibited by both parties, the difference is modest in practical terms.[8] In percentage terms the public is situated nearly exactly in the middle between the Conservatives on the one hand, and Labour and the Liberal Democrats on the other. Nevertheless, a clear majority favours devolution for Scotland. Further analyses (not shown) indicate that despite perhaps a bit more public opposition in Scotland, the majority in support of Scottish devolution holds throughout Scotland, Wales and England. Moreover, the partisan differences in the views of the politicians persist across the three nations.[9]

The succeeding panels of Table 4.1 set out in turn the results from questions asking about support for devolution for Wales, Northern Ireland, London and the regions of England.[10] Taken together they show a slow drift downwards in support for devolution among all the groups as one works through the panels. Nevertheless, the overall picture remains one of a clear partisan divide among the politicians, with the public in the middle. Throughout the panels the Liberal Democrats generally report greater enthusiasm for devolution in all its forms than do Labour, but these differences are of little consequence, as politicians from both parties show overwhelming support for all aspects of devolution.[11] Among Conservatives support also generally drops as we work through the panels: standing for devolution remains in every instance a minority viewpoint. The overall picture, however, is of a strong partisan divide on the issue of devolution no matter who the beneficiary may be. The public remains in the middle throughout. It is important to note, however, that the views of the public at large move from clear support on devolution for Scotland to modest majority support in the cases of Wales and Northern Ireland. But when it comes to support for devolution to London and the regions of England only a minority of the British public concur. And so in practical terms, the public sides with Labour and the Liberal Democrats regarding Scotland, Wales and Northern Ireland but with the Conservatives on London and the regions. Thus Labour seems ahead of public opinion on the last two aspects of devolution.[12]

2: Attitudes towards rights protection instruments

The Human Rights Act was passed in 1998. Two years on, Britons gained a right to information, albeit with exceptions, with the Freedom of Information Act (fully enforced only from January 2005). One oddity of the BRS data involves its question about reform of the House of Lords. Although Lords reform is sensibly presented by McDonald and Hazell as part of the theme of democratic reform, the BRS under the influence of Charter 88 posed the question of an elected House of Lords in terms of its contribution to protecting rights. Accordingly, it will be considered here as part of the citizen rights theme.[13] Although reform of the House of Lords began in 1999, this endeavour remains a work in progress: the party is committed to further changes to the composition and power of the Upper House.

Respondents to the BRS were asked their views of such matters through a sequence of questions about the usefulness of a Bill of Rights, a freedom of information Act and a reformed House of Lords in protecting rights and liberties. These items asked for a rating scale ranging from 0 to 10, where higher scores indicate greater regard, and presumably corresponding support, for the mechanism. To aid in interpretation, the results for these queries reported in Table 4.2 include not only mean scores but also an indication of confidence intervals around the means (as well as the standard error term used in the calculation of the intervals).[14]

Again, each panel of the table indicates clear partisan lines among the political sample. Viewing mean scores, the extent of partisan divide may be less immediately obvious than the percentage differences on the devolution items, but it is nonetheless real as the confidence intervals attest. On each of the three rights instruments the partisan differences are clearly etched. Once again, the Conservatives are less enthusiastic regarding the reforms than either Labour or the Liberal Democrats, but on two of the measures all three groups of politicians place themselves on the more supportive side of the 0–10 scale. The three panels of Table 4.2 set out the specifics.

Table 4.2: Mean support for constitutional reforms among political leaders (by party) and the public

A Bill of Rights

Sample group (sample size)	Mean	Std error	95% confidence interval	
			Lower boundary	Upper boundary
Con (324)	6.343	0.109	6.128	6.557
Lab (335)	8.113	0.108	7.902	8.325
Lib Dem (301)	9.166	0.114	8.943	9.389
Public (1,987)	6.678	0.046	6.588	6.786

A freedom of information Act

Sample group (sample size)	Mean	Std error	95% confidence interval	
			Lower boundary	Upper boundary
Con (330)	6.939	0.084	6.774	7.105
Lab (337)	8.955	0.083	8.792	9.119
Lib Dem (301)	9.349	0.088	9.176	9.522
Public (2,045)	7.745	0.044	7.659	7.831

An elected House of Lords

Sample group (sample size)	Mean	Std error	95% confidence interval	
			Lower boundary	Upper boundary
Con (328)	4.256	0.133	3.995	4.518
Lab (336)	8.345	0.132	8.087	8.604
Lib Dem (300)	8.007	0.139	7.733	8.280
Public (2,007)	6.578	0.058	6.486	6.670

In the first panel, reporting views on a British Bill of Rights, all three parties show majority support, prefiguring perhaps the all-party support on the Human Rights Act in 1998. Still, obvious partisan differences are on display. But as a foretaste of their later complaints about the Human Rights Act, Conservative politicians are least supportive. The Liberal Democrats are the most enthusiastic, with Labour politicians much closer, as expected, to the latter than the former. The public once more find themselves between the parties. Yet even though they are much closer to the Conservatives in terms of mean scores, even the lower bound of the confidence interval of nearly 6.7 for the public is well above the middle score on the scale. As such, it would be fair to view this as majority support.

The second panel of Table 4.2 reveals greater support for a freedom of information Act than for a Bill of Rights among the citizenry and among both the Conservative and Labour partisans. The only exception to this is for the Liberal Democrats, whose confidence intervals for the two questions cross, suggesting that they probably support both measures equally. As to the bigger picture, the data indicate support, at least in principle, for a freedom of information Act in all quarters given scores that exceed the midpoint of the scale for all concerned. Nevertheless, Conservative politicians are less keen on the idea than their colleagues in the other major parties, perhaps consistent with Conservative preference under John Major for a non-statutory code. Again, the public falls between the extremes and, as on the Bill of Rights question, somewhat nearer to the Conservatives than the other parties, but still above the midpoint.

Table 4.2's third panel contains results from the item about electing the House of Lords. Recalling that the question was framed in terms of its contribution to rights protection, there appears to be less enthusiasm for an elected House of Lords than for a Bill of Rights or a freedom of information Act. Perhaps this foreshadows the difficulties Labour's actual proposals faced or maybe simply greater difficulty among respondents in viewing this as a mechanism for guaranteeing rights.[15] In any case, it is here that the partisan divide becomes most evident on any of the three rights protection instruments. Conservative politicians score well below the midpoint and Liberal Democrat and Labour ones well above, with no overlap in the confidence levels. The citizens in this case find themselves closer to the views of the Liberal Democrats and of Labour than to the Conservatives. Again majority support for the proposal seems evident.

3: Attitudes towards democratic restructuring
In delineating a third dimension of reform in Britain, McDonald and Hazell discuss New Labour's achievements along three fronts: referendums, pro-portional representation and electoral regulation. The BRS included questions pertinent to the first two of these, but not the third. There is an additional question in the data set concerning the representation of women and minorities in Parliament that also warrants analysis. It touches upon an unrealised aspect of reform – extending democratic representation – that

complements those discussed in Chapter 3 as based in a more pluralist concept of democracy.[16]

Turning first to the matter of referendums, the first panel of Table 4.3 demonstrates that referendums are endorsed as a means of settling complex political issues by only a minority of each group of politicians. Even so, there are notable differences along partisan lines. Most obviously, the views of the Conservatives diverge from those of the other two parties. Nearly eight in every ten Conservatives prefer Parliament to resolve important political matters rather than turning to a referendum. This represents significantly less support for referendums as a decision-making device than we observe among either Labour or the Liberal Democrats, who do not in turn differ significantly from each other. But even among these partisans, support for referendums is never more than a minority viewpoint. In this respect all three groups of partisan political leaders differ from the public at large. And the difference here is not merely statistically significant; it is substantively so in that a clear majority of the British public favours the use of referendums in deciding complex political issues.[17] We might fairly conclude from these results that the public was not only supportive but substantially ahead of all three major political parties in favouring this aspect of democratic reform.

Turning to the second panel of Table 4.3, we see that among politicians proportional representation is, without a doubt, the most divisive question in this or any theme of reform. The Conservative politicians are nearly all arrayed against proportional representation while the Liberal Democrats are almost unanimous in rejecting the first-past-the-post (FPTP) system in favour of proportional representation.[18] Labour politicians are split down the middle on the question.[19] Perhaps a further indication of what Kenneth MacKenzie terms Labour ambivalence over proportional representation is the relatively large percentage of Labour politicians who resort to the 'don't know' option in answering the question. Considering the electoral fortunes of the three parties at the time of the survey, these results make eminently good sense. Conservatives firmly support an electoral system that brought them to national power, the Liberal Democrats want to change the same system that locks them out of power and Labour politicians are ambivalent about a system which had kept them out of power at Westminster since 1979 but which had yielded somewhat better results in local government. The public is, of course, also divided on the matter, yet a narrow majority favours proportional representation over the current FPTP arrangement for selecting MPs.

Table 4.3: Support for democratic reforms

Support for resolving important political matters by referendum as against in Parliament

| | Political leaders | | | Public |
	Con	Lab	Lib Dem	
Referendum	17.2%	33.5%	40.9%	61.2%
Parliament	79.5%	63.2%	54.2%	35.4%
Don't know	3.3%	3.3%	5.0%	3.4%
(sample size)	(331)	(337)	(301)	(2,055)

Support for proportional representation

| | Political leaders | | | Public |
	Con	Lab	Lib Dem	
PR	5.4%	45.5%	98.3%	52.0%
First past the post	94.0%	47.6%	0.7%	44.5%
Don't know	0.6%	6.9%	1.0%	3.6%
(sample size)	(331)	(334)	(301)	(2,056)

Support for minority and female MPs

| | Political leaders | | | Public |
	Con	Lab	Lib Dem	
Yes	19.0%	67.0%	74.2%	42.8%
No	78.5%	29.8%	23.1%	51.6%
Don't know	2.5%	3.3%	2.7%	5.6%
(sample size)	(326)	(336)	(299)	(2,047)

Although the BRS did not contain any questions on electoral regulation, an aspect of democratic restructuring that is covered appears in a series of questions asking about whether the respondents thought Parliament should ideally be more representative of women and racial or ethnic minorities.[20] The final panel of Table 4.3 shows that this particular rendering of democratic representation produces a familiar partisan divide. The Conservatives are primarily on the 'no' side, while Labour and Liberal Democrats generally express support for Parliament reflecting the population at large, at least in terms of ethnic, racial and gender distribution. In these data, any difference between Labour and the Liberal Democrats is more apparent than real in that there is neither a statistical nor a practical difference in their stand on support for minority MPs.[21] Interestingly, the public is divided on the issue but with a slightly greater percentage opposed to the ideal of proportional gendered and racial parliamentary representation. There is little suggestion in these figures of public pressure for reform on this front.

4: Attitudes regarding judicial reform

The judicial reforms were a late addition to the reform programme – they were passed into law in the Constitutional Reform Act 2005 – and so it is perhaps not surprising that there are no questions in the 1992 BRS asking about support for a new Supreme Court, a new method of appointing judges or reform of the office of Lord Chancellor. Nevertheless, there are several questions contained in the data that touch upon attitudes towards the judiciary and its relationship with Parliament. Together they may offer a glimpse of public and partisan attitudes relevant to judicial reform, but the results must be considered preliminary at best.

The first of these questions asks respondents, again using a scale ranging from zero to ten, to rate the fairness and impartiality of British judges. Presumably, low ratings on fairness and impartiality should correspond to greater support for judicial reform whereas high ratings probably signal less support for judicial reform. The results appear in the first panel of Table 4.4. Again, confidence intervals are presented along with mean scores to assist in making comparisons.

The highest ratings of British judges come from Conservative politicians. And the lowest ratings are from Labour. This difference is in no way likely to be due to sampling error, evident in that the likely ranges of true mean scores (the respective confidence intervals) do not come anywhere near overlapping. Moreover, one might even discern some degree of enthusiasm for judicial reform among Labour in that their mean score is comfortably below the midpoint of the scale. The mean for the Liberal Democrats lies between the Conservative and Labour positions, although it is somewhat closer to Labour's. The British public's mean score, while lower than that of the Conservatives and higher than that of the Labour politicians, does not differ much from that of the Liberal Democrats. The overlap in their respective confidence intervals indicates that this slight difference between the public and the Liberal Democrats could well be due to sampling error. More sub-stantively, the public's scores are above the midpoint of the scale, indicating ratings more positive than negative of its judges. Nevertheless, the public's ratings are closer to those of Labour than to those of the Conservatives. It may be difficult to discern much enthusiasm for judicial reform in the public's rating of its judges, but it is also difficult to see much public enthusiasm for judges in the middling score they earn here.

Table 4.4: Attitudes towards the judiciary

British judges: fairness and impartiality

| | | | 95% confidence interval | |
Sample group (sample size)	Mean	Std error	Lower boundary	Upper boundary
Con (327)	7.606	0.101	7.406	7.805
Lab (334)	5.144	0.100	4.947	5.341
Lib Dem (298)	6.128	0.106	5.919	6.336
Public (2,004)	6.071	0.047	5.979	6.163

British courts: defending liberties

| | | | 95% confidence interval | |
Sample group (sample size)	Mean	Std error	Lower boundary	Upper boundary
Con (331)	7.287	0.100	7.091	7.483
Lab (336)	5.607	0.099	5.413	5.802
Lib Dem (300)	6.207	0.105	6.001	6.412
Public (2,044)	6.523	0.044	6.437	6.609

Prefer British courts, European Court of Human Rights or no difference

	Political leaders			Public
	Con	Lab	Lib Dem	
Prefer ECtHR	12.7%	57.3%	43.7%	26.2%
Prefer British courts	21.6%	2.4%	2.7%	16.6%
No preference	65.7%	40.4%	53.6%	57.3%
(sample size)	(329)	(337)	(300)	(2,049)

The results presented in the second panel of Table 4.4 largely echo those in the first. Again, ratings range from zero to ten, only this time they report a rating of the British courts in terms of protecting rights. The Conservatives once more stand out in rating the courts most highly. And from this one might reasonably infer that Conservative politicians would be least likely of the political groups to support calls for judicial reform. Labour politicians once more post the lowest average rating with Liberal Democrats again taking up the middle ground. The range of mean scores indicated by the confidence intervals suggests that these partisan differences are unlikely to be due to sampling error. The public again fall in the middle.

The final panel of Table 4.4 offers a different perspective on the courts and the theme of judicial reform, but its results essentially confirm much of what we have already seen. The findings are fashioned from two questions touching on the relationship between the courts and Parliament, each question asking whether Parliament or a court should have the final say. The questions differ with respect to whether British courts or the European Court of Human Rights (ECtHR) is pitted against Parliament. The results in the top two rows in the third panel of Table 4.4 report whether the respondent shows any preference for either the British courts or the ECtHR. The bottom row combines those who reveal no preference for either the British or European courts by selecting either Parliament or the court on both questions. Again the politicians sharply divide, with the public falling somewhere in the middle. More specifically, Labour politicians are most likely to prefer the ECtHR while the Conservatives are least likely to do so. The Liberal Democrats and the public again fall between these extremes. Based on these results, it is again not an unreasonable inferential stretch to see Labour as most likely, and the Conservatives as least likely, to support court reforms. It is more difficult, however, to discern either majority public support for judicial reform or resounding support for British courts in these results. The public may reasonably be seen as permissive of reform.

Patterns of response

The first point to make about the findings thus far comes from examining the data obtained in interviewing the political leaders. The overarching pattern emerging in the results for all four themes of constitutional reform is that of partisan difference. This is, of course, hardly surprising in so far as the issues at hand are drawn from an openly partisan, and hence often divisive, political agenda. Nevertheless, recognition of this reality is necessary before turning to examine the possible origins of politicians' views in a culture of rights. Any analyses aiming to ground the political class's attitude towards constitutional reforms in values implicit in a culture of rights must also reckon with the partisanship.

The second point to emerge is that the reforms seem to be broadly responsive to public preferences. With a few notable exceptions, all of the constitutional reforms of the last decade enjoyed majority popular support even before New Labour came to power in 1997. The exceptions are themselves instructive. Regarding the first theme of decentralisation, the three major elements of the devolution agenda, Scotland, Wales and Northern Ireland, all had clear majority support. The majority, however, did not seem enthusiastic for devolution either for London or the regions of England. On the second theme, both the Bill of Rights and freedom of information aspects of the rights protection agenda appeared to have majority support. So too did reform of the House of Lords and those elements of democratic reform that were pursued, albeit in a limited way, by New Labour, namely referendums and proportional representation.[22] Interestingly, this seems to be the case even at a time when Labour politicians themselves appear to be opposed and/or ambivalent to these reforms. Moreover, increased minority representation in Parliament, an aspect of democratic restructuring not endorsed by a majority of the public, was not pursued despite broad support among Labour politicians. As to the final theme of judicial reform, it is more difficult to assess the extent of public support, in part because of the equivocal results and in part because of the temporal and consequent conceptual gap between the available measures and the eventual reforms. Nevertheless, the findings might be seen to be indicative of a permissive attitude towards reform. Taking the four themes of reform as a whole, it is fair to say that, generally speaking, New Labour's reforms were backed by majority public support.

Underlying values and constitutional reform

Beyond the partisan differences evident thus far in the BRS data, why do some politicians and some elements of the public favour reform while others do not? Nothing like a complete answer will be attempted, but a model of the values underpinning support for British constitutional reforms will be offered to gain some insight into the basis for reform in rights culture. In identifying which values might play a central role in what has been described as a rights culture, the focus here is on the values of liberty, equality and authority. Other values might be selected but these are broadly consistent with those identified in the influential post-materialist perspective.[23] The name derives from its emphasis on a decline in materialist orientations since the end of World War II as basic needs for physical security and material well-being have been increasingly met in Western societies. Consequently, the thinking goes, more people now place higher priority on the values of individual liberty and social acceptance than respect for authority and tradition, which are on the decline. This change in values is viewed as engendering a greater empathy for, and greater political involvement by, previously marginalised groups, including ethnic minorities, homosexuals and women, leading to their greater participation – a process often called the 'new politics'. Implicit in the present analysis is the contention that the changes in values provide the grounds for the elements of the new constitutional settlement we have witnessed since 1997.

The BRS was inspired by the Canadian Charter Project in its overall inspiration and design as well as in some of its measures.[24] So questions typically used to describe respondents in the post-materialist literature do not appear in these data. Yet the available survey items do speak to the value placed by Britons on authority and tradition, as well as their acceptance of various groups as equals and, of course, their endorsement of individual rights and freedoms.

Figure 4.1 sets out in schematic fashion a basic notion of rights culture lying behind attitudes regarding the four themes of constitutional reform. Consistent with conventional practice, the ellipses in the diagram represent abstract concepts each of which is based on a number of specific indicators in the form of individual questions.[25] The double-headed arrows connecting the values of liberty, authority and equality indicate a simple association among them. These are typically estimated as simple measures of association that report the strength and direction of the relation between the two values. The single-headed arrows running from the three values to the four themes of reform indicate a hypothesised direct effect or causal relation such that value preferences lead to support for the reforms. Statistical estimates of these direct effects present the net influence of one variable on another by taking account of the other variables in the model. For example, estimates for the path running from liberty to devolution in the figure control for the effects of the values both of authority and of equality as well as any inter-correlation among these values.

The central idea here is that people's values regarding questions of liberty, authority and equality fit together and influence their attitudes for and against their views on devolution, rights protection instruments, democratic restructuring and judicial reforms. More specifically, consistent with post-materialist thinking that support for liberty and equality should go together, the survey results should show liberty and equality positively associated with one another and each negatively (inversely) related to authority. We might expect all four themes of constitutional reform to be related positively to support for the values of liberty and equality and negatively to support for authority.

Figure 4.1: Values and support for four dimensions of constitutional reform in Britain

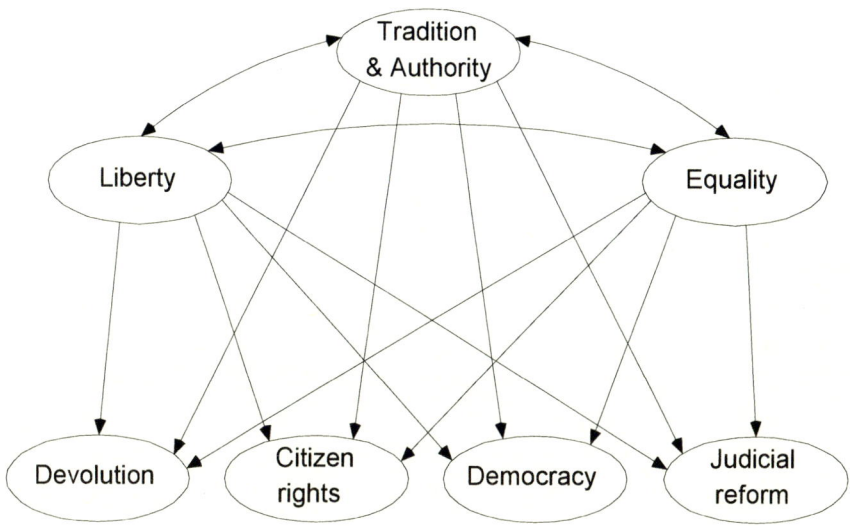

Each value dimension is further explored by examining the responses of Britons and the samples of their political leaders to a range of questions. To measure liberty there are items about free speech, freedom of assembly and the right to silence. Support for authority is measured using questions about the value of traditional ideas of right and wrong and the importance of respect for authority. Equality is indexed by a general question about the promotion of rights as well as more specific questions about support for the equality of women, equal rights for gays and the protection of ethnic minorities.[26] And people's views on each of the four themes of constitutional reform are gauged using the relevant questions discussed earlier.[27]

In order to appreciate partisan differences among the politicians, as well as to estimate the connections depicted in the model shown in Figure 4.1 for the British public, a simultaneous multi-group estimation procedure was used.[28] Accordingly, each group of political leaders is treated as a separate sample in the analysis, plus a group for the general population sample, yielding four groups in all. This approach highlights the similarities and differences among the citizens and political leaders for each of the three parties.[29] Moreover, it confirms that the model reflects what the data tell us.[30] More specifically, this means that the pattern of relationships observed in the BRS corresponds closely to the structure of inter-connected values and attitudes towards reform identified in Figure 4.1.

Three major implications flow from the close fit of the model to the data. The first is that McDonald and Hazell's conceptualisation of New Labour's constitutional reforms as falling into four more or less coherent themes receives substantial empirical support.[31] A second implication is that it supports the understanding advanced here that the values of liberty, authority and equality are inter-related in such a way that they may reasonably be viewed as an expression of an emerging culture of rights. And finally, the model demonstrates the extent and ways in which, even taking into account party differences, attitudes towards the themes of reforms are effectively rooted in this common structure of values or culture of rights. In other words, the unifying foundation of New Labour's four themes of constitutional reform is not in any single political idea or value. Instead, the unifying theoretical framework consists of a coherent structure of inter-related values.

The three panels of Table 4.5 present statistical information on the estimated linkages among the variables.[32] The first estimates the extent of inter-correlation among the four themes of constitutional reform identified by McDonald and Hazell.[33] In all but two instances the coefficients are positive, which means support for (or opposition to) one theme of reform implies a corresponding response to the other themes as well.[34] Nevertheless, the relationships are not all of the same magnitude, producing something of a patchwork of strong and weak correlations. This is perhaps most evident among Conservative and Labour politicians but it appears as well among the Liberal Democrats and the public. Attending closely to this pattern in the first panel reveals several specific areas of particular coherence in views towards the four themes of reform. For example, attitudes towards rights protection instruments and democratic restructuring are notably consistent across sample groups. Thus for all three partisan groupings and the general public as well, agreement with one set of reforms reliably predicts agreement with the other. And opposition likewise goes with opposition. A similar cross-group pattern of inter-correlation holds for democratic restructuring and judicial reform. Two further relationships, both involving devolution, hold for three of the four sample groups. And in each case the fourth group's lack of correlation

Table 4.5: Linkages among values and themes of reform

Linkages among dimensions of constitutional reform

Correlation among reforms	Conservatives			Labour			Liberal Democrats			Public		
	Rights	Democracy	Judicial	Rights	Democracy	Judicial	Rights	Democracy	Judicial	Rights	Democracy	Judicial
Devolution	*0.11*	**0.49**	**0.20**	**0.29**	-0.08	**0.15**	**0.40**	**0.34**	**0.15**	**0.22**	**0.39**	**0.17**
Rights	—	**0.40**	0.07	—	**0.52**	-0.01	—	**0.34**	0.03	—	**0.55**	**0.14**
Democracy		—	0.43		—	**0.37**		—	**0.39**		—	**0.40**
Judicial			—			—			—			—

Linkages among values

Correlation among values	Conservatives		Labour		Liberal Democrats		Public	
	Authority	Equality	Authority	Equality	Authority	Equality	Authority	Equality
Liberty	**-0.50**	**0.37**	**-0.48**	**0.50**	**-0.43**	**0.44**	**-0.55**	**0.56**
Equality	0.00	—	**-0.28**	—	**-0.24**	—	**-0.22**	—

Predicting support for constitutional reforms from values

	Support for devolution				Support for rights protection instruments			
	Con	Lab	Lib Dem	Public	Con	Lab	Lib Dem	Public
Liberty	*0.32*	**0.43**	0.11	**0.15**	-0.16	-0.06	0.09	0.07
Authority	0.00	-0.05	**-0.22**	-0.03	0.09	0.08	0.02	**0.12**
Equality	0.09	-0.03	**0.19**	**0.26**	**0.49**	**0.41**	**0.31**	**0.45**
Explained variance (R²)	0.13	0.19	0.15	0.14	0.23	0.14	0.14	0.23

	Support for democratic restructuring				Support for judicial reform			
	Con	Lab	Lib Dem	Public	Con	Lab	Lib Dem	Public
Liberty	-0.20	-0.19	*0.28*	0.37	-0.08	*0.28*	0.09	0.09
Authority	*-0.30*	-0.54	-0.42	-0.09	**-0.30**	**-0.33**	**-0.43**	**-0.36**
Equality	0.61	*0.42*	0.51	0.19	-0.05	0.01	-0.02	0.01
R²	0.36	0.46	0.40	0.30	0.13	0.27	0.23	0.17

Significant coefficients are in **bold**. Marginal significance is indicated by *italics*.

Sample sizes: Conservatives 331, Labour 337, Lib Dem 301, Public 2,060 makes sense in light of what we have already seen. Supporting devolution goes with support for rights protection for everyone except the Conservatives, because they generally support devolution but only half-heartedly support the rights instruments.[35] And devolution goes with democratic restructuring for everyone except Labour politicians, who are at best ambivalent towards it.[36] Apart from these two obvious cases, the other modest and weak inter-correlations in the first panel involve judicial reform. Of course, the indicators used to measure attitudes towards judicial reform are the least direct and hence the least conceptually adequate of those used in the analysis. So findings based upon these measures must be taken with a pinch of salt.[37] Though far from comprehensive, there is a considerable degree of overall consistency in both partisan and public attitudes towards the four themes of constitutional reform. So we have some fairly clear evidence that the reforms introduced by New Labour were seen by both politicians and the British public as a set of more or less coherent political reforms well before their introduction.

The second panel of Table 4.5 addresses the coherence among the values theorised to influence attitudes towards the reforms. It presents the inter-relationships among the values of liberty, authority and equality. With just one exception, it depicts coherence among values much as one anticipates using a post-materialist perspective on value change. In all four groups the values of liberty and authority are, for example, negatively correlated. And these relationships are consistently strong. This indicates that, irrespective of whether one is an ordinary citizen or a politician, or whatever party a politician may sit for, the more value a person places on liberty, the less he or she will value authority and vice versa. This fits with the post-materialist outlook describing a decline in the value placed on authority and the rise of liberty as a value.

Moving to the relationship between liberty and equality, the model estimates indicate a substantial positive correlation for all groups, but the magnitude of the relation varies somewhat across them. But the differences here are more of emphasis than of kind. For Conservatives, and to a lesser degree Liberal Democrats, liberty and equality are not as tightly bound together as they are for Labour and citizens. Nevertheless, the relationship takes the same general form. The more value one places on liberty, the more value is also placed on equality. Again, this is broadly consistent with the post-materialist view that the ascendant values of liberty and equality go hand in hand. Here the evidence suggests this is true across the political spectrum. Where a notable difference in linkages among values does emerge is in the connection between equality and authority. For three out of the four groups there is a modest inverse relationship between authority and equality. This is again consistent with mainline thinking on value dynamics. The more one values social equality and acceptance the less value one should place upon tradition and authority. And this is just what we see for Labour, Liberal Democrats and the British public. For Conservative politicians, however, authority and equality are uncorrelated. This means that knowing their views on either of these values tells us nothing whatsoever about views on the other. Thus among the Conservatives, placing a high value on authority is just as likely to be associated with strong support for the value of equality as it is to be associated with little or no support for equality. The two values are, for Conservative politicians, separate and unconnected. Couched in the terms of value change, a lack of connection here suggests that the views of Conservative politicians may cut distinctively against the grain of the dominant value reorientation in democratic societies. This difficulty faces conservatives throughout the West.[38] Its basis may lie, as is the case elsewhere, with an attempt by Conservatives to embrace equality while simultaneously continuing to value tradition and authority. There is some indication that this may also be a challenge, albeit less severe, for the other political parties and for citizens more generally in that relationships between authority and equality are weaker than between authority and liberty for all four groups. But the complete incoherence of the values of authority and equality among Conservatives is apparent in the total absence of a relationship. Aside from this revealing exception, the values of the British public and their political leaders otherwise appear to form an essentially coherent political culture in line with post-materialist expectations. And this structure of values in turn provides the basis for support among politicians for each of the three major parties, as well as among the public at large, for the four related themes of constitutional reform in Britain.

The third panel of Table 4.5 provides information on the connections depicted as single-headed arrows in Figure 4.1. As such, it provides evidence on the underpinnings of attitudes towards the four themes of constitutional reform identified by McDonald and Hazell. And it does so in terms of the values of liberty, equality and authority, which are at the heart of the post-materialist perspective on value change. Overall, what we see is that, beyond the parry and thrust of partisanship debate, support for the reforms is rooted in a greater emphasis on liberty and equality and a corresponding lesser value is placed on traditional authority, as hypothesised by post-materialist thinking.

In this panel standardised parameters similar to regression coefficients summarise the influence of each of the three values on attitudes towards the four themes of reform.[39] The proportion of explained variance (R^2) for each dimension of constitutional reform is indicated at the bottom of the respective columns. It shows in percentage terms the extent to which the combined influence of the three values accounts for variation in attitudes towards each reform theme within each group. Naturally, there are differences across themes and groups, but each group's views on all four sets of constitutional reforms are rooted in their values well beyond what one would find by chance. And for the politicians, in particular, this suggests that beyond the value commitments entailed in holding political office under a particular party banner, views on constitutional reform are grounded in basic values of liberty, authority and equality.

In assessing the relative importance of these values in predicting support for constitutional reform in each of the groups, it remains useful to differentiate between attitudes towards the four themes of reform. The detailed pattern of results differs across the themes.[40] And for each theme there is also some variation among the partisan groups. Nevertheless, for the most part, support for constitutional reform is related to the values in accord with the post-materialist outlook. That is to say, the values of liberty and equality tend to promote support for the reforms while support for the value of authority militates against them. Of course, the details vary by both theme and group.

Looking first at the results on support for devolution among the Conservative and Labour parties, the impact of the value of liberty on support for devolution is clear and positive. By comparison the roles played by authority and equality are insignificant, in both statistical and practical terms. So among politicians in these parties, support for devolution moves in accord with the value placed upon liberty. Among Liberal Democrats, the story differs in detail but the effect is the same. For Liberal Democrats equality and authority go toe to toe, the first pulling towards support for devolution, the second pulling against. Again, support for devolution is consistent with a rise in equality and decline in the values of tradition and authority. For the public, liberty and equality both contribute to explaining support for devolution. This is perhaps not surprising given that different partisan leaders base their own support for devolution on these values. In any case, the more value the average citizen places on either liberty or equality (or both), the more likely he or she is to support devolution. Although the details differ somewhat, the overall picture of support for devolution is based on the greater emphasis on liberty and equality and less concern for traditional authority, fully consistent with post-materialist thinking.

A different value profile underpins attitudes on the rights protection instruments, but still the results are essentially in line with the post-materialist approach. Nevertheless, it is particularly striking, and perhaps somewhat ironic, that the value placed upon liberty has negligible influence on support for the rights protection instruments.[41] The influence of authority is also generally marginal, except among the public, but even there it remains a secondary influence in the model. Intriguingly, its sign is positive, the lone exception to post-materialist thinking in our findings. It suggests that among the public, at least at the outset, attraction to rights protection instruments is based in part on support for, and not opposition to, the values of tradition and authority.[42] In sharp contrast to the weak role played by both liberty and authority in explaining support for new rights protection instruments, the role of equality is obviously predominant. Across all four groups, the value of equality has a strong, positive bearing on respondents' views of the reforms and innovations in rights protection.[43] This major effect is, of course, also broadly consistent with the view that the reforms are based on post-materialist values embedded in a rights culture. But its specific form is revealing. The reforms in the area of citizen rights are almost entirely based upon the ascendant value of equality, with virtually no input from liberty.[44]

Turning to the third theme of reform – democratic restructuring – partisan attitudes rest primarily upon a trade-off between equality and the value of traditional authority. Again liberty has little effect for the politicians. Only among Liberal Democrats does the value of liberty play a tertiary role in support of democratic reform. As with the other parties, support for democratic restructuring is primarily grounded in support for equality and resisted by deference to traditional authority, consistent with our theoretical outlook. Interestingly, the citizens' perspective differs from politicians' in two ways. Unlike the politicians, authority plays no significant role in the public's attitudes towards democratic reform. In its stead liberty plays a central role in that their support for democratic restructuring rests primarily with the value placed on liberty, and only secondarily on equality.

The model's explanation for variation in attitudes towards the judiciary, and by extension towards its reform, does not differ much across the four samples. Irrespective of partisanship among the politicians, or whether one is an ordinary Briton, attitudes towards the judiciary depend essentially upon one value – authority. The negative signs on the coefficients for authority indicate an inverse relationship such that the less one values traditional authority the more one will support judicial reform and vice versa. This, too, is consistent with the dominant thinking of value change in that support for judicial reform comes as a result of the decline in the value of tradition and authority. Among the Labour politicians there is some secondary influence of liberty, in the expected direction, but otherwise attitudes towards the judiciary are an expression of the value one places on authority.

Modelling the basis of support of the four themes in British constitutional reform reveals that their common basis lies not in a single value but in the inter-play among a trio of related values. Thus, controlling for partisan differences, proponents and opponents of these reforms ground their views in the importance they place upon the ascendant values of liberty and equality and the decline in respect lent to traditional authority. In tracing the sources of support (and opposition) for these reforms to this inter-related set of values, the model identifies an essential coherence behind these reforms in an emerging culture of rights. But it also sheds some light on why the coherence is not always immediately evident. Much of it lies behind the ongoing political debate and rests in the set of relationships among these correlated political values. Adding a further layer of complexity, some of the themes of reform have their underpinnings in distinct elements of the three inter-related values.

Consider, for example, the results for the Conservatives presented in Table 4.5. The issue of devolution turns for them almost entirely on the value of liberty. Those who are more supportive of fundamental freedoms of speech, association and assembly are more likely to support devolution. And those who place less emphasis on these same values are less supportive. In contrast, rights protection instruments such as the Human Rights and Freedom of Information Acts primarily engage the value they place on advancing equality for women, gays and minorities and not at all in their views of fundamental issues of liberty.[45] Matters of judicial reform turn on yet a third concern – the value Conservatives place upon traditional authority. And democratic reforms, such as referendums and proportional representation, pivot on a trade-off between the value placed on equality and that on authority.

To the extent that different themes draw on the same values, there is some obvious coherence. The rights instruments and democratic reform, for example, both draw on equality. And judicial and democratic reforms both have some basis in authority. So there is some relatively clear coherence in the common causes of these reforms. But another aspect of coherence among the reforms is perhaps less obvious. Support for devolution is based on the value of liberty while support for the rights protection instruments is rooted in equality. To appreciate the connection between devolution and citizen rights reforms requires some digging into the connections among the values. And in so doing, the connection between liberty and equality, even among the Conservatives, provides a clear linkage. The common root of support for devolution and citizen rights reforms lies with the connection between liberty and equality, even among Conservatives.

Much the same can be said about Labour and Liberal Democrat politicians. For these two partisan groups there are perhaps a few more common elements in the bases for their respective attitudes towards the reforms and a bit more consistency in their values. So the underlying coherence may be somewhat more evident, both in terms of support for the reforms and in underlying values. Even so, the correlations are less than perfect and so appreciation of the linkages among the reforms understandably remains only partial until one probes beneath the surface of political debate into the realm of underlying values. In doing so, one comes to appreciate that the deepening and widening of democracy entailed by the reforms that their parties have pursued is premised on the increased importance placed on liberty and equality and the decrease in concern for traditional authority that comes with post-materialist value change.

Citizens differ little from the politicians in any of these respects. Moreover, the patterning of results suggests that, well before the onset of New Labour's reform initiatives, the British public had as good a grasp of the value concerns underlying the impetus for the constitutional reforms as any of the politicians. On two of the four themes, the public's views on reform are primarily influenced by the same value considerations as are the views of the politicians. On the theme of citizen rights, for example, the public appreciates that the core value at stake is equality and not liberty. And regarding the public's views on judicial reform, the primary value fulcrum is traditional authority, just as it is among the politicians. The match is somewhat weaker on democratic restructuring and devolution but still the public responds largely in terms of the ascendant values of liberty and equality, both of which figure prominently in the thinking of the politicians. Where the public differs from the politicians is in the role of traditional authority. For the public, it is not a significant consideration on devolution or democratic restructuring, while it is for the politicians. And interestingly, despite frequent messages to the contrary, the public views the rights protection instruments as consistent with the values of tradition and authority.

Summary

This chapter has been guided by McDonald and Hazell's thematic analysis of British constitutional reforms pursued by New Labour since 1997. They identify four dimensions of reform: decentralisation, protection of citizen rights, democratisation and judicial reform. The analysis here looks at public opinion data to discern the views of politicians from the three major parties as well as of the British public towards some key aspects of each dimension of reform. Despite identifying sharp cleavages among the partisan leaders, the data show that most of the reform agenda had majority public support well before Labour took office in 1997.

The chapter has examined the foundations of attitudes towards each theme of constitutional reform using a multivariate statistical model. The analysis here confirms that the British public, as well as politicians for each of the three major parties, perceive the reforms as essentially falling into the four broad categories as identified by McDonald and Hazell. It further traces support for constitutional innovation to a common set of values reflective of an emerging culture of rights. In doing so, it has described the way in which the four themes are essentially related due to their common basis in inter-related values of liberty, equality and authority. More specifically, the reforms are shown to be grounded in key values at the heart of rights culture – rising levels of support for liberty and equality and a corresponding decline in deference to authority.

Modelling the basis of support for the constitutional reforms also sheds some light on why the coherence of these reforms remains controversial. The unifying constitutional cement that binds the reforms together is not to be found in a single value. Yet the reforms hang together because the values on which they are based are themselves inter-correlated. Few of the reform's defenders have focused on this fact. And so the debate about their coherence persists.

Fundamental value change may offer fertile ground for a new constitutional settlement. Yet it also provides considerable scope for controversy rooted in these very same values. There are, and will likely remain, substantial differences in the value placed on liberty, equality and authority in Britain, and these differences will continue to be exploited by the major political parties. In so far as the reforms are based upon value differences, we may expect them to remain the source of political argument.[46]

Part III

Process

5

How the reforms came about

Kenneth MacKenzie

Within a year of the Blair government taking office, one of the more erudite British political commentators was accusing it of presiding over 'a frenzy of constitutional reform' which needed 'to be underpinned by some unifying political vision'.[1]

This chapter describes how that situation came about and how the programme got off to such a flying start despite – or perhaps because of – its lack of coherent political vision. The government showed little appetite for contemplating or presenting constitutional change in the round and found some of the consequences of its own reforms to be a source of embarrassment or frustration. Nevertheless they have transformed the landscape of governance in Britain beyond recognition and probably, irrevocably. Their achievements in this area ought to be a significant part of their monument as an administration.

I will examine the origins of the process as I remember them as Head of the Cabinet Office Constitution Secretariat from 1997 to 1998 and how they affected each of the elements of the constitutional reform programme. That, of course, makes this an essentially individual view based on personal observation and within the bounds of confidentiality. I will, however, also describe more briefly the stages which followed my personal involvement in formulating the policies as Parliament passed the necessary legislation and government departments, local authorities, other public bodies, the media and the chattering classes geared up for the implementation of what Vernon Bogdanor has described as 'the quiet constitutional revolution' that was about to overtake the country.

Before dawn: pre-election period

My starting point must be the period of the mid-1990s, when the

Conservative government's fortunes were in severe decline. There was a smell of death around as John Major's government approached the end of its term, the last possible moment for which, under the Parliament Acts, worked out at a date in May 1997. The Tories clung on in the hope that something would turn up so there was – unusually for Britain – a long run-up to that election and a six-week campaign. The strong evidence of the opinion polls was that there would be a notable New Labour victory though few expected a landslide on the scale which ensued.

Against this political background – and after eighteen years of continuous rule by the same party – the civil service was particularly conscious of its duty to be well prepared for a change of government and to gear up to implement the new administration's policy programme. It had been apparent for some time that this would include a large measure of constitutional reform. Both New Labour and the other main opposition party, the Liberal Democrats, were keenly interested in this, partly no doubt on the merits of the case for modernising Britain's uncodified constitution, but also because it proffered useful sticks with which to beat the Conservatives.

Thus freedom of information campaigners argued for more transparency than the government's non-statutory code afforded; the European Convention on Human Rights (ECHR) could be prayed in aid against a number of Tory policies and the unfairness of recourse only to the European court at Strasbourg was demonstrable; a nod in the direction of electoral reform, however cautious, proved attractive to the Liberal Democrats; and the restoration of democracy to the Greater London area had much local appeal. Most audible of all was the cry to remedy the democratic deficits in Scotland and Wales, where Conservative ministers ruled but with their party in a minority bordering upon extinction.

Scottish – and to a perhaps surprising extent UK – politics had been much affected by the failure to implement the previous Labour governments' attempts at legislative devolution to Scotland and Wales in the 1970s. Following successive Conservative election victories in the UK as a whole – but not in Scotland – there had been increasing frustration with allegedly unrepresentative and undemocratic Tory rule north of the border. That was compounded by the apparent unwillingness on the part of the government to respond. True, the Secretary of State for Scotland brought the Scottish Grand Committee of the House of Commons (which consists of all the Scottish members of Parliament) to various Scottish towns and cities so that our elected representatives were seen to be meeting in Scotland. He also arranged a theatrical ceremony to mark the return of the Stone of Scone (on which the Scottish Kings were traditionally crowned) 700 years after Edward I of England took it to Westminster Abbey. But these were regarded as cosmetic gestures and in no way an adequate response to the expressed wishes of the electorate.

Since 1989 a Scottish Constitutional Convention with Labour and Liberal Democrat participation (but boycotted by the Conservatives and Scottish National Party) had harnessed the efforts of civic society – the churches, local authorities, trade unions, universities, business community, ethnic minorities and the voluntary sector – to produce a blueprint for devolution. Its report, *Scotland's Parliament, Scotland's Right*, was published on St Andrew's Day, 30 November 1995. This approach had survived the change of Labour leadership in 1994 despite much public wrangling within the party, especially on the necessity for another referendum to ease any Bill's passage through Parliament. New Labour's intentions were confirmed in the authorised talks between the civil service and opposition spokesmen which now precede a general election in Britain. In 1996 the plans were made public and were set out in detail in the March 1997 report of the Joint Consultative Committee on Constitutional Reform, which had been established by New Labour and the Liberal Democrats.

A key figure in what then happened was the Cabinet Secretary, Sir Robin Butler, now Lord Butler of Brockwell. As the country's top civil servant, he led the talks with the opposition but even before they started he had drawn up his contingency plans. He was acutely aware that constitutional reform was not an active policy area for Major and his colleagues much beyond open government and improving public accountability. Devolution was to be confined to Northern Ireland for reasons peculiar to that province although the Prime Minister had invested a good deal of time, effort and political capital in it. Major was also anxious to maintain the integrity of the United Kingdom by resisting separatist tendencies in Scotland and Wales. In 1993 he had published a White Paper promoting various measures like the touring Grand Committee. Later he made arrangements within government to include the territorial departments (which administered Scottish, Welsh and Northern Irish affairs) more effectively in the process of decision-making in London.

As the high priest of that process, Butler knew that the Cabinet Office would need to be equipped to handle any constitutional reform proposals better than had been the case in the 1970s, when its overcentralist approach was partly blamed for the failure of the Callaghan government's plans. He had no significant existing capability on the subject but the remit of the Economic and Domestic Secretariat included constitutional matters in so far as they arose and the management of the government's legislative programme. In 1995 he took the opportunity to allow for the contingency of constitutional reform by looking for someone to appoint as its head who was familiar with devolution and other issues but who would ensure that the game was played according to the normal rules of collective Cabinet government.

I was therefore summoned, almost literally like Cincinnatus from the plough – I had been in charge of the Scottish Office Agricultural and Fisheries Department – to lead the Economic and Domestic Secretariat and thereby gain street credibility in Whitehall to add to my familiarity with Scotland. My deputy, Bill Jeffrey, was also a Scot but had served throughout his career in the Home Office, supposedly a bastion of orthodoxy. There was more to this, however, than simply putting a kilt round things. Scottish Office staff had a sound reputation for being able to work flexibly across departmental boundaries – both institutional and subject matter – in their smaller-scale and more federal administrative environment. That attribute would be much needed. Late in 1996, it was becoming clear from Butler's contacts with the opposition that they would be looking for rapid progress with devolution as the foretaste to an ample diet of constitutional measures. So, we quietly dusted down the material prepared by our predecessors in 1992 that advised how to implement what would have been the Kinnock government's devolution proposals had the Labour Party won that election.

Another ready and valuable source of advice and information across most of the elements in the constitutional reform programme was a series of studies produced by Professor Robert Hazell's Constitution Unit. Notable among them were their 1996 reports *Delivering Constitutional Reform* and *Scotland's Parliament: Fundamentals of a New Scotland Act.*

The awakening: the 1997 election campaign

All this prepared the way for what appeared in the 1997 manifesto, *New Labour: Because Britain Deserves Better.* It has been customary over many years for the civil service to study the manifestos of the major parties so that departments can act swiftly in support of new ministers, no matter which party or parties form the next administration. This enables departments to draw up plans to adjust their internal structure in order to cope with changed priorities and to join ministers in 'hitting the ground running', as they predictably put it. Every department is expected to prepare at least three sets of notes for incoming ministers, allowing for the possibility of minority parties working in coalition in the event of a hung Parliament. With New Labour tipped as the hot favourite the party's manifesto was greeted with a particularly keen sense of expectation.

This document confirmed that devolution would be the aperitif to a much larger menu of wide-ranging, radical constitutional change for a whole parliament and beyond with heavy demands on legislative time. The constitutional reform passages were similar though not identical in the UK and the Scottish versions. In the former they appeared in a chapter entitled 'We Will Clean Up Politics' – an obvious swipe at Major's administration. With equal devotion to what would catch the eye of its readers, the Scottish version of the same chapter was headed 'We Will Trust the People – A Parliament for Scotland'.[2]

The overall emphasis in both versions was on restoring democracy, decentralisation and asserting the rights of citizens. The order of headings in the UK version was as follows:

- A modern House of Lords
- An effective House of Commons
- Open government
- Devolution: strengthening the Union
- Good local government
- London
- The regions of England
- Real rights for citizens
- Northern Ireland.

It is fair to suppose that this chapter owed much to the undoubted drafting skills of the then shadow Lord Chancellor, Lord Irvine of Lairg, who was subsequently put in charge of clearing its implementation within the new government.

At this point we were considering how to support the collective consideration of a whole programme of constitutional reform. The obvious options were:

1. a 1970s-style centralised Cabinet Office Constitution Unit to own and manage the whole thing while merely consulting the policy subject departments;

2. a proactive secretariat, modelled on the Cabinet Office secretariat that deals with European business, with a strong policy-coordinating remit and a good deal of clout but with lead responsibility and ownership remaining firmly with the policy subject departments;

3. a more reactive style of secretariat based on the Economic & Domestic model, simply servicing Cabinet committees with a limited role in implementation, leaving a good deal of the initiative to policy subject departments.

Option 1 would have been a radical departure from the Cabinet Office's normal role of coordinating policy-making towards directing it. It gradually emerged that New Labour was tending towards option 2 but this was not a foregone conclusion and so the Constitution Secretariat had to be appointed behind closed doors, ready to be wheeled out immediately after the election.

I was therefore given a confidential list of high flyers nominated by their permanent secretaries as suitable candidates from which to choose six or seven in a mix of grades and experience to staff the new secretariat. I interviewed them alone and swore the successful candidates to secrecy even from their immediate superiors so as not to be overanticipating the outcome of the election. This meant that we all had to be replaced in our existing jobs the morning after the results came through. My troops came from a range of departments: the Home Office, the Treasury, the Scottish Office, Environment, Education and the Cabinet Office, and were shortly joined by a couple of able lawyers selected by the Treasury Solicitor.

Before they arrived, we had drawn up a plan for handling the whole programme including the possibility of being asked to produce an overarching White Paper. This was considered by an inter-departmental working group of officials representing each department likely to be affected. Attention inevitably focused on devolution and there was much predictable apprehension on the part of the more centralist-minded departments about the proposals as set out in the manifesto. Those who dealt frequently with European business were particularly concerned about compatibility with UK obligations under the various EU treaties and directives. They were also interested in comparisons with the position of devolved legislatures in other member states. Some of this was echoed both individually and collectively when we unveiled the plans to permanent secretaries.

This exercise revealed that some departments – notably the Home Office and the Scottish Office – had made substantial preparations for the activity which a new government, elected on these manifesto pledges, would generate. The others, including the Welsh Office, had studied the manifestos for themselves and had earmarked staff resources on a contingency basis but to nothing like the same extent. Drawing on its experiences in the 1979 and 1992 elections, *Scotland's Parliament, Scotland's Right* and its separate discussions with the Labour opposition in Scotland, the Scottish Office was ready with detailed position papers setting out options on all the issues which seemed likely to arise within government and when the legislation went through Parliament. It was able to put staff on to this even before the election was called by assembling a shadow team of talented individuals in key posts at the centre, some of whom were already engaged in supporting the Secretary of State, Michael Forsyth, in his efforts to defend the status quo. Their familiarity with the subject matter – albeit from the politically opposite point of view – served well when Donald Dewar arrived as Secretary of State, enabling him to make an immediate start on implementing his pledges. They worked for ministers from both parties with equal loyalty and zeal, as the Civil Service Code requires them to do.

Glad confident morning: from election to referendum

On the day after the May 1997 election we were summoned to meet Sir Robin Butler and the newly appointed Lord Chancellor, Lord Irvine. They confirmed that the Constitution Secretariat should spring into action immediately and the staff came together for the first time later that same day. The Prime Minister and Irvine also accepted our proposals for the initial configuration of Cabinet committees, details of which were, of course, published as they were set up.[3] These committees were:

- Ministerial Committee on Constitutional Reform Policy
- Ministerial Committee on Devolution to Scotland, Wales and the English Regions
- Ministerial Committee on Incorporation of the European Convention on Human Rights
- Ministerial Committee on Freedom of Information
- Ministerial Committee on House of Lords Reform.

The Lord Chancellor chaired all these committees with the exception of Constitutional Reform Policy, which was chaired by the Prime Minister. One might expect that this committee would have performed the overarching function across the whole programme but it met only twice between 1997 and 1998 and then only to deal with specific points requiring resolution at that level.

In time-honoured fashion, a number of official committees were also set up to prepare the ground for ministers. These provided extensive networks which helped to clarify technical arguments, narrow down points of difference and concentrate ministers' time on what they alone could decide. Policy responsibility rested with lead departments so they produced the papers for discussion and then drafted White Papers leading to instructions for the draftsmen of the Bills. The secretariat worked alongside them, probing, prompting, supporting, brokering deals with other interested departments and securing what consistency was seen as necessary across the programme as a whole. Our position was described by one Cabinet Secretary as 'a ringside seat for which people would pay money'! Despite this being a much more proactive role than the usual Cabinet Office coordination, it was largely welcomed by the departmental participants. We kept them in the picture, presented the arguments fairly and avoided charges of bias or of having an agenda of our own. There were murmurings later on from some departments which had let the full implications of the programme pass them by at the time, that the Scots in particular had got away with murder but even they recognised that they had only themselves to blame.

The process was under way within a week of the May 1997 election so that the Devolution Referendums Bill would be ready for introduction immediately following the Queen's Speech the week after that. The Bill was a short enabling measure prepared by the draftsmen on a contingency basis with a draft money resolution to authorise the expenditure. The manifesto commitment to hold the referendums 'not later than the autumn' – whenever that might be in Scotland or Wales – meant that the Bill had to be passed and White Papers produced before the summer recess at the end of July.

It was clear to us even as early as that first weekend that ministers were strongly influenced in their approach by the following guiding principles:

- Deliver on John Smith's legacy – a party imperative;
- Avoid the mistakes of the 1970s – when the centralist Cabinet Office Constitution Unit failed through lack of ownership on the part of the affected policy departments;
- Keep adequate control of the process – a New Labour watchword;

- Handle the business within the context of the Blair project – i.e. the modernisation and empowerment elements of the New Labour agenda;
- Get ahead with it quickly.

The last point probably explains a good deal of what happened. Ministers rightly suspected that there was little electoral mileage in constitutional reform as such and so they were anxious to discharge their manifesto commitments, especially the Scottish and Welsh referendums, before their (at that time) unbelievable luck at the polls ran out. Moreover, on the face of it, these were all measures which could credibly (if in some cases mistakenly) be assumed to be deliverable within the Chancellor of the Exchequer's strict policy of absorption of policy initiatives within the frozen existing budgets of those doing the initiating. That meant that they could be introduced and legislated upon fairly quickly and kept well clear of the public expenditure debate, thereby diminishing the scope for inter-departmental controversy. Speed and thrift also help to explain the bold decision to give lead responsibility to those departments whose policy areas and budgets were principally affected rather than attempt to impose the detail of the reform measures from the centre.

The next eleven weeks were both exhausting and exhilarating, with coordinating the preparation of papers, briefing the chairman – often by 8 a.m. – and hitting our target of circulating the minutes of meetings within twenty-four hours. Securing collective agreement on the devolution White Papers in that timescale presented a formidable challenge. Admittedly some things went through virtually on the nod, reflecting the limited extent of ministerial interest:

- retention of the staff in the Scottish Executive and Welsh National Assembly in a unified civil service by contrast with the separate Northern Ireland civil service; this was seen as a means of preserving professional standards and integrity and as part of the glue of the union;
- retention of the post of Secretary of State for Scotland, which was intended as a temporary measure to ease the transitional process rather than as a permanent device to safeguard UK interests in Scotland and vice versa;
- the additional member system for proportional representation in elections to the Scottish Parliament and Welsh Assembly, as recommended by the Scottish constitutional convention;
- adoption of administrative concordats to regulate dealings between the

Scottish and Welsh departments and their UK or English opposite numbers in London rather than have a formal code of conduct enshrined in statute law.

At the same time, a raft of potentially contentious issues had to be brokered at some speed among ministers and the outcomes written into the draft White Papers in appropriate terms. These included:

- defining the devolved powers in the White Papers and draft Bills by reference to a reserved list of areas other than which everything was to be regarded as devolved, according to the precedent of the Government of Ireland Act 1920, instead of the open-ended approach adopted in the 1978 legislation, which embodied lists of devolved areas;
- rejecting the Scottish Constitutional Convention's recommendation that the devolution legislation should be entrenched so that no subsequent parliament could repeal it;
- addressing the question of Scottish and Welsh members of Parliament remaining eligible to vote on issues affecting England which had been devolved to the Scottish Parliament or Welsh Assembly so far as their own constituents were concerned;
- deciding how disputes about what was devolved or reserved were to be resolved;
- retaining the population-related formula for calculating incremental changes to the Scottish and Welsh budgets on the basis of changes in comparable programmes in England;
- deciding how the tax-varying powers of the Scottish Parliament should be applied;
- prescribing the role of the devolved administrations in relation to the European Union;
- prescribing the relationship between the devolved administrations and the Queen as head of state;
- agreeing rules and procedures for the conduct of the referendums;
- settling a host of detailed but sensitive subject issues such as abortion law, higher education student funding, the operations of Great Britain bodies like the Forestry Commission and cross-border bodies like the rivers Tweed and Solway estuarial fisheries boards.

Meanwhile, the rest of the constitutional reform programme was taking off.

Mainstream Cabinet committees considered draft consultative documents prior to legislation on London government and regional development agencies to promote economic expansion in England. We had also started work on incorporation of the ECHR and freedom of information. These efforts were not quite so frantic as for devolution but there was heavy pounding throughout the autumn on issues which needed to be resolved collectively. Work on House of Lords reform started soon after that.

In what I gather is still a unique phenomenon for this government, given Tony Blair's alleged preference for a sofa-and-coffee-table style of transacting business, the classic Cabinet committee system proved fit for purpose and passed the acid test that 'what matters is what works'. That it did work is largely due to our ability to come up to speed rapidly and deliver against the principles set out above. It owed much also to its proving an acceptable way of working to the Lord Chancellor, whose commanding position at that time in relation to the Prime Minister and his colleagues, including those who have survived as lasting big hitters, was crucial. The system even enabled ministers to neutralise their erstwhile allies among the Liberal Democrats by creating a joint consultative committee between the leaderships of the two parties. This was intended to bring the third party in from the cold and give them a privileged opportunity for dialogue with senior ministers on matters where they held a common view. These turned out to be precious few apart from constitutional reform and so the committee devoted most of its time to monitoring and maintaining progress on the various elements without ever being allowed to stray into articulating an overriding vision for the programme as a whole, though the Liberal Democrats were keen that it should. This committee was finally wound up at the 2005 general election.

Revelation of the details of these Cabinet committees' deliberations must presumably await the publication of the minutes and papers from 2027 onwards. Some general observations may, however, be made. The Lord Chancellor's chairmanship was characteristically brisk but at no time bullying. If he appeared to be giving a minister a hard time, it was to enable him or her to make the case as convincingly as its weight would bear and equal rigour was applied to the opposite view. He and the secretariat enjoyed great mutual rapport and we had access to him whenever we needed it.

Understandings had clearly been reached outside committee with the big beasts of the government such as the Deputy Prime Minister, the Chancellor of the Exchequer, the Foreign Secretary and the Secretary of State for Education and Employment; most other ministers were much too preoccupied with mastering their own portfolios. This influenced the conclusions but did not stifle discussion. The Prime Minister kept himself well informed of developments on a weekly basis with the secretariats and, behind the scenes, through his main political adviser on constitutional issues, Pat McFadden. McFadden, whom he had acquired from the Scottish Secretary, Donald Dewar, kept a cool head in brokering issues which had given rise to sudden controversy. We worked harmoniously with him and found him an invaluable source of help and ideas.

High noon: from manifesto to implementation

From the summer of 1997 the process quickly broadened out from the hothouse of Cabinet committee meetings with Green and White Papers entering the public demesne as the basis for widespread consultation with backbenchers, interest groups and (in the cases of devolution to Scotland, Wales and London and, later, of elected mayors) the electorate.[4] Legislation quickly followed, absorbing an enormous amount of parliamentary time including a good deal of debate on the floor of both Houses. This permitted much more detailed scrutiny and refinement of the schemes than had been possible in the initial rush. Concurrent preparations for implementation required further consultation with future key players and affected parties. This public exposure phase chimed well with the government's rhetoric about greater openness and citizen participation. It may also have produced a readier acceptance of constitutional change and raised greater expectations of more to come. Enhanced civic engagement was probably a factor in the success of the measures since it made them more transparent to the people affected and thereby more acceptable. That in turn encouraged the new institutions to conduct their affairs more openly.

Nor did any of this prevent the target timetables being achieved. For example, within two years of the May 1997 election, the Scottish Parliament and National Assembly of Wales were ready to be elected and commence business. To give a flavour for the various phases of the operation it is useful to consider some of the main components.

Implementation: devolution to Scotland

Scottish devolution was undoubtedly the flagship of the constitutional reform programme and the centrepiece of the legacy of John Smith. Failure to deliver in essence what the Scottish Constitutional Convention had recommended would have been regarded as a gross betrayal and extremely damaging to the new government. That did not inhibit the scrutiny to which most of the proposals in the White Paper on Scotland's Parliament were subjected. They were certainly not nodded through just because they emanated from the Convention. The acid test, especially on matters of powers or the resolution of disputes was whether they would be sufficiently robust to withstand the doomsday scenario of a Conservative government in London facing down a Scottish National Party administration in Edinburgh − a contingency that so far appears to be remote.

In the event, the tight manifesto target date for the referendum, preceded by a White Paper, was met. It was held on 11 September 1997 despite some public pressure to postpone it following the death of the Princess of Wales on 31 August. The result was a decisive majority in favour of the principle of a Scottish Parliament and a smaller, but nevertheless comfortable, majority in favour of the tax-varying power. Once the referendum was in the bag, the policy was a fait accompli and there was a distinct change of gear. There was less collective activity, at least in ministerial meetings as distinct from correspondence, and so the process assumed a lower profile and became preoccupied with detailed but necessary legal arguments. The Ministerial Committee on Devolution's diet consisted mainly of legislative competence and other points referred to it for decision in the course of preparing instructions to the draftsman of what became the Scotland Bill. Similar proceedings took place when the Bill was going through Parliament and ministers had to respond quickly and with a collectively agreed line to amendments as they were tabled.

By comparison with its predecessor twenty years before, the Scotland Bill had a reasonably easy parliamentary passage, at least in the Commons, where Donald Dewar, as Secretary of State, frequently participated personally and with characteristic authority. It took longer to get through the House of Lords, where the minister of state at the Scottish Office, Lord Sewell, performed creditably.[5] Nevertheless the Scotland Bill was passed in time for the first elections to be held in May 1999 and the new legislature became fully operational from 1 July of that year.

By that time Whitehall departments were waking up to the implications of devolved administrations for the future conduct of business. The conundrum of fellow members of a unified civil service working for a different set of political masters in a coalition embracing one of the UK opposition parties on comparable but devolved subjects took some time to assimilate. On the basis of guidance produced by the Constitution Secretariat, a series of concordats between individual departments and their opposite numbers in Scotland and Wales were hammered out with varying degrees of difficulty over a period of about eighteen months. In December 2001 these arrangements were incorporated in a memorandum of understanding published by the Cabinet Office.[6]

Because ministers from the devolved administrations could not take part in UK Cabinet committees, the logical next step was a forum in which respective ministers could exchange information and ideas and present a united front or else devise a modus vivendi for adopting different approaches. A joint consultative committee chaired by the Prime Minister including the First Ministers from Scotland, Wales and Northern Ireland was constituted, mainly as an act of statesmanship but with the potential for serving as a court of appeal if the going got rough. So far it has not featured prominently in that guise and it currently lies disused. Equivalent bodies for subject areas lasted a bit longer. The whole liaison system was policed at first by the Constitution Secretariat in a quasi-executive role but the amount of business proved insufficient to justify a separate unit so its coordination responsibility reverted to the Economic and Domestic Secretariat after the 2001 general election. Liaison with the devolved administrations passed elsewhere in the Cabinet Office while the Deputy Prime Minister was based there and ended up with the Lord Chancellor's Department and, now, with the Department for Constitutional Affairs.

From all this the devolved administrations have developed a much more solid and accepted position than their predecessors, the territorial departments. Cynics might suggest that, from the vantage point of Westminster or Whitehall, they are easier to ignore if they go their separate ways. But there have been embarrassments and tensions over, for example, tuition fees and care for the elderly in Scotland and the abolition of prescription charges in Wales.

Implementation, of course did not stop with the break from London. The Scottish Office had the double task of creating a Parliament from scratch at the same time as converting itself from a department of state into a mini-government as the Scottish Executive. To do this it set up a consultative steering group under Henry McLeish, a minister of state at the Scottish Office and later, First Minister. This and its finance sub-group pulled in all the talents from the spheres of politics and governance to devise and recommend procedures, institutions and processes of accountability for the new legislature to adopt. In so doing they drew widely upon the same kind of cross-section of Scottish society and opinion – churches, trade unions, the business community, local authorities, voluntary sector, minority representatives and public consultation – as did the Scottish Constitutional Convention in the early 1990s.

The Scottish Office had the immediate tasks of finding a temporary home for the Parliament, recruiting its initial staff and planning for its long-term accommodation and other needs. I say nothing here about the saga over the cost of the new Parliament building because it simply did not feature on our radar screen in Whitehall. Contrary to the conspiracy theories which still circulate in Edinburgh, there was no diktat from Downing Street. The matter was entirely one for Dewar to decide as he saw fit provided he found the money from within his existing budget, which is precisely what happened.

There are, however, rocks not far below the surface of the settlement:

- the effects of any economic downturn;
- the future of the budget-setting formula;
- the impact of EU enlargement;
- the future of the unified civil service;
- growing resentment at the frequent use of legislative consent motions;
- aspirations of the Scottish Executive to extend its influence on reserved matters such as immigration policy and international relations;
- cracks in the coalition as revealed at the 2006 Dunfermline by-election (where the Liberal Democrat Scottish Transport Minister's proposals to increase tolls on the Forth road bridge were disowned by the Chancellor of the Exchequer);
- the coincidental timing of the May 2007 Scottish Parliamentary election with the tercentenary of the Union.

Each of these factors impinges on the likelihood of maintaining the relative harmony between London and Edinburgh which has prevailed since 1999. Their several impacts in Scotland and on its potential viability as an independent country point in different directions but the cumulative effect could well be to fuel Scottish separatism.

Implementation: devolution to Wales

It was quickly apparent in the Ministerial Committee on Devolution that the Welsh scheme in the manifesto had not had the benefit of detailed debate and wider consensus-building which the Scottish Constitutional Convention had provided. Realising the much weaker position in which the Secretary of State for Wales thus found himself, the Lord Chancellor as architect of the whole programme took particular care to assist him in his task and set aside special meeting days to concentrate on the Welsh White Paper. Nor had the Welsh Office been able to build up its staff capability to the same extent as the Scots and so there was much more mentoring on the part of the Constitution Secretariat to enable a respectable White Paper to be produced in time.

The Welsh referendum was a narrow squeak for the government and there were claims of confusion in the counting of ballot papers. Nevertheless the Government of Wales Bill went ahead, taking nearly as long to get through the House of Commons as the Scotland Act but much less time in the Lords. The government had tried to speed things up by splitting the committee stage in the Commons between a Committee of the Whole House (CWH) and a standing committee. They eventually reached a compromise with the opposition which treated the Bill as of first-class constitutional importance but confined its committee stage to seven days. Thereafter events followed the Scottish pattern: there were negotiations with Whitehall and Westminster and the preparation of the way for the election of the first Welsh Assembly.

Implementation: London

The 1997 commitment to restore democracy to London by holding a referendum on a Greater London Authority (GLA) and a directly elected mayor was clearly seen as being a constitutional issue rather than a local government one. Nevertheless, for reasons of speed and convenience, internal consideration of the legislation both for the referendum and for the GLA itself was remitted to a London sub-committee reporting jointly to the Ministerial Committee on Devolution and to the Ministerial Committee on Local and Regional Government. The commitment was duly delivered of a positive outcome largely obscured by the government's embarrassment over the election of Ken Livingstone as mayor. But it can – and did – take credit for returning local democracy to the people of London. A by-product, with the potential to transform the local government scene across England, as envisaged in the 1997 manifesto, was the use of plebiscites in thirty cities in 2002 to determine whether they wanted to have elected mayors.

Fuelled by the high profile and influence of the mayor, not least in the campaign to bring the 2012 Olympic Games to London, there has been renewed speculation about further devolution. The 2005 New Labour manifesto contained an unexpected commitment to a review of the powers of the GLA, which was launched in November 2005. Livingstone had already published proposals for extra powers on training, waste disposal and capital investment in housing. The Office of the Deputy Prime Minister's consultation paper largely followed the mayor's agenda.

Implementation: electoral reform

Electoral reform first received collective attention in the summer of 1997 in the joint consultative committee with the Liberal Democrats. One tangible and predictable outcome was fulfilment of the pledge to set up what became the Jenkins Commission on Electoral Reform. Its completed but unimplemented report allowed the government to make a much watered-down commitment in the 2001 manifesto to 'assess whether changes might be made to the electoral system for the House of Commons' subject to a referendum.[7] It is ironic that the proportional representation bandwagon has stopped in its tracks at the gates of the Palace of Westminster after rolling steadily forwards for the European Parliament and the devolved legislatures. New Labour's vested interest in the first-past-the-post system which delivered its large majorities may help to explain its ambivalence towards constitutional reform. The issue of proportional representation remains a live one for local government and especially for the Liberal Democrats, who have used their powerful influence in the Scottish coalition to achieve the introduction of the single transferable vote system for local elections there.

Nevertheless the government's door remained open to measures of electoral reform, which would counter the prevailing cynicism about voting and its declining significance in public respect for the political process. Hence a raft of legislation in this general area has gone through: the Recognition of Political Parties Act 1998, which also set up the Electoral Commission; the European Parliament Elections Act 1999, changing the voting system to the regional list there; and the Representation of the People Act 2000, experimenting in new voting methods to make voting easier, which were extended to European Parliament and local government elections in 2004. After the 2005 general election, the government passed an Electoral Administration Act to reform electoral registration, tackle electoral fraud and improve regulation of donations to political parties.

Implementation: a modern House of Lords

Of all the constitutional questions it was clear from the start that this would be much the most difficult to resolve, always accompanied by the seductive temptation, embraced by so many other administrations since 1910, to leave well alone. In fairness to the government, perhaps the 1997 manifesto was, in retrospect, too specific in looking beyond the removal of the hereditary peers to what a reformed chamber might look like. Certainly there was no lack of energy on the part of the Lord Chancellor, fertile with his own ideas of what should be attempted. He persuaded the Prime Minister to let him and Lord Richard, Leader of the Lords, make a start in committee in the autumn of 1997. In the absence of a policy department which would accept the subject, the Constitution Secretariat prepared a good deal of the research material for the committee and took the lead. A wide cross-section of opinion was canvassed. This, however, is a field where the deeper you plough the more convincing are the arguments for doing nothing – certainly nothing which would upset the sensitivities of the elected House of Commons or the status of existing life peers. That of course is the net result so far despite the efforts of successive bodies to which the government has batted the issue.

The only significant change has been the House of Lords Act 1999, which removed most but not all of the hereditary peers. The consequence of tackling that long-standing issue, however, has been to enhance the legitimacy of the Upper House sufficiently to encourage them to make increasing, but not full, use of the powers they already have, to the frequent annoyance of the government. In its first eight years, the Blair government never lost a single vote in the House of Commons. In the Lords, by contrast, they were defeated on 353 occasions. In the 2004/5 session, more than half the divisions resulted in a government defeat.

In its 2001 manifesto New Labour took to the high ground of maintaining the traditional primacy of the Commons and seeking to implement the report of the Wakeham Royal Commission as effectively as possible. There followed another White Paper in 2001. That, in turn, was followed by a Green Paper in 2003 after a Gilbertian fall-about over votes on options from a joint committee of both Houses in the 2002/3 session. For a time it seemed as though progress might prove impossible because the government's own MPs were divided over the merits of an appointed versus an elected House. The renewed pledges in the 2005 manifesto were echoed in the subsequent Queen's Speech and a new parliamentary joint committee was set up in May 2006 to consider the practicality of codifying the conventions governing the Lords' relationship with the Commons. The composition of the Upper House was to be the subject of separate inter-party discussions and further free votes on the chamber's composition were to follow in 2007.

Implementation: an effective House of Commons

When it came to modernisation of the Commons, the government had the alibi that it was for the House to undertake a rolling programme of work to renew itself. Little emerged before Robin Cook became Leader of the House in 2001 but his legacy in reordering the parliamentary timetable and introducing separate but concurrent debates in the adjacent Westminster Hall chamber is generally regarded as having improved the effectiveness of the place. Cynics may say that the government's willingness to accept such an apparently radical package demonstrated the irrelevance of Parliament. If so, they have had their point proved since the 2005 election. The only legislative contribution to reform of the House of Commons has been to allow clergymen (and members of the Irish Parliament) to sit as MPs.

More interesting and significant, however, is the way in which the sheer volume and pace of the government's constitutional reform programme have generated lasting procedural changes in the House of Commons. In order to accommodate the flow of constitutional Bills from 1997/8 onwards, even with a large majority, the government's business managers had to challenge the convention that Bills 'of first class constitutional importance' must have their committee stage taken entirely by a CWH. This absorbs prime time on the floor of the House and leads to a second reading level of debate on the main clauses of principle leaving much of the detail not discussed or scrutinised at all. As already noted, CWH procedure was accepted for the Government of Wales Bill (after fierce exchanges with the opposition), the Scotland Bill (with an agreed timetable in a programme motion), the Northern Ireland Bill 1998, the Human Rights Bill in the same year, the House of Lords Bill 1999 and the Constitutional Reform Bill 2005.

As an alternative, the government tried to gain acceptance for splitting constitutional Bills at their committee stage, taking the main clauses of principle on the floor and the rest in standing committee upstairs. This approach started with the Greater London Authority Bill 1998 followed by the Political Parties, Elections and Referendums Bill 2000 and the Regional Assemblies (Preparations) Bill 2003. It allows for more hours at committee stage and more amendments to be debated hence greater scrutiny albeit by a smaller and less wide-ranging group of MPs. A related development has been the increased number of specialist committees which have contributed their expert scrutiny to the general scrutiny of constitutional Bills. Most important of these since 2001 has been the Joint Committee on Human Rights. This has been a powerful addition and one of the few ways in which Parliament has been strengthened during this period.

There have been other by-products of the constitutional reform programme's own progress which have improved the effectiveness of the House of Commons. Building political consensus has been used as part of the preparation for some of the big constitutional changes introduced. New Labour's participation in the Scottish Constitutional Convention, cross-party talks in Northern Ireland and with the Liberal Democrats and joint parliamentary committees on Lords reform are obvious examples.

Harnessing expertise not available to the House itself has also been extensively used for constitutional reform, notably the Jenkins Commission on electoral systems, the Wakeham Commission on House of Lords reform and the Richard Commission on the government of Wales. These were each in themselves a useful vehicle for widespread consultation on their subjects and engaging the public was a recurrent theme. The rapid development of pre-legislative scrutiny has been a particularly prominent feature. Publication of draft Bills as the basis for public consultation to shape legislative proposals at a formative stage had been repeatedly commended by the Commons Modernisation Select Committee. The Lords Constitution Committee has also recommended that draft Bills should become the norm rather than the exception with committees empowered to take evidence from interested and informed parties.[8] The government has acted positively in response to these recommendations in publishing more draft Bills. The referendums, of course, constituted the widest consultation of all.

Implementation: incorporation of the ECHR into domestic UK law

To the Lord Chancellor personally and others such as Lord Lester QC who had long campaigned for incorporation of the ECHR into domestic law, this was the real jewel in the crown of the programme. A draft White Paper was rapidly prepared in the summer of 1997 between the Lord Chancellor's Department (LCD) and the Home Office. This went through the relevant Cabinet committee with enviable speed to secure an early place in the first session's legislative timetable. The government chose a model fitted to the UK's situation by bringing access to the enforcement of human rights closer to the people in a way that ostensibly did nothing to disturb the separation of powers or the supremacy of Parliament. So, if the courts found that a law or its interpretation breached the convention, they could not strike down the offending provision but should recommend its amendment to Parliament in terms that would in practice brook no delay. In Scotland such a judgment on an enactment by the Scottish Parliament or on an action by the Executive would automatically render it invalid as being beyond the powers vested in the Parliament by the Scotland Act 1998.

The Human Rights Bill was deliberately first introduced in the House of Lords with its judicial capacity in mind and the Lord Chancellor – despite other pressures – took a leading part at all stages. It reached the statute book by the close of the 1997/8 session. At the same time it has to be said that this was the sleeping giant of the constitutional reform programme in that few beyond the cognoscenti fully appreciated its potential impact. Incorporation profoundly affected the business within and well beyond the law courts. It has proved an inconvenient and expensive rod for the government's own back, although to perhaps a lesser extent than might have been expected. Many predicted that it would rapidly become embedded in the national culture. Certainly, human rights considerations understandably now pervade the conduct of all sorts of relationships and transactions, generating activity for lawyers and the laity in pursuing disputes or proofing proposals against them. Ministers have thus found themselves on a gibbet of their own devising in such areas as asylum seekers, prisoners' anti-social behaviour, anti-terrorism legislation, speed cameras and, in Scotland, policy on youth crime. In fairness, however, the record shows that many of the key decisions which have constrained the government did not emanate from the domestic courts but from Strasbourg, where the UK remains bound by its international obligations to uphold the convention irrespective of whether there is a domestic Human Rights Act or not.

The widespread impact was foreseen by the legal profession, which arranged an extensive programme of awareness seminars and other education about what it would mean for various client groups. The Constitution Secretariat presided over inter-departmental moots to draw up procedures for examining existing legislation and judgements in order to alert departments to their implications and also to proof future legislative and administrative action against challenge on human rights grounds. The government followed this up during 1998 and 1999 with a very intensive training programme for judges, magistrates and government lawyers. Implementation began first in Northern Ireland from 1998 with the establishment of a Human Rights Commission as a result of the Good Friday Agreement between the parties there.

For their part, the courts exercised their power to reinterpret statutes to make them compliant with the Human Rights Act in just ten cases during the first five years of the Act's enforcement. Ten declarations of incompatibility have so far been upheld.[9] In response, the government has taken remedial action in every case by either repealing or amending the offending provision. Implementation of the Human Rights Act has engendered partnership and dialogue among all three branches of government. The parliamentary Joint Committee on Human Rights has played a central role, producing more than ninety reports after scrutiny of legislation for compliance with the convention. In 2007 the new Commission for Equality and Human Rights will be created under the Equality Act and the Scottish Parliament is also legislating for a new Human Rights Commissioner.

In July 2006 the government published the report of its review of the operation of the 1998 Act. This review was set up in response to growing criticism of the Act following such incidents as the murder of Naomi Bryant by Anthony Rice, to whose early release into the community some misapplication of the Human Rights Act may have contributed. Far from vindicating the growing army of critics, the report concluded that the Act's impact on UK law and policy-making has been largely beneficial. The government says it will now seek to ensure that the public are better informed about its benefits and that officials applying it should place appropriate emphasis on public safety.

Implementation: open government

Freedom of information (FoI) also presented awkward consequences for the government but the genie had already been let out of this particular bottle in John Major's non-statutory Code on Access to Official Information. The FoI Committee was in many ways the most interesting Cabinet committee to observe since there was genuine debate among its members, which increasingly reflected their practical experience as ministers. That was in contrast to some of the earlier committee meetings, which were more like the continuation of a conversation which the ministers must have had when they were still in opposition. There was criticism in many quarters when FoI did not appear in the first Queen's Speech – a conspicuous and suspect absentee from a star cast of constitutional reform pledges. The propitiatory White Paper did not appear until December 1997 and the retreat from that high point of liberty hall, which confounded even seasoned FoI campaigners, was long and painful. This retreat was reflected in the transfer of responsibility from the Cabinet Office to the Home Office in 1998. In 1999 there was pre-legislative consultation on a much more restricted draft Bill which did not become law until 2000 following concessions by the government both before its formal introduction and on its way through Parliament. Even then, full implementation was deferred until January 2005.

Again, as with ECHR, the ramifications of open government for all public bodies and particularly for individual casework as distinct from state secrets took time to percolate. The Scottish Parliament passed a slightly more liberal regime in 2002 which came into effect in January 2005. Take-up there has been heavy, particularly from political journalists. The internal upheaval and financial consequences for public bodies generally were probably underestimated. Nonetheless, for the first time Britain now has legislation endowing individual citizens with a statutorily enforceable right to information no longer regarded as something in the gift of government. That represents a significant and irreversible change in the way public administration is conducted in Britain.

Conclusions: tears before bedtime?

What conclusions, then, can we draw about how the Blair government achieved so much on constitutional reform and whether its programme added up to more than the sum of its parts?

Given the build-up before the 1997 election as I have described it, one could be forgiven for thinking that the new government might well want to implement or at least to present its entire constitutional agenda as a coherent whole and to set up machinery to achieve that. Contrary to that expectation, the government decided early on not to contemplate an overarching White Paper. The Lord Chancellor's explanation was: 'We have the equivalent of a White Paper in the election manifesto. We are well capable of dying in a surfeit of unnecessary paper, so why on earth should we want more?'

There was much comment and scepticism about the government's lack of an overall approach to this programme, both at the beginning and for some time after. Whitehall watchers as eminent and seasoned as Professors Peter Hennessy and Robert Hazell quickly drew attention to the absence of any all-embracing linkage of the whole rolling process. Media commentators were not far behind. The failure of the Prime Minister or any minister other than the Chancellor of the Exchequer and the arguably less political Lord Chancellor even to make a speech about the proposed programme was also the subject of early criticism.[10]

Various theories have been advanced as to why this might be. The most plausible is that most senior ministers either did not believe in constitutional reform, or they were not interested in it, or they did not understand it but if they had appreciated the programme in toto, they might well have recoiled from it. Certainly constitutional reform is about process rather than product and there are few votes in the former outwith the chattering classes.

The then Lord Chancellor was chief architect and publicist for the whole programme. His fullest defence of the position was in his Constitution Unit lecture in December 1998:

> I dispute any proposition that our programme lacks coherence. We made conscious choices about precisely which aspects of our constitution needed earliest attention, and on what basis. We are conscious of the way different elements of any constitutional settlement can impact on each other. Nonetheless many elements of the package are not inter-dependent. Nor is there any reason why they should be. Many of the measures are responses to particular problems which are the product of lengthy and complex prehistories of their own.
>
> Each strand of our constitutional reform programme is well justified on its own merits. The strands do not spring from a single master plan, however much that concept might appeal to purists. *Non sequitur* that they are incoherent. There are uniting themes and objectives – modernisation, decentralisation, openness,

accountability, the protection of fundamental human rights, the sharing of authority within a framework of law – all of which will fundamentally change the fabric of our political and administrative culture. In a sentence: our objective is to put in place an integrated programme of measures to decentralise power in the United Kingdom, and to enhance the rights of individuals within a more open society.[11]

That the government has delivered on the programme, with the understandable exceptions of the second stage of House of Lords reform and a referendum on proportional representation for the Commons, cannot seriously be denied. Its significance in changing the landscape whether intentionally or not is also acknowledged by most informed observers. This will therefore feature prominently, perhaps dominantly in what Tony Blair's administration is remembered for in fifty years' time. Peter Hennessy commented in 1998:

> There is no precedent since 1688 for such a concentrated and deliberate rebuilding of the constitutional architecture. It equals, perhaps even surpasses, the nineteenth- and early twentieth-century surges of franchise reform. Above all else it distinguishes this government from any of its predecessors. And yet its scope and substance lack the central position they deserve in the popular impression of this most image-conscious of administrations.[12]

At the same time as Hennessy was making this assessment, the *Economist*'s columnist Bagehot was raising the nagging question as to why this 'frenzy of constitutional reform' was not 'underpinned by some unifying political vision'. His explanation was that the government had made a virtue of ad-hoccery in order to get each element right in its own terms and disposed of quickly. Hennessy put it rather differently: 'Ministers and the political class generally are treating the government's constitutional reform programme as a restructuring of an *existing* political culture rather than seeing it as the cultural transformer it is almost certainly going to be.'[13]

Both views have merit. On balance, defending the absence of a White Paper was probably less of a distraction than writing one but you can never prove a negative. Most ministers realised very early on that devolution was something they had at least to be seen to have done but then that would be the end of it in crude electoral terms – as distinct from the verdict of history. They need have no regrets but can expect no early political credit. They displayed no abiding pride in their achievement as each brick fitted into the wall of the reformed constitution but rather exhibited a sense of frustration and some embarrassment at the consequences. There is the obvious paradox of a government open to charges of control-freakery while actually giving away so much power through devolution, through emphasis on individuals' rights and through FoI. I would put this down to pressure of time and other preoccupations rather than deliberate intent.

With events crowding in upon them, there have been so many more pressing things to think about, not least public service delivery, European issues, conflicts in Kosovo, Afghanistan and Iraq, as well as the war on terrorism. Is it any wonder that no one but successive Lord Chancellors in their peculiar eminence has been prepared to embrace and champion the programme? In fairness there has been a more conscious effort to integrate the handling and presentation of constitutional reform and to tidy up arrangements within government. By 2001 the range of activity had sufficiently broadened out to allow the separate Constitution Secretariat to be wound up and its residual functions to revert to the Economic and Domestic Secretariat. Following the 2001 reshuffle of ministers, there was an accretion within the LCD of the former constitutional responsibilities of the Home Office and the Cabinet Office. These included relations between church and state, the monarchy, the Channel Isles and Isle of Man, elections, referendums and party funding, FoI and data protection, human rights and Lords reform. Policy on the judicial system and responsibility for running the courts was already vested in the LCD.

Paradoxically, when the pilot was dropped with the departure of Lord Irvine from the government in June 2003, a symbolic step was taken in reconstituting his department as the Department of Constitutional Affairs. It includes a Constitution Directorate with a formal remit to pull the programme together and keep up the momentum of delivery with a sense of strategic direction. A significant achievement already has been the Constitutional Reform Act of 2005, establishing a Supreme Court and Judicial Appointments Commission as well as reforming (but not abolishing) the office of Lord Chancellor.

Yet even now, with most of the original programme in place, there is still no single point of ministerial responsibility. After the 2005 general election, the Cabinet committee dedicated to devolution policy was subsumed in the present Constitutional Affairs Committee, chaired by the Leader of the House of Commons, Jack Straw. It has sub-committees on electoral policy, parliamentary modernisation and FoI. Ministerial responsibility for English regional policy including London government now lies with the Department for Communities and Local Government. Any change to the settlements elsewhere would be for the Scotland, Wales or Northern Ireland Secretaries of State to lead for as long as their posts continue to exist. Perhaps the creative tension which has imbued the process from the start remains to assure us that the quiet constitutional revolution is not yet over.

Part IV

Meaning

6

Judicial reform: the emergence of the third branch of government

Kate Malleson

Forty years ago the judiciary in the UK was regarded as an essentially legal institution, occupying a 'place apart' from the political order. The requirements of the overriding principle of parliamentary sovereignty were interpreted as limiting the remit of the courts to a relatively narrow or legalistic application of the law as passed by Parliament. The concept of judicial independence was consequently understood in restricted terms as a notion which related to the individual judges in their role as adjudicators and not to the judiciary as a collective institution or branch of government. Today, these basic assumptions are in the process of long-term revision as the role of the judiciary undergoes a change more radical than at any time in recent history.

The roots of this development are both recent and longstanding. Its immediate origins are found in the first round of constitutional reforms instituted by the Labour government – the passage of the Human Rights Act 1998 and the devolution of political power to Scotland and Wales. An immediate and predictable effect of these changes was to give the courts a new role, firstly in determining a wider range of cases raising fundamental rights issues, and secondly in adjudicating on boundary disputes between central government and the regional powers. Both of these functions have more traditionally been associated with federal systems in which strong constitutional courts interpret and apply the terms of a written constitution and a Bill of Rights. But the roots of the expanding role of the judiciary go back much further than 1997 and are to be found in the growth of judicial power arising from the gradual development of judicial review, through which the legality, rationality and reasonableness of official action can be challenged in the courts.

It was the existence of this mature judicial review jurisdiction which allowed the provisions of the Human Rights Act to impact so quickly and significantly on such a wide range of official decision-making.

The combined effect of these recent and long-term developments is that where once power struggles within and between a wide range of governmental and public institutions would have been resolved in the political arena, it is now increasingly likely that they will come before the courts for the judges to determine. The courts have thus been drawn into politically sensitive areas previously beyond their scope, as a result of which the judiciary now plays a more central role in the British constitution. This new judicial role in mediating and adjudicating the boundaries of the constitution is still developing, but it is clear that the effect of this trend will be to reshape the relationship between the judiciary and the other branches of government.

The provisions of the Constitutional Reform Act 2005

It is against this background that the Constitutional Reform Act 2005 was passed, reforming the office of Lord Chancellor, establishing a new Supreme Court and restructuring the judicial appointments process. These provisions, constituting the second phase of the constitutional reforms introduced by the Labour administration, were intended to secure the independence of the judiciary by 'redrawing the relationship between the judiciary and the other branches of government' and putting it on a 'modern footing'. The immediate impetus for the changes was undoubtedly the first phase of reforms outlined above, which served to highlight the potential weaknesses in the institutional arrangements which governed the relationship between the judiciary and the other branches of government and to bring into relief the potential dangers of the close inter-connection between them.[1] But just as the origins of the expansion of judicial power lie in changes taking place over a much longer timescale, so concerns about the relationship between the judiciary and the other branches of government predate 1997. Where once there had been a general consensus that the Lord Chancellor's three roles as member of Cabinet, head of the judiciary and Speaker of the House of Lords enhanced the functioning of the political system and strengthened judicial independence, they increasingly came to be regarded as a potential for the abuse of executive power. In particular, the Lord Chancellor's responsibility for appointing judges became a source of growing concern as the role of senior judges in scrutinising government decision-making increased. Likewise, the presence of the top appellate court in Parliament had once been widely regarded as an effective means of drawing on the legal expertise of the top judges during the law-making process, so enhancing the quality of legislation. By the 1990s, however, many Law Lords themselves had come to regard the lack of separation between the two as problematic as the same senior judges who participated in passing the laws were increasingly asked to decide on the conformity of those Acts with basic human rights.

By the late 1990s, far fewer voices were heard in support of the argument that these overlaps between the branches of government were a source of its stability. Increasingly, the inter-connection was seen as endangering judicial independence, breaching basic constitutional principles and being out of step with the rest of Europe. By the start of the Labour government's second term in 2001, the long debate about these issues had slowly generated broad support across the political spectrum for a 'clearer and deeper' separation of the functions and powers of the judiciary from the other branches of government. The decision to embark upon extensive institutional reform was therefore not a surprise, but the provisions set out in the Constitutional Reform Act were unusual in a number of respects. First, they ran counter to the trend of recent political developments in that they represented a conscious shift of power away from the executive. Second, they were forward-looking, seeking to construct a new constitutional model which anticipated future needs rather than responding to an immediate perceived problem. In introducing the reforms the government made clear that there was no suggestion that the overlapping constitutional roles of the Lord Chancellor or the presence of the Law Lords in the House of Lords had, in practice, undermined judicial independence, but rather that the present system held inherent structural weaknesses which might give rise to such abuse in the future. The third surprising feature of the reforms is that they explicitly sought to promote constitutional principle above pragmatism.[2] While accepting that the previous arrangements had worked effectively, the changes were designed to restructure the relationship between the judiciary and the other branches of government so that it would conform more closely to the concept of the separation of powers. This elevation of principle above pragmatism would be surprising enough given the traditional value ascribed to 'what works' in the British constitution.[3] It is even more unusual in view of the fact that the particular principle of separation of powers is one which has been almost universally dismissed by constitutional scholars, judges and politicians as a 'rickety chariot for the conveyance of fallacious ideas'.[4]

In some respects, therefore, the provisions of the Constitutional Reform Act were novel, just as they were surprisingly radical in scope. Neither of these qualities was, however, stressed by the government when they were introduced. Instead, it sought to play down the far-reaching nature of the changes. While keen to talk up its radical reforming credentials in policy areas such as health and education, the Labour government, paradoxically, preferred to understate the impact of its far-reaching constitutional programme. By entitling the White Paper which introduced the Human Rights Act 'Bringing Rights Home', the government sought to suggest that the provisions did little more than give the British public rights in the UK courts which they already enjoyed in Strasbourg. Similarly, the rationale behind the Constitutional Reform Act was presented as clarifying the role of the judiciary so as to enhance transparency and public confidence in the working of the system rather than engineering substantive changes in the distribution of constitutional power. The rushed nature of the proposals, put together in the context of a Cabinet reshuffle in 2003, may partly explain the lack of any detailed exposition of the likely longer-term impact of the changes.[5] But it was also clear that the new Lord Chancellor, Lord Falconer, sought to build support for the changes by emphasising the limits to their scope and impact. The result was to give the impression that the changes concerned constitutional form rather than substance and that the former would have little effect on the latter. Yet the history of the creation and evolution of constitutions around the world tells us otherwise. While the provisions of the Constitutional Reform Act are indeed an attempt to bring the institutional relationships of the judiciary into line with its changing role and the growth of judicial power in the constitution, there is little doubt that their effect will be, in turn, to contribute further to the emergence of the judiciary as a distinct branch of government.

The office of Lord Chancellor

The problems which flowed from the government's failure to address the likely implications of the changes set out in the Constitutional Reform Act were most starkly illustrated in relation to the proposals for reform of the office of the Lord Chancellor. Of all the elements of the reforms, these were the least thought through, the most bitterly contested and ultimately some of the most far-reaching. Initially proposing the complete abolition of the office of Lord Chancellor and its reformulation into the post of Secretary of State for Constitutional Affairs, the first draft of the Bill was silent as to who would take over the role of head of the judiciary. The apparent neglect of such a fundamental question inevitably fuelled legitimate concern over the future of judicial independence under the new system and led to intense opposition to the proposals in Parliament. After long debate, it was accepted by the government that the title and the office of Lord Chancellor should remain, albeit in much reduced form, and that the Lord Chief Justice should become the head of the judiciary as President of the Courts of England and Wales.

The notion that transferring the role of head of the judiciary from a member of the executive to the judiciary should be seen as posing a threat to judicial independence is one which might reasonably perplex observers from outside the British system. This apparent contradiction makes sense only in the context of the unique role played by the office of Lord Chancellor. Its most striking feature, beyond the obvious one of its overlapping roles, is that it managed simultaneously to bring together and keep apart the branches of government. Variously described in terms of a link, a bridge or a form of constitutional 'hinge', a key element of the office was to facilitate under-standing of the position of the judges to the executive and vice versa. At the same time, the role was also often characterised as being that of a 'buffer', holding the executive at arm's length from the judges: 'armed with a long barge pole to keep off marauding craft from any quarter'.[6] This unusual push-me-pull-you quality meant that, by definition, the breaking-up of the multiple functions of the office of Lord Chancellor required the respective roles of linchpin and shock-absorber to be reallocated to different and clearly defined places. The test of the success of this element of the changes will be whether in the future both aspects of the Lord Chancellor's role could be equally effectively performed elsewhere.

During the passage of the legislation it was the Lord Chancellor's buffering function in defending the judiciary from attack that attracted the greatest attention. There were strong concerns about the loss of such a powerful voice representing judicial interests within government, not surprising given that, paradoxically, the removal of the office of Lord Chancellor was proposed at a time when relations between the two branches of government appeared to have reached an all-time low. In particular, the reaction of the then Home Secretary, David Blunkett, to Home Office defeats in the courts suggested a weakening respect within the executive for their role. Blunkett claimed in

2003, for example, that he was 'fed up with having to deal with a situation where Parliament debates issues and the judges overturn them'. It is not easy to tell whether these sorts of comment represented a long-term change of approach with implications for the success of the provisions of the Constitutional Reform Act. As the senior judges themselves recognise, a degree of tension between the executive and judiciary is not only inevitable but healthy and that it is when there is a state of 'perfect harmony' between the judges and executive that citizens need to worry.[7] The difficulty is distinguishing the short-term ebb and flow of the relationship from long-term trends, since it is clear that the degree to which disgruntled Home Secretaries criticise the judiciary when they receive unfavourable decisions is partly a reflection of different personalities. Both the Conservative Home Secretary, Michael Howard, in the 1980s and Blunkett were quicker to criticise and less measured in their response than most. Blunkett's successor, Charles Clarke, by contrast, was far more respectful and restrained in response to equally challenging defeats in the courts. Nevertheless, the general trend in recent years has inevitably been towards greater tension between the branches as the courts' scrutiny of executive action has increased in frequency and intensity. It is not in the least surprising that Lord Irvine of Lairg reported that when Lord Chancellor he had to argue in Cabinet in support of judicial independence on 'many, many occasions'.[8] Nor is the need for such support likely to diminish. The critical question, therefore, is whether under the new arrangements future Lord Chancellors will be in a position to provide this support for judicial independence.

Opponents of the Bill hoped that by salvaging the office of Lord Chancellor to a degree, albeit stripped of its judicial functions, the role of protector from within government could be preserved. This hope is both forlorn and misguided. While it is true that the office of Lord Chancellor will continue and that the government's concession in retaining the title of Lord Chancellor may have comforted traditionalists, it cannot alter the fact that the nature of the office has fundamentally changed. Future Lord Chancellors will not enjoy the constitutional status which previously attached to that office by virtue of its position at the junction of the three branches of state. Not only is the Lord Chancellor no longer head of the judiciary, she or he need not be a member of the House of Lords nor even a lawyer by background. Lord Chancellors have traditionally been drawn from an elite corps of very senior lawyers respected or at least accepted by both politicians and the judiciary. The future holders of the post, in contrast, are very likely to be professional politicians and may well be non-lawyers with limited affiliation to or understanding of the role of the judiciary.[9] But perhaps more significant in terms of the impact of the changing role on judicial independence is the changing nature of the office in terms of career hierarchy. In the past, the office of Lord Chancellor was the pinnacle of a distinguished legal and political career. This fact might have encouraged some to hang on to their place on the Woolsack longer than they should have done, but it had the advantage that the occupant had nothing to gain or lose in terms of promotion by standing up for the judiciary and suffering unpopularity among his ministerial colleagues or even with the Prime Minister. In future the position will be different. The Lord Chancellor may be a mid-career politician inevitably looking for promotion to one of the higher-ranking departments. Some occupants may be first rate, others may be more mediocre. Either way, it is unrealistic to expect that a passing minister, in post until the next Cabinet reshuffle, will be willing or able to defend the judiciary against attacks by more senior Cabinet colleagues in the same way as Lord Chancellors have done in the past.

One way in which the government sought to address this problem was to reduce the danger of threats from the executive by translating the political obligation on the executive to respect judicial independence into a legal one by including in the Act a provision that the Lord Chancellor and other ministers involved in the administration of justice must respect judicial independence.[10] While these provisions represent a welcome recognition of the importance of reaffirming the principle of judicial independence, they can only have very limited effect. They may serve as a useful reference point for judges to turn to at times of conflict in the hope of reminding politicians of their obligations, but the provisions cannot of themselves ensure that judges are protected from improper political pressure in their decision-making on a day-to-day basis. Nor can the provisions assist with the perennial problem of determining what constitutes a breach of judicial independence. Extreme actions such as bribery or seeking to influence the outcome of litigation will always clearly amount to a breach. But the disputed ground will continue to be, as it has always been in modern history, the extensive grey area of critical press briefings by the executive, attempts to reduce the jurisdiction of the courts and tightening the budget for the administration of justice. The question of what constitutes acceptable boundaries in these areas is ultimately determined by the political culture, and judicial independence will only be safe where there is a basic culture of mutual respect between the branches of government. What is clear is that dismantling the office of Lord Chancellor in its traditional form will mean that new methods must be established for mediating and negotiating the relationship between the two branches.

The concordat

A key element of this new relationship is set out in what has come to be known as the concordat.[11] This vital constitutional document establishing the future division of powers between the executive and judiciary has passed almost unnoticed outside legal circles. Between 2003 and 2005 the Lord Chancellor, Lord Falconer, and the then Lord Chief Justice, Lord Woolf, met regularly in private to determine how the many roles previously undertaken by the Lord Chancellor would be carried out.[12] Their final agreement was incorporated directly in the Constitutional Reform Bill with almost no public debate and during the passage of the Bill the provisions attracted very little attention. This neglect is surprising, given that the way in which judicial independence is promoted in practice will largely be determined by the terms of the concordat. Before 2005, it was generally unnecessary to articulate whether the Lord Chancellor was acting in his judicial or executive capacity when carrying out a particular function. It was not clear whether, for example, decisions concerning the deployment of judges was a task which the Lord Chancellor performed as the head of the judiciary or a member of the executive. Under the terms of the concordat, incorporated into the Constitutional Reform Act, it is now explicitly established that this role is for the Lord Chief Justice and therefore falls within the control of the judiciary. The implications of this sort of decision-making in terms of judicial independence are obvious. But perhaps the most interesting aspect of the concordat is that it was not simply a carve-up of power between the branches of government but was intended to create a form of partnership, in which the two branches of government share in the decision-making affecting the governance of the judiciary and the running of the courts through the allocation of decision-making powers 'with appropriate constraints and mutual consultation'.[13] Most decisions concerning the management of the courts and the judiciary are now formally ascribed to either the Lord Chief Justice or the Lord Chancellor, but in almost all cases there is a duty to consult with the other or obtain their agreement. For example, the overall number of judges is to be determined by the Lord Chancellor after consultation with the Lord Chief Justice because 'real and effective partnership between the

Government and the Judiciary is seen as paramount, particularly in this area'.[14] Similarly, the Lord Chief Justice has responsibility for judicial discipline but may only warn or reprimand a judge with the agreement of the Lord Chancellor.[15] What has been created is an institutional relationship which envisages two separate but equal branches working together to manage the courts and judiciary. How in practice this will work in the future remains to be seen. The concordat was drafted by two individuals who shared similar career backgrounds, values and priorities. Given the changing role of the office of Lord Chancellor, it will need to be robust enough to function effectively in the context of a Lord Chief Justice and a Lord Chancellor who stand clearly in different branches of the government. For this new 'separate but equal' system to work, substantial changes are therefore needed to the governance structure of the judiciary.

The governance of the judiciary

The transfer of such a wide range of roles into the sole or joint responsibility of the Lord Chief Justice requires a major change in the nature of the judicial support system. Whereas the Lord Chancellor has an entire government department at his disposal, until recently the Lord Chief Justice has had only minimal management and administrative back-up. The traditional approach to judicial governance has been one which is informal and light-touch. As the court system has expanded rapidly, the administrative roles undertaken by judges have grown in an ad hoc fashion. By and large, senior judges have simply absorbed additional management roles on top of their adjudicative functions on an ex-officio basis with very limited administrative support. Nor has there been a formal or permanent structure for collective decision-making within the judiciary. This situation arose not simply as a result of lack of resources or a failure by a greatly expanded judiciary to catch up with its governance needs. Rather the arrangements were partly a consequence of a particular vision of judicial independence, one which prioritises the need for judges to be free, not just of external interference, but of interference from other judges. It was for this reason that Lord Taylor when Lord Chief Justice objected to the introduction of performance appraisal in the judiciary on the grounds that it would 'clearly endanger the fundamental independence of individual judges, not only from the executive *but also from each other*' (emphasis added).[16] Thus although the judiciary is a rigidly hierarchical structure in terms of the authority of adjudicative decision-making, it has always pursued an ideal of a flat management structure in which the individual judges retain the greatest possible degree of autonomy over their working lives. While in practice it has been recognised that the Lord Chancellor and the Lord Chief Justice were required to make management decisions for the judiciary as a whole, this has been regarded as a task performed by them as 'first among equals'. For this reason, the judiciary has traditionally been highly sensitive to claims that any senior judge speaks for the judiciary collectively. Indeed, the notion that there is such a thing as 'the view of the judiciary' is widely rejected by many judges, who pride themselves on the fact that the only area that they agree upon is that of judicial pensions.

Yet despite this strong culture of individualism, the move to a more structured governance within the judiciary had begun before the Constitutional Reform Act. By necessity, the rapid expansion in size of the judiciary had led to the expansion in the number and formality of senior administrative positions with named and appointed posts, such as the vice-president of the Queen's Bench Division, Deputy Lord Chief Justice and the Head of Civil Justice. Similarly, the Judges' Council, which until relatively recently was a virtually moribund institution, has been revitalised in order to play a central role in the new governance structure. Because membership is drawn from all the different levels of the judiciary, including more recently members of the House of Lords/Supreme Court,[17] the council has the potential to play a vital role in representing the interests of the judiciary as a whole. Equally important is the newly formulated Judicial Executive Board, made up of seven senior judges which appears to be envisaged as a sort of judicial cabinet. It meets monthly and its core function is to enable the Lord Chief Justice to make policy and executive decisions through it. Administrative back-up will now be provided through a new body, the Judicial Office of England and Wales, which will have sixty staff including a communications office.

The relatively ad-hoc creation of this governance structure from a mixture of new and refurbished institutions raises a number of questions about both judicial accountability and judicial independence. What, for example, are the respective remits in terms of policy making of the Judges' Council and the Judicial Executive Board? How do their roles relate to each other? Where are the rules governing their powers and membership laid down? Who determines these? What is the process for selecting the representatives from each judicial level for the Judicial Council? Are they elected or appointed? If the latter, what are the criteria for selection and who chooses them? None of these vital issues are currently the subject of public debate. Clearly many questions remain about the new judicial governance structure, but what is certain is that the overall result of the changes will be a greater concentration of power in the hands of the senior judiciary. This outcome is probably inevitable and may also be desirable as a means of securing judicial independence, but it is not unproblematic in terms of both judicial independence and accountability. These alterations represent significant structural and ideological changes within the judiciary, which, it would appear, are being implemented with little input from outside the senior judiciary and the Department for Constitutional Affairs. The implications of this lack of transparency for a powerful institution consciously seeking to enhance public confidence are obvious.

The judicial appointments process

By contrast, lack of transparency and public debate is not a criticism which can be levelled against the Act's provisions on judicial appointments. The proposals for transferring the power to appoint judges from the Lord Chancellor to two new appointment commissions were the subject of full and detailed debate both before and during the legislative process, and the changes attracted broad support in principle. The details of the new process were, however, highly contentious. In particular, there was deep division over the question of what role, if any, the executive should play in the new system. Under the previous arrangements the power of appointment had, in practice, rested with the Lord Chancellor, who made his decision after consultation with the senior judges. For appointments to the Court of Appeal and the House of Lords, the decision formally rested with the Prime Minister on the advice of the Lord Chancellor, but the extent to which different Prime Ministers engaged with the process was hard to assess since the process of consultation between the Lord Chancellor and Prime Minister was always regarded as confidential.

It was in relation to these upper-rank judicial appointments that opinion was most sharply divided over the new provisions. Many members of the judiciary argued that it was essential to remove all executive involvement in selecting the senior judiciary since it was at this level that the pressure to manipulate would be greatest. Others argued that it was precisely in relation to these appointments, where the judges were engaged in high-level decisions with policy-making implications, that there should be some real link to the democratic process and that the Lord Chancellor should be more than just a rubber stamp. Initially the government supported the latter view in relation to the Supreme Court appointments and the Bill provided that the Supreme Court commission would nominate between two and five names for the Lord Chancellor to choose from, so ensuring a genuine degree of political input. In the end, however, the government conceded this point and both the Supreme Court commission and the Judicial Appointments Commission were given the ultimate decision-making power, being required to recommend one name which the Lord Chancellor could reject only in limited circumstances. The effect was to remove the danger of improper political interference from the system but it also removed the opportunity for democratic involvement in the selection of public decision-makers.

One way in which the democratic deficit caused by the removal of the executive from the appointment process might have been countered would have been to include the legislature in the process. Currently, Parliament plays no role in judicial appointments, though it has the ultimate responsibility for removing errant senior judges. This power relates solely to judges of the High Court and above, who can be dismissed by the monarch if both Houses of Parliament vote for their removal, though this is a power which has been exercised only once, in 1830, when an Irish judge was found to have embezzled court fees. In theory, there is no reason why Parliament should not be given the power to call judges before it as part of the appointments process. This would represent no more than an extension of the current and increasingly common practice of taking evidence from senior judges before select committees on a wide variety of matters relating to the law and the justice system. Yet Parliament itself has rejected this option.

The explanation for this rejection lies in a widely held view of US Senate confirmation hearings as invading the privacy of individual candidates and undermining judicial independence. Clearly the widespread objections to the hearings of Clarence Thomas and Robert Bork on these grounds have some basis. Moreover the highly partisan nature of the US judicial appointments process is such that the hearings can sometimes be merely a choreographed dance in which very little useful information is revealed. Yet the very particular context of the United States should not lead to a blanket rejection of some sort of legislative hearing. In a different political culture, it is quite possible that such hearings would provide a valuable means of injecting some democratic scrutiny into the process while allowing the wider public some sense of the people chosen to sit on their highest court. The Canadian Parliament decided to introduce nomination hearings for its Supreme Court judges in March 2006 as part of a reform designed to reduce party political influence, illustrating the growing awareness of the need to enhance democratic accountability while at the same time removing political patronage from the system. The debate in Canada before the change almost exactly mirrored that which took place in the UK. If the solution which the Canadians have adopted to the dilemma of balancing independence and accountability in judicial selection proves successful, we may well look back at the British decision to reject any parliamentary involvement as a missed opportunity.

The other effect of removing any substantive input from the executive in the judicial appointments process was to increase the significance of the membership of the commissions and in particular the role of the lay members. Their function is a vital one in balancing the interests of the legal and judicial members of the commissions and mitigating the danger of cloning, which inevitably arises when an appointment is made by those already doing the job. Since the need for greater diversity in the composition of the judiciary was a driving force behind the decision to establish the new system, the lay members' ability to challenge established approaches and develop innovative means of drawing high-quality candidates from beyond the traditional judicial backgrounds into the recruitment pool will be a key measure of the success of the commissions. In particular, the decision that the chair of the Judicial Appointments Commission would be a layperson was an important step in establishing the central role of the lay membership. The appointment of the highly respected former First Civil Service Commissioner, Baroness Prashar, as the first chair of the commission in 2006 is likely to have ensured that the new system will not be overly dominated by judicial and legal interests.

The Supreme Court

Whereas the provisions for the reform of the post of Lord Chancellor and the judicial appointments process involve an explicit redistribution of power, those for establishing the new Supreme Court, in theory, do not. The new court will exercise the same formal powers as the Appellate Committee of the House of Lords and it will take on the devolution powers of the Judicial Committee of the Privy Council. The first Supreme Court judges will be the existing Law Lords. On the face of it, therefore, the creation of the new Supreme Court is the least radical aspect of the constitutional reforms. In practice, however, the removal of the top court from the legislature and its reformation as an autonomous institution is likely to have a significant and long-term effect on its constitutional role. The current changes need to be understood in the light of the changing role of the UK judiciary discussed above and also of the development of a global community of increasingly powerful constitutional and supreme courts.

At a formal level, the most fundamental change to the powers of the top courts in the UK in recent history was the passage of the European Communities Act 1973, which gave the UK courts the power to declare an Act of Parliament invalid if incompatible with European legislation. This potentially dramatic revision of the principle of parliamentary sovereignty was highly controversial at the time. But in practice its effect has been limited and its occasional application by the courts has not shaken the constitutional foundations as critics feared. For supporters of a traditional conception of parliamentary sovereignty, the threat lies not in the growing role of the EU but closer to home with the increasing domination of Parliament by the executive and the knock-on effect this has had on the role of the judiciary. Since the 1980s, the election of strong governments both on the left and right with large majorities in Parliament has given rise to claims that the only effective opposition lies in the House of Lords and the courts. Fears that the concentration of power within the executive might threaten basic constitutional and political norms have led members of the senior judiciary to talk of a 'higher law' which would require them to strike down legislation that sought to undermine basic principles such as the rule of law. In 1994 the then Lord Chief Justice, Lord Woolf, made clear that if, for example, Parliament 'did the unthinkable' and removed the courts' power of judicial review he would consider it necessary to 'mak[e] clear that ultimately there are even limits on the supremacy of Parliament which it is the courts' inalienable responsibility to identify and uphold'.[18] However, having dipped a toe in these dangerous waters, the senior judiciary then drew back from the brink. Lord Steyn articulated a widely held view in his statement that

> the relationship between the judiciary and the legislature is simple and straightforward. Parliament asserts sovereign legislative power. The courts acknowledge the sovereignty of Parliament. And in countless decisions the courts have declared the unqualified supremacy of Parliament. *There are no*

exceptions ... the judiciary unreservedly respects the will of Parliament as expressed in statutes.[19]

But despite such assertions, it was never likely that the genie could be put back in the bottle and in the intervening years the underlying political conditions which gave rise to the debate on the proper limits of judicial power have not changed. Indeed, they are if anything more acute as the power of the executive in Parliament has continued to strengthen. Moreover, the passing of the Human Rights Act has significantly increased the likelihood that courts will be called upon to consider whether an Act of Parliament conflicts with a 'higher constitutional law', giving the judges the role of applying principles of constitutionality 'little different from those which exist in countries where the power of the legislature is expressly limited by a constitutional document'.[20] In 2004 the question of how far courts might go when faced with such a challenge to fundamental constitutional principles came close to being tested when the Government proposed legislation which would have removed the courts' jurisdiction in certain asylum and immigration appeal cases. Senior judges and academics suggested for the first time that the courts might be entitled to ignore an Act of Parliament if the legislation was passed.[21] As Woolf asked: 'What areas of government decision-making would be next to be removed from the scrutiny of the courts? What is the use of courts if you cannot access them?'[22] In response to such opposition, the government backed down and removed the offending clause of the Bill. But the underlying question of the limits to parliamentary sovereignty was revisited in 2005 when the House of Lords was asked to rule on whether the Hunting Act 2004, passed under the 1949 Parliament Act, was a valid statute. The context may have been less confrontational than the debate over the provisions of the Asylum and Immigration Bill removing the courts' jurisdiction, but its implication for parliamentary sovereignty was equally significant. Although the Lords upheld the legality of the Hunting Act, it concluded that there were indeed limits to the law-making power of Parliament:

> In exceptional circumstances involving an attempt to abolish judicial review or the ordinary role of the courts, the Appellate Committee of the House of Lords or a new Supreme Court may have to consider whether this is a constitutional fundamental which even a sovereign Parliament acting at the behest of a compliant House of Commons cannot abolish.[23]

This important judgment should be seen as the latest step in the process of refining the notion of parliamentary sovereignty.[24] What is clear is that the relationship between the courts and Parliament is in a state of transition between parliamentary sovereignty and constitutional supremacy. To properly understand the nature of this evolution, it is necessary to place the emergence of the Supreme Court and the determination of its powers in the context of the wider trend of increasing power among Supreme Courts and constitutional courts around the world. What we are seeing is the emergence of a global community of senior judges.[25] They are drawn from countries with different court structures and constitutional arrangements; some have the power to strike down legislation and others do not. But increasingly they see themselves as engaged in a global conversation about the interpretation of basic human rights and the relationship between elected and unelected branches of power. They read one another's judgments and speeches; they meet at conferences and share thoughts on their roles and functions. The UK Supreme Court will undoubtedly be a leading and respected member of this community of top jurists, which is likely to have the effect of enhancing the new Supreme Court Justices' views of their role. Baroness Hale, for example, has described the role of the new Supreme Court, as being to bridge the gap between law and society and to protect democracy. It is hard to imagine that any Law Lord thirty years ago would have seen such a broad mission statement as an accurate or acceptable view of the Appellate Committee of the House of Lords.

Exactly how the new Supreme Court will develop is still uncertain. What is clear, however, is that the current trend around the world is for increasing power and authority to be vested in supreme courts and the creation of an autonomous Supreme Court in the UK, housed in its own building with an independent budget and staff and a distinct identity, is likely to follow that trend.

Conclusion

Critics of the provisions of the Constitutional Reform Act claimed that they elevated theory above practice, breaking a sound and functioning system for the sake of conformity with a theoretical ideal. This claim is misguided. It is certainly true that the changes were not a knee-jerk response to an immediate crisis. They were instead a rare and commendable example of a longer-term recognition of the need to change institutional arrangements in order to bring them into line with the reality of changing constitutional power relations. These institutional readjustments are, however, likely in turn to impact on those power relations by promoting greater judicial confidence and thus authority. The changes therefore need to be understood as both a response to, and a driver of, the expanding role of the judiciary in the British constitution. As such, they will bring about long-term changes in the relationships between both the judiciary and the executive and the judiciary and the legislature as well as a redefinition of the nature of judicial independence in the British system. They should not, therefore, be seen as a sideline to the rest of the constitutional reforms, but rather as part of the wider project of modernising British constitutional arrangements to make them 'fit for purpose' for the twenty-first century.

A central question addressed in this chapter concerns the nature and degree of conflict between the judiciary and the other branches of government that we can expect to see in the years ahead. The idea of a partnership as expressed in the concordat may well provide a basis for the future relationship, but it would be unrealistic to expect it to be a partnership without tensions and confrontation. The consequence of a more active judiciary with greater autonomy will inevitably, and rightly, be a more dynamic relationship between the branches of government. Without the Lord Chancellor to mediate that relationship, the judges themselves will need to learn quickly to defend themselves from criticism and to ensure that the proper resources and support for the courts are in place. This can only be done if a new vision of judicial independence is adopted, one in which the judiciary itself is understood as requiring institutional and collective independence.

The effect of the reconstruction of the judiciary as institutionally separate from but functionally inter-connected with the other branches of government will be to move it closer to being a distinct third branch of government. Whether or not this is a positive development is ultimately a political judgement. Where the balance should lie in weighing the disadvantages of unelected judicial power against its capacity to check the 'elective dictatorship' is a question of political preference. There are sound democratic reasons for objecting to the expansion of judicial power; but the real answer to concerns about the growing influence of the courts lies in reversing the declining effectiveness of Parliament so that the judges are not called upon to fulfil the role of an unofficial opposition and to provide the sole check on abuse of executive power. Until the question of the revitalisation of Parliament is seriously addressed, the expansion in the role of the judiciary is inevitable. The result is that the provisions of the Constitutional Reform Act have an important role to play in establishing clearer boundaries between the branches of government and taking the negotiations, tensions and conflicts between them from the private corridors of power into the public arena. The need for greater visibility and public awareness of the increasingly powerful judiciary is acute. The governance structure of the judiciary, the role of the Supreme Court and the judicial appointments process are areas of vital constitutional importance which need ongoing scrutiny and debate. They are too important to be left to lawyers.

7

A porous and pragmatic settlement: asymmetrical devolution and democratic constraint in Scotland and Wales

Ailsa Henderson[1]

Upon its election in 1997 New Labour honoured its promise to reform political institutions, bringing in legislation to establish a Scottish Parliament, a Welsh Assembly and an elected authority in London. It signed the Good Friday Agreement to bring about devolution in Northern Ireland and introduced reforms to the House of Lords. These developments are significant for they represented a clear step away from unitary government and signalled a commitment to democratic reform. They are, however, an example of adaptation rather than a wholesale transformation of the character of the British state: more radical options might, for example, have included republicanism or federalism. Indeed it is striking that the 'greatest creator of federal systems in world history'[2] has so consciously avoided federalism within its own borders.[3]

The Blairite programme of constitutional change has been the subject of considerable interest and observers have debated whether it is a coherent plan or a grab bag of popular options designed to reward particular groups of voters for their support in 1997. The different elements of the programme point in contradictory directions: some reforms appear to shore up the principle of parliamentary sovereignty while others appear to weaken it. The reforms also employ more than one strategy, devolving power while pursuing legislation to improve citizen access to politicians and political information. The comprehensive nature of the reform seemingly explains its lack of coherence. This chapter examines one of these reforms, asymmetrical devolution in the UK and its origins and development, focusing primarily on Scotland and Wales.

Governments in unitary states which have decided to loosen their hold on power at the centre have at their disposal several options that stop short of federalism. These include the 'four Ds' of deconcentration, decentralisation, delegation and devolution. They can deconcentrate power at the centre by including a broader range of individuals in executive decision-making processes. They can decentralise power, for example by dispersing public authorities across the country. A delegation of power sees a transfer of decision-making authority, often to municipal councils or local unelected bodies. Here, the central government retains formal authority and sets the boundaries under which delegated authorities may perform their roles. Last, central authorities can devolve power, by giving decision-making authority to regional or sub-state levels of government. Here, the sub-state levels have exclusive jurisdiction over their assigned areas of competence. In the first two options, the executive still performs the same role that it occupied previously, but it either includes a wider range of individuals or relocates decision makers throughout the state. In the third and fourth options, however, the centre no longer performs certain roles that it did before, ceding power to other authorities.

After the 1997 election New Labour implemented elements of deconcentration, decentralisation and devolution. The invitation for Liberal Democrats to come onto a joint consultative committee with Cabinet ministers can be seen as an example of deconcentration. The establishment of an elected authority in London is an example of decentralisation. The establishment of legislatures in Scotland, Wales and Northern Ireland are deemed examples of devolution. But the three devolution settlements provide varying levels of autonomy and reflect the diverse goals of devolution campaigns and differing appetites for reform among the three electorates. Devolution is thus not one technique but has been applied differently in three cases and contains within it a range of departures from 'politics as usual'.

How can we account for the diversity of the devolution settlements and their current institutional arrangements? Despite the range of agents seen to be responsible for devolution – the electorates, the nationalist parties and civil society – two things are apparent. First, the nature of the current settlement and the practice of devolution owe their existence to the Labour Party.

Second, the behaviour of Labour, and later New Labour, can best be understood in the context of democratic constraint. Here, the behaviour of political actors can be explained by the anticipated obstacles of legislative rules, public opposition or electoral competition. But before explaining why the devolution arrangements are so diverse, it is useful to determine the extent of their asymmetry.

Asymmetrical devolution

The Scottish Parliament has the power to pass primary legislation in certain areas of jurisdiction and thus its role is akin to that of a US state or a Canadian province. There are two important restrictions on this power. First, its fiscal power is limited to varying tax by three pence in the pound. Second, Westminster retains sovereign authority. Because the Scottish Parliament was created by an Act passed at Westminster, it can be disbanded by similar legislation. Although the new Parliament has authority to legislate, its Acts can also be ruled *ultra vires*, outside the competence of the legislature. The Westminster Parliament could also decide to overrule legislation of the devolved institution for more partisan reasons. Before 1999, most observers argued that this power, although formally retained, would matter little, as it would not be in the interests of a Westminster government to disband or overrule a Scottish Parliament backed by the will of a Scottish electorate.

The Welsh Assembly, by contrast, has no power to pass primary legislation. Instead it can pass secondary legislation within the scope of statutes passed at Westminster. The assembly has no fiscal powers and so it is entirely dependent on the block grant it receives from Westminster. In some respects, the creation of the Welsh Assembly seems a policy of delegation rather than devolution, for the centre still retains decision-making power, the Assembly more an implementation arm of the Westminster executive. Unlike in Scotland, where the campaign for a devolved legislature was characterised by calls for political renewal, calls for a Welsh legislature emphasised the impact of devolution on economic renewal and development.[4] In this the creation of the Welsh Assembly appears more similar to devolution as we normally understand it, as a method of empowering government at the local level. Devolution to Scotland was qualitatively different, more akin to arguments for federalism. When devolution campaigns argued for a Scottish legislature they grounded their arguments in the presence of a democratic deficit and the necessity of democratising administrative devolution. The assumption that a separate political space already existed in Scotland, that it merely required a democratic decision-making body, suggests that the federal notion of separate but equal authorities might have been palatable to devolution campaigners. A different settlement was sought and established in Wales.

The legislature in Northern Ireland has powers similar to those of the Scottish Parliament. The Good Friday Agreement, which outlined the structure of the devolved legislature, also provided shared sovereignty on certain issues with the Republic of Ireland and the possibility of a referendum in which residents of Northern Ireland could opt to leave the UK. These two developments represent a significant constraint on the principle of parliamentary sovereignty, for they suggest two ways in which Westminster's authority could be challenged, first by another sovereign body and second by the public.

Just as the constitutional arrangements for the three legislatures vary, so do their internal structures. Northern Ireland uses the single transferable vote electoral system while Scotland and Wales use a mixed compensatory system similar to that employed in Germany. The Good Friday Agreement required republicans and loyalists to share power within the Northern Ireland Executive. The larger proportion of list seats in Scotland provides a near guarantee of coalition government, while the smaller proportion of list seats in Wales makes one-party government possible. Each of these features can be expected to have an impact on political developments in the devolved territories, for they suggest differing levels of access to decision-making authority.

The diversity of the three devolution settlements can be described as asymmetrical devolution. Asymmetry is not uncommon within federal systems.[5] The UK is not, of course, a federal system – it is quasi-federal at best – but the shift from a unitary state has led researchers to explore federalism research to see whether there are any lessons there for British political development.[6] Certainly there is considerable evidence of asymmetry in the world's federations. Fiscal powers among sub-state units such as provinces or *Länder* can vary. The range of jurisdiction can vary, so that some have control over health, education, community government, non-renewable resources and immigration and others manage a more restricted set of responsibilities. Representation in upper houses also varies. In some federations sub-state units have equal numbers of representatives, as in the US Senate, while in others representation varies by population. It is important to distinguish between *de jure* asymmetry, which is written into the settlement, and asymmetry in practice, which is what we find when administrative units exercise various opt-out clauses, or decide not to exercise their full jurisdictional autonomy.

In terms of asymmetrical devolution in the UK, two features are worth noting. First, asymmetry is not new to the UK. As Archie Brown remarks, 'A fetish with symmetry has never been apparent before.'[7] For fifty years Northern Ireland had a devolved legislature while other constituent parts of the UK did not. Within Westminster, institutional reforms – including the creation of territorial secretaries of state with supporting ministries – were granted in differing forms and at different dates. Indeed the UK pattern of institutional accommodation of its constituent nations has been characterised by its ad hoc nature. Devolution may be asymmetrical but it is consistent with Britain's approach to institutional reform.

Second, asymmetry is not set in stone.[8] In the absence of a written constitution, asymmetry within the UK is only as permanent as the will of Parliament. Change is likely, for asymmetry tends to encourage aspirations on the part of those with more minimal institutional arrangements: 'It is in the very nature of such asymmetrical arrangements that they invite the less autonomous territorial polities in an uneven constitutional framework to "catch up" with the pace setters.'[9] Certainly the experiences of the autonomous communities in Spain confirm this. Efforts to reopen the Scotland Act, or the introduction of any future Governance of England Act might make more symmetrical the asymmetrical arrangements that have, since the 1920s, characterised devolution within the UK. Indeed, efforts to remove some of the current asymmetry in the settlement can be seen in the Government of Wales Act 2006. This gives new powers to the Assembly, including the prospect of primary legislative capacity, should it be approved by two thirds of the current Assembly, and by a simple majority in both Houses of Parliament and in a public referendum. Proposed changes to the institutional structure of the Assembly better distinguish between the powers of the legislature and the executive and establish a commission comparable to the corporate body of the Scottish Parliament. The statute is a step towards greater symmetry in the political structures of the UK.

The devolution settlement has been described as unusual, both for what it is (many things at once) and for what it is not (a clear adjustment to a federal system). But how might we account for the asymmetrical nature of devolution, and what impact does it have on political developments in the UK? Part of the answer lies in our understandings of democratic constraint.

Devolution and democratic constraint

In his investigation of institutional design, Johan Olsen observed that reformers do not always get what they want.[10] The best of intentions can be waylaid by the rough-and-tumble world of democratic politics. Institutional reform is thus like any other policy, subject to the influence of stakeholders, opposition parties and divisions among reformers. Views of civil society or a suspicious electorate must be taken into account. Each of these groups might have rival visions to those presented by reformers. Indeed they might house within them differences of opinion on the best way to proceed. These rival visions act as a form of constraint on reformers and the eventual settlement should be seen as a product of negotiation among key actors.

In established democracies, the chief negotiation among rival visions occurs within the context of partisan competition. In their bid to win votes political parties might back more popular reforms and shy away from unpopular ones. They might champion forms of change otherwise at odds with their partisan principles. The arena of partisan competition serves as a constraint, structuring how parties perceive their roles as agents of change. If, as Olsen argues, reformers advocating solution X must also contend with rivals who want solutions Y or Z, we should be aware that the decision to back X was initially informed by the cost–benefit environment of electioneering; parties might adopt policies on institutional reform that suit their electoral purposes as much as their ideological leanings.

The arena of democratic politics provides several different forms of constraint, each of which might push or pull institutional reformers towards or away from particular goals. This is as true for political parties as it is for non-partisan or cross-party coalitions of reformers. The democratic context provides institutional, partisan, electoral and public constraints. These constraints can have two possible consequences. First, they might encourage reformers to temper their initial goals, to compromise with opponents to drop claims they believe to be unpopular. Second, reactions to constraints might encourage advocates to increase their support or to make demands in excess of their original goals, akin to a runaway train. This vision of constraints is useful for it helps to clarify the relationship between wishes and outcomes. Rather than viewing successful institutional design as the summary of reformist intention it is useful to view it as a process containing multiple accommodations that later structure the influence of the institutions. This is more controversial than it sounds, for it suggests that what the settlement looks like at the end is not the determining factor in its influence. Instead, the accommodations of various groups and the extent to which goals are subject to constraints affect the way different actors view the institution and in turn affect the potential development of the institution.

Two institutions with similar structures might develop in different directions so that for successive political generations they appear remarkably dissimilar. This development is informed by people who inhabit positions of power within the institutions, their behaviour influenced in part by the process through which the institutions were created. Even when legislation outlines the structures of institutions, unwritten conventions can bend and twist settlements. The constraints present at the time of institutional creation, in addition to those present during the period in which institutions settle into a consistent working culture, can affect institutional development. The number of constraints is less relevant than their perceived influence over reforms. Different political actors will be more or less susceptible to different influences. For politicians eager to secure re-election, electoral politics presents a significant constraint. For advocates of a particular cause or committed members of certain types of political party, ideology might serve as a constraint on behaviour. An example of practical constraints helps to illustrate this point.

The failed devolution projects in the 1970s can be seen as the result of multiple political constraints. Constraints were partisan in that the Labour Party was divided and could not pass the original Scotland and Wales Bill of 1976 without accommodating internal dissenters. They were electoral in that Labour, already in a weak position (and thus very attentive to internal division), lost the 1979 election to an anti-devolution Conservative Party. Institutional constraints included the principle of parliamentary sovereignty, which prevented more radical options of reform. The final constraint was public: the electorates in Scotland and Wales failed to provide the necessary degree of support for devolution. Identifying constraints within the context of a failed devolution experience can be misleading, though, for it encourages us to view constraints as obstacles to reform. We should also acknowledge that successful reforms may exist because of constraints. Democratic, partisan, public and institutional constraints have each affected both the tenor of the devolution settlement in the UK and the manner of its implementation. Both are affected by two features. First, the dominance of the Labour Party is itself a significant constraint on the tenor of democratic reform and second, current administrations in Edinburgh and Cardiff exist within an arena of partisan constraint.

The Labour Party dominated the pre-devolution landscape of Scotland and Wales. Labour might not have earned a majority of votes in either Scotland or Wales but since the 1970s it has earned more support than any other single party, which in turn provided a majority of seats. For Gerry Hassan, this dominance meant that Labour's goals and values became the goals and values for a civil society and state.[11] This is most evident in the Scotland and Wales devolution debates. Labour support for devolution was a reliable vote getter in Scotland and Wales during the lean years of partisan support in England. Its dominance in the devolution campaign was perhaps most evident in Wales, where the institutional arrangements for an eventual Assembly were not debated within a public forum, nor arrived at by cross-party consensus, but were the product of policy conversations within the Welsh Labour Party.[12] In Scotland, where the Scottish Constitutional Convention provided a forum in which to debate both the principle and practice of devolution, this cross-party body was dominated by Labour representation and rhetoric. The overall tenor of the devolution settlement – the electoral system, the number of representatives, the structure of committees, the treatment of gender issues – can be linked to the Labour Party. Where a range of policies addressed a similar issue, it is the Labour Party policy that most closely approximated to the post-devolution settlement. It is not just that a Labour government introduced the Government of Wales Act and the Scotland Act in the UK Parliament. The entire devolution settlement bears the stamp of the Labour Party, its dominance the chief constraint on institutional arrangements.

New Labour exists within an arena of democratic constraint. These constraints vary by locus, time and object: those occurring at the UK level are different from those facing parties in a devolved setting; constraints after devolution are different from those before; and Labour encounters different constraints as a single-party government, as part of a coalition government and as a party. At the UK level, its chief rival is the Conservative Party but in a regionalised electorate New Labour faces the potential constraint of internal division if the parties in Scotland and Wales feel their electoral environments make it difficult to follow the UK line. The chief institutional constraint for UK New Labour is an electoral system that tends to produce majority govern-ments, although any New Labour government faces competing institutional constraints in the form of EU membership and the associated enlarged role for the judiciary on the one hand, and the construct of parliamentary sovereignty on the other.

At the devolved level, the Scottish and Welsh Labour parties faced different constraints pre-devolution than they do post-devolution. Before 1997, the Scottish and Welsh Labour parties faced weaker parties on the right and nationalist parties on the left. The demography of the two nations makes their electorates look more like the industrial heartlands of England, which also affects the policies that might win popular support. Partisan constraints are therefore twofold: one right–left, one separatist–unionist. Post-devolution, the expanded number of smaller parties on the left/nationalist end of the political spectrums represents another new constraint.[13] The electoral system – an institutional constraint – makes single-party government unlikely in Scotland and only a possibility in Wales.

Any devolved government, of any stripe, encounters additional constraints, most of them institutional. Governments are financially dependent on the block grant, although in the Scottish case the Parliament may expand its financial autonomy by exercising its right to vary tax. They are constrained by the limited jurisdiction of their own legislatures and the Judicial Committee of the Privy Council, which may rule devolved legislation *ultra vires*. The potential for additional constraint on Wales is obvious. A Westminster government that wishes to produce legislation that is complete and specific can leave less room for innovation in implementation than one whose legislation addresses first principles and broad goals. Governments in both Scotland and Wales are further constrained by UK membership of the EU and by the lack of formal access to EU decision-making, though access in practice exists for Scotland.

Three conclusions may be drawn from these constraints. First, New Labour in the UK faces fewer constraints than do the Labour parties in either Scotland or Wales. Second, the number of constraints faced by the Scottish and Welsh Labour parties has expanded since devolution. Third, any devolved Labour government – whether in coalition or not – faces an additional layer of constraints. Of course all parties face the ultimate constraint at the hands of the electorate, an electorate that is often informed about parties by a political media that may be indifferent or hostile to the party. Persistently negative political coverage, or the absence of coverage, can also be seen as a constraint. Particularly within Scotland, Westminster MPs have complained about the marked reduction in the coverage they receive, while those in Holyrood have felt persecuted by an unsupportive press.

Given the patterns of constraint, we might ask two questions. First, what impact did the Labour Party have on the asymmetrical devolution settlement? Second, what impact has the Labour Party, in its various regional incarnations, had on the emerging practice of devolution?

'What matters is what works': Labour pragmatism and asymmetrical devolution

The dominance of the Labour Party is central to our understanding of devolution. Seen as part of a conscious plan, devolution under New Labour is described as a principled bid for pluralistic partyless democracy.[14] Seen as part of an effort to win electoral favour, devolution becomes the ultimate act of pragmatism.[15] The true position, most likely, lies somewhere in between these two extremes. The Labour Party has exhibited varying support for Scottish and Welsh devolution since the 1960s.[16] The initial calculation might have been made purely in an effort to win votes in the periphery but pragmatism should not be seen as the absence of support for devolution.[17] It is reasonable to assume that devolution was made possible by a certain amount of practical pragmatism. Whatever the original decision, few would doubt that within Scotland there is, among elected politicians of the Labour Party, majority support for the principle of devolution and support for its success. Within Wales, Labour was more divided in 1979 than in 1997 but inconsistent support for devolution has appeared at times as a significant rather than just a theoretical obstacle to its successful implementation. Within England, support for devolution to Scotland and Wales is more guarded, and references to the West Lothian question more common. (Labour MP Tam Dalyell once remarked that in the event of devolution it would be unfair for English MPs to be denied the opportunity to comment on policy in Scotland if Scottish MPs, and thus the West Lothian voters who elected him, were able to influence policy in England.) Labour support for devolution has thus varied over time, within the party, and across regions.

Whatever its origins, support for devolution did not become a litmus test of Labour support. It did not occupy Labour minds in the way that, for example, Liberals have long advocated home rule. Constraints are more important for pragmatic advocates of policy than they are for ideologues. Because devolution was not a point of great principle it has become a policy like any other, to be shaped by internal party pressures and assessments of electoral advantage. As Brigid Hadfield argues, devolution was a pragmatic response to 'local demands' rather than a point of principle.[18] This in turn produced the current asymmetrical outcomes, the resultant Bills and settlements a response to local pressures and opportunities. The different types of constraint operating in Scotland and Wales served to shape the different settlements.

The post-devolution reaction of certain politicians at Westminster further attests to the fact that devolution was marked by pragmatism. Scottish and Welsh Labour MPs have, at times, expressed scepticism about the principle of devolution and have shown themselves to be frustrated by the perceived poor quality of representation from members of the new legislatures and the degree of media attention enjoyed by the devolved legislatures. One Scottish Labour MP referred to Holyrood as an 'odds and sods parliament' whose members did not work as hard as those at Westminster.[19] Lack of support is best seen in the abhorrence for some of the most likely consequences of devolution: policy divergence and non-coterminous electoral constituencies. Indeed the creation of rival political spaces, surely the most predictable of consequences, appears particularly disappointing to some of the Labour MPs from Scotland and Wales. Free personal care for the elderly in Scotland, portrayed by advocates as an example of the Scottish Parliament accurately judging the demands of electors, can be seen also as an expensive policy that places a burden, uniquely, on the public finances in Scotland. Such opposition is not limited to politicians. The repeal of Section 2A in Scotland, which prohibited the education curriculum from 'normalising' homosexuality, while the equivalent provision (Section 28) remained in England and Wales, was described in one report as an 'awkward situation'.[20] The point of devolution, if there continues to be an expectation of identical policy across the UK, is not clear. At times it appears that devolution was supposed to produce different policy processes but identical policy outcomes. It is possible, of course, that confusion about devolution, or discontent with its consequences, merely betrays a pre-existing level of opposition to devolution, but this does not appear to be the case. Levels of support for devolution in Scotland were high among both the electorate and the political class. While many of the current critiques of devolution stem from the inadequate way in which the first few cohorts of representatives have discharged their duties, it is equally possible to find critiques grounded in the principle of devolution, something that we would not expect to find among supporters who based their calls for change in principled arguments for home rule or subsidiarity.

The pragmatic approach to devolution helped to produce, then, an asymmetrical arrangement because the level of internal dissent and voter support differed in Scotland and Wales. And yet when it promoted devolution, New Labour suggested it was in recognition of the principle of subsidiarity. This argument was strengthened by the fact that devolution was 'delivered' to three parts of the UK at roughly the same time. The Welsh electorate was far less supportive and far more divided than voters in Scotland. In fact support was so modest in Wales that New Labour might have delivered devolution in Scotland and chosen merely to expand the scope of administrative devolution that already existed in Wales. This, however, would have prevented New Labour from arguing that devolution was in recognition of the principle of subsidiarity, rather than a pragmatic effort to reward voters while undermining nationalism.[21] Even the use of principles, then, has been governed by pragmatism.

The porous settlement

Since 1999, Labour influence on the practice of devolution has been affected by the presence of several constraints. The settlement itself is relevant, for asymmetrical and pragmatic devolution has served to heighten Labour influence; the pragmatic settlement brought a level of asymmetry that discouraged the rigid identification of roles and tasks. The presence of Labour or Labour-led administrations in London, Edinburgh and Cardiff provided no additional incentive for clearly articulated boundaries. In this context Labour reaction to constraints has served to create a porous settlement, one where the boundaries around institutions are less clear than they might have been. We might expect a porous settlement in Wales, where secondary legislation lends itself to fluid relations with Westminster, but we can see it in Scotland as well. Two things are worth noting here. First, the asymmetrical nature of the institutional arrangements had a direct effect on the porous nature of the settlement. Second, it had an indirect effect for it heightened Labour influence, which in turn provided no incentive for the boundaries between institutions to solidify. Although the division between devolved and reserved areas is not watertight, the settlement appears more porous in operation than it might have been.[22] This is best seen in relation to party relations, legislative consent and the treatment of reserve matters.

The political experiences of politicians in the devolved legislatures always guaranteed a degree of Westminster influence.[23] The initial First Ministers of Scotland and Wales were both former secretaries of state for their respective nations. Labour members of the initial ten-person Scottish Executive included three members with Westminster seats at the time of their election to Holyrood, while the smaller Welsh executive contained two.[24] This influence was not confined to the government benches. There were, in total, thirteen of these dual-mandate members in the Scottish Parliament, six from the SNP. That Labour, Liberal Democrat, SNP and Plaid Cymru politicians with leadership roles had cut their political teeth in Westminster must be considered a constraint on the development of a distinct political culture within Scotland and Wales.[25]

New Labour's efforts to influence developments within Scottish and Welsh Labour have been explicit and well chronicled, as have reactions to that involvement. Before the devolved legislatures were established there was an expectation that New Labour would exert considerable control over its devolved Labour counterparts. The *Economist* warned, for example: 'Unless Mr Blair can impose discipline in Scotland, a Scottish parliament could become one of his biggest headaches.'[26] One academic noted: 'From the vantage point of Millbank Tower, they want to keep a watchful eye on what the party gets up to in all the new institutions being created in Edinburgh, Cardiff and London, and ensure they do not depart too radically from the approved Blairite line.'[27] Certainly New Labour attempted to exert influence.[28] David Baker reports rumours that a member of the Scottish Executive withdrew from a leadership contest because of central influence,[29] and the UK Labour Party was clearly involved in the selection of Labour candidates for the Scottish and Welsh elections.

Efforts to control political developments in the devolved legislatures were not always successful. New Labour picks for the top post did not enjoy long reigns[30] and Welsh voters apparently punished Labour in the 2003 Assembly elections because it was seen to be a puppet of UK New Labour.[31] The 2001 British general election provided the most explicit example of devolved activity in Westminster politics. Devolved politicians of all parties were prominent within the Westminster campaign. Members of coalition executives in Scotland and Wales were surprisingly active, prompting some commentators to suggest that they were shirking their duties as Cabinet ministers.[32] One week before the Westminster election there were only seventy-two MSPs in the chamber to vote, a smaller proportion than usually appeared in the 129-member legislature. Although the Scottish Parliament published eleven reports or inquiries in April and nineteen in June, only four were published the month of the May election.[33] Increasingly, though, the devolved legislatures appear to be pursuing their own paths, not least in leadership selection. Emerging challenges stem from the imprecise distinctions between reserved matters addressed by Westminster and the devolved jurisdiction of the new legislatures. Recent public disputes about the Skye

Bridge tolls and Scottish Water have led to public debates in the media about who determines public policy in Scotland. Nevertheless, in Scotland and Wales we have an example of very close relations between the UK party and its devolved counterpart.

If the relationship between UK New Labour and the devolved incarnations of the party in Scotland and Wales provide evidence of a porous devolution settlement, the behaviour of the Labour-led administrations offers further examples of the contingent nature of devolution. The difference is thus between the activities of Labour as a party and Labour administrations. Here, the Labour-led administrations have not established impermeable boundaries around the institutions. Although Westminster retains, by virtue of parliamentary supremacy, the right to disband any of the devolved legislatures, or even legislate in devolved areas, those writing before devolution pointed out that doing so would be seen as a no-win situation.[34] In an effort to generate a convention that Westminster would only legislate in devolved issues if asked to do so by Holyrood, the Labour-led administration in the Scottish Parliament has taken to introducing motions whenever it wants to request or permit Westminster legislation. These legislative consent motions, also known as Sewel motions, have been used increasingly since 1999.[35] The Scottish Parliament passed thirty-nine legislative consent motions in the first session. The rate at which such motions were passed increased marginally in the first two years of the second session. These motions are not seen as something that could imperil the status of devolution. Even the SNP, a party we would expect to police quite judiciously the boundaries of devolution, has supported a small number. On its own the occasional legislative consent motion could hardly damage devolution but the extent of their use has surprised those who suggested Westminster's sovereignty was theoretical rather than practical.

Of course, financial decisions provide additional evidence of the Parliament deliberately clipping its own wings. Despite its ability to vary tax by three pence in the pound the Labour-led executive has chosen not to exercise this option. This decision can be interpreted in two ways. First, it can be seen as an example of prudent financial management from an administration keen not to overburden its electorate with additional tax at a time when public moneys appear to meet demanded expenditure. Alternatively, it can be viewed as evidence of a government hesitant to employ the full range of powers made available in the Scotland Act. That the Parliament is able to rely solely on moneys transferred from Westminster to fund policy created in Edinburgh is further proof of the less-than-rigid boundaries between the two levels of government.

If Westminster attention to devolved matters provides one example of hazy boundaries, so too does devolved attention to reserved matters. The Scottish Parliament in particular devotes a significant amount of time to reserved matters. Often this has less to do with the Labour/Liberal Democrat executive and more to do with non-executive parties who have chosen to use some of their party motions to debate issues outside the competency of the Scottish Parliament. There is nothing wrong with this tactic, in the sense that it is not proscribed by the Scotland Act, nor does it stem from imprecise distinctions between reserved and devolved areas. Expectations that devolved politicians would start to see themselves as the political voice of a nation, representatives of an 'entire range of citizen concerns' not bound by divisions between reserved and devolved powers, were clearly correct.[36] The topics addressed by cross-party groups provide further proof of the attention paid by devolved politicians to reserved powers. In Wales, where the groups may cover 'any subject relevant to the assembly', all focus on devolved topics. In Scotland, where the rules governing their creation indicate they must identify issues of 'genuine public interest', groups on Cuba, Malawi, Palestine and Tibet demonstrate the attention of parliamentarians to international concerns beyond the remit of the Parliament.

The behaviour of representatives in devolved legislatures has contributed to the imprecision concerning institutional boundaries. Partly this is possible because of the asymmetrical nature of the settlement. The settlement was born of pragmatism. That very pragmatism prevented the introduction of a seismic shift in the UK political system and instead introduced an asymmetrical settlement. Consequently devolution has come to be seen as something which has been advanced in a piecemeal matter, where the constraints present at any one time have prompted reactions and shaped behaviours. In part it is to this that we can attribute the poorly developed structure of inter-governmental relations between Westminster, Holyrood and Cardiff.[37] Given the degree to which parliamentarians in Westminster support parliamentary sovereignty it is understandable that they would not want to formalise procedures that might undermine this principle. The presence of small, careful and ad hoc shifts taken only when absolutely necessary can, in this sense, be seen as a way of preserving the character of the UK Parliament in the face of limited change. The only problem with such an approach, however, is that devolution is not a limited change, and only appears partial when compared to symmetrical federalism. Radical change may have been an unlikely candidate under the circumstances, but the pragmatic approach to the attainment of devolution has coloured the behaviour of political actors post-devolution.

Thus far we have discussed the presence of constraints. The absence of constraints is also relevant. We might recall that there are several constraints pushing and pulling political actors towards particular action. Within the devolved polities, Labour-led administrations might face civil society, the media or electorate as potential constraints. None of these is operating as it might in devolved politics. A civil society active in the 1980s and 1990s has either transformed itself into interest groups to be incorporated as policy stakeholders or found its members currently occupied by political positions within the wider political network. A media that at times has been unsupportive of the principle of devolution also serves as an unreliable check on Labour administrations. Particularly in the early days, the media was so consistently critical of devolution and of the first cohort of representatives that it failed to address valid concerns about policy. The public, while still supportive of devolution in principle, has shown lower degrees of support for devolution in practice. The electorate appears disengaged, if we use turnout as a guide.[38]

We might think of the various constraints as a tug of war, encouraging parties to adopt pragmatic approaches to policy that serve median levels of support. In the complete absence of constraints parties would be free to pursue their ideologically determined goals. A more likely situation, however, would prove to be an uneven tug of war. This is what we find in post-devolution Scotland and Wales. There are considerable constraints on the Labour-led administrations that encourage an ad hoc approach to institutional development. What is lacking are constraints which might encourage the administrations to chart a different course, although this appears to be changing slowly. In the absence of these more typical constraints on the executive the legislature itself serves as an effective constraint. Each successive leadership transformation, each Cabinet reshuffle strengthens the position of the legislature vis-à-vis the executive. It moves executive members to the back benches, reducing the skills gap between the executive and other representatives. It brings backbench members to the executive, giving power to those beyond the initial cohort of politicians with Westminster experience. It also temporarily destabilises Labour, thereby strengthening the position of opposition parties. Each change thus destabilises the executive at the expense of the legislature and in so doing brings the legislature closer to the vision of new politics espoused by some advocates of devolution, one where there is a less obvious division between the executive and opposition parties.

Both the presence and absence of constraints is relevant. We should, however, distinguish between types of constraints. We can identify push constraints, which would encourage the devolved Labour parties to follow closely the behaviour or wishes of the UK Labour Party. We can also identify pull constraints, which would encourage devolved Labour to chart an independent course. It is not just that constraints have been present or absent post-devolution, but that the types of constraints helped to create a porous devolution settlement. In the first session following the 1999 elections, the presence of push constraints facilitated closer relations with Westminster. This then established a precedent for Westminster behaviour, setting expectations within New Labour about the type of influence possible or perhaps even welcomed by devolved Labour. That the administrations in Edinburgh and Cardiff were either Labour executives or Labour-led coalitions also served as a push constraint, leading to decreased vigilance in the patrolling of institutional boundaries.

Throughout the first session, however, a number of pull constraints emerged, encouraging the Labour-led executives to distance themselves from the New Labour government at Westminster. These included the presence of coalition governments in Edinburgh and, later, in Cardiff. The necessity of forging policy that reflected the interests of coalition partners served to distance devolved Labour from New Labour. At times the coalitions provided a convenient excuse for devolved Labour when it pursued a policy distinct from that promoted in London but deemed to be more popular with the devolved electorate. Scottish legislation on tuition fees can be seen as one example of this. In addition, the second devolved elections in 2003 provided voters with an opportunity to cast a ballot in an election which was wholly within the context of the devolution settlement. In 1999 the legislatures were not yet operating and so there was no opportunity for voters to base their choices on the behaviour of devolved parties in a devolved context; the legislatures had not yet provided independent grounds on which to cast a ballot. We should of course be cautious with this interpretation. Even in the absence of devolved legislatures voters in Wales and Scotland might have had a sense of how the parties, when campaigning in Wales and Scotland, emphasised different policies than in the UK-wide campaigns. It is also open to question whether voters in the second devolved elections cast their ballots purely on devolved matters, or whether they were influenced more by issues relevant to Westminster.[39] Support for parties without seats at Westminster, or indeed for parties that could never hope to lead executives at Westminster, points to an independent electoral contest. James Mitchell and Jonathan Bradbury note a shift in Welsh politics from one of the policy of process to more distributive concerns, which also confirms the operation of a rival political space.[40] This would have served as a pull factor on the devolved Labour parties, well aware that their electoral rivals were different in Holyrood and Cardiff from those faced in Westminster elections. Jack McConnell, the Scottish First Minister, has shown an interest in charting an independent path but he has met with considerable difficulties. The headline in which he declared, 'Actually, I am in charge' pointed both to his efforts and his need to make such a statement given New Labour control.[41]

In Wales, we have started to see a desire to 'catch up' with the devolution settlement in Scotland, although north of the border there appears little appetite for an expansion of authority.[42] The Richard commission recommended the acquisition of primary powers, a separation of executive authority within the Assembly and an increase in the number of Assembly members, all changes that would bring the Assembly closer to the institutional arrangements of the Scottish Parliament. Reaction to the commission points to the emergence of pull constraints as diverse pressure groups and non-executive parties supported the adoption of these recommendations. If the dominance of Welsh Labour in the devolution debate was itself a considerable constraint on the creation of devolution, debates about the future of devolution appear to include a more diverse cast. Whether the Government of Wales Act 2006 will serve to distance any future Labour-led administration from UK New Labour is doubtful. The new institutions will more closely approximate the institutional structures of the Scottish Parliament. While this will transform the Welsh legislature from an example of delegation to one of more typical devolution, the strengthened role for the executive will not necessarily distance any prospective Labour-led administration from its UK counterpart. What is likely, however, is that the more symmetrical arrangements might prompt an examination of the institutional arrangements among the various legislatures and in so doing might make explicit debates about roles and boundaries.

Conclusion

The pragmatism with which New Labour implemented devolution was both the product of pre-existing constraints and later served itself as a constraint on the practice of devolution. New Labour, aware of the risks of internal dissent, eager to reward pro-devolution voters for their support and keen to implement significant change, devised a programme of devolution that ensured its success and its asymmetry. Both the pragmatism with which it was accomplished and the asymmetry that resulted failed to produce a seismic change that encouraged political actors to identify clear and marked boundaries around the various levels of political authority. As a result, the desires of New Labour to exert a degree of influence within devolved politics were met with less resistance than they might have been. There are, of course, different types of constraint. Some might compel actors to define clearly the boundaries between institutions and in so doing serve to distinguish the separate roles of the Labour Party in its various incarnations. These we might consider pull constraints. Push constrains, by contrast, might encourage administrations to leave hazy the boundaries between institutions, to take advantage of the informal and partisan networks in order to meet legislative ends. In the early days of devolution, the strength of push constraints and the relative absence of pull constraints encouraged close relationships between New Labour and the Labour-led devolved administrations. Thus it is not so much that asymmetry pushed the administrations together, but that the absence of a seismic and symmetrical shift towards federalism did not necessitate a clear enunciation of the boundaries around institutions and administrations. In the absence of such an enunciation, problem-solving or dispute resolution has occurred on an ad hoc basis; a pragmatic interest in achieving ends has not encouraged the development of mechanisms that could become lightning rods for jurisdictional disputes. The devolved adminis-trations had little to push them to test the limits of the devolution settlement.

The Scottish Parliament, with its primary legislative powers, was more likely to establish clearer boundaries than was the Welsh Assembly. Through the activities of its Labour members and the use of legislative consent motions the Labour-led administration in the Scottish Parliament has restricted the potential scope of its activity at a time when its non-executive parties have sought to broaden it beyond the limit of devolved jurisdiction. The emergence of pull constraints has encouraged further signs of independence, though this, coupled with earlier behaviour, has served to reinforce the extent to which pragmatic and asymmetrical devolution has created a porous settlement.

8

Britain and Europe: a tale of two constitutions

Craig Parsons

British citizens have heard more talk of constitutions in recent years than in any period in living memory. They have participated in (or been subjected to) not one but two explicitly constitutional discussions. Almost simultaneously with the domestic reform agenda that is the topic of this book, the European Union launched a process to draft a European constitution. The discussions often seemed to run in parallel and mutually supporting directions. Reform discourse in the two arenas shared many themes: rights, transparency, devolved powers in multi-level government, and attempts to bring politics closer to the people. At a broad level, each step in the domestic reform agenda also seemed to bring Britain closer to the norms of continental European states. New Labour proposed to take one of Europe's most centralised states, with a distinct tradition of rights, conservative courts, an anachronistic role for hereditary title holders, and an atypical electoral system, and on each of these counts to 'modernise' it in ways that moved closer to the European middle ground. None of these changes were presented as part of an EU agenda, but they seemed to correspond implicitly to Tony Blair's foreign policy goal to put the UK 'at the heart of Europe'.

And yet few would suggest that the European and British constitutional reforms are part of a common process, and the Blair government has avoided any explicit suggestion that 'modernisation' equates to 'Europeanisation'. The government and British political actors and observers have tended to regard domestic constitutional reform and EU issues as separate policy realms. This chapter considers why, and also tries to tease out some ways in which the EU has nonetheless helped to create the context for domestic constitutional reform. The EU's constitutional reform process has had little direct bearing on the British reforms. But the earlier consolidation of a de facto EU constitution by the early 1990s helped pave the way for those reforms. In the 1980s and 1990s change in the EU served to encourage advocates of domestic constitutional change, showing them that they were moving with the tide rather than against it.

The chapter first traces the EU constitutional narrative. By the early 1990s legal scholars began to see an implicit EU constitution in the consolidation of a powerful legal architecture. But the subsequent process to acquire the label explicitly – making a constitution into a Constitution – was pursued by EU advocates for presentational reasons. The reforms focused more on codifying the EU order than on changing it, employing grand rhetoric to awaken citizens from their traditional Euro-apathy. It ended in the Constitution's spectacular failure in French and Dutch referendums in 2005 – and it still left behind a constitution (with a small C). The chapter then focuses on the relevance of this implicit EU constitution to Britain's domestic reforms, notably judicial empowerment, citizens' rights and devolution. It concludes by explaining why the European and domestic reforms have been managed – politically and bureaucratically – as two distinct policy realms.

Consolidation of a European constitutional order

In common parlance a constitution is a body of fundamental law. It defines basic rights and obligations, trumps lower-level law, and is typically entrenched, rendering it difficult to amend.[1] Even in the UK, where the unfettered parliamentary sovereignty of the classic Westminster model suggested that a majority could alter anything by the same procedure with which it passed an ordinary law, the point of designating certain principles as 'constitutional' has always been to underscore that changing them invites special scrutiny.

The EU was designed to be more 'constitutional' than any previous contract between sovereign states. For its initial advocates in the early post-war period, the key novelty of what became the EU project was that it would bind member states in fundamental, hard-to-alter ways. They hoped a constraining supranational framework would bring deep integration, ending any possibility of war within Europe, tempering nationalism, fostering economic dynamism and creating a powerful European voice in world affairs. The European Economic Community (EEC) treaty of 1957 that laid the foundation for today's EU emphasised the delegation of sovereignty to formally independent central institutions. They were modelled on federal states, not diplomatic organisations: an executive European Commission, a bicameral legislature with a European Parliament (EP) and senate-like Council of Ministers, and a European Court of Justice (ECJ).[2] Like most national constitutions but unlike every preceding international treaty, the EEC's founding treaty included no procedure for a state to withdraw. The main device by which these institutions would bring integration was a broad mandate to establish a common market with freedom of movement for persons, goods, services and capital. Europe's founding fathers hoped their construct would imitate the history of the United States, where gradual market integration and institutional centralisation melded diverse states into a greater whole.

These ambitions were hotly contested and initial delegations of policy-making power to the EEC were limited. Even among its leading advocates, no serious politicians favoured the rapid creation of a federal United States of Europe. They remained national leaders with national loyalties and constituencies, and only envisioned a federalising project as a gradual, long-term goal. Thus the EEC's institutional powers would be phased in over a twelve-year transition period. At the end of this period member states would retain the ability to block most important decisions in the Council of Ministers. The treaty language on the binding nature of EEC law was vague. Moreover, even with these built-in limitations, opponents of supranationality sought to weaken the treaty deal as it was implemented. In particular, Charles de Gaulle, who was resolutely opposed to the Community's supranational ambitions, returned to power in France shortly after the treaty was signed. He surprised everyone by agreeing to meet the EEC commitments, but then did his best to downgrade the community into a more conventional diplomatic organisation. He blocked the direct election of the EP and later forced the retention of national vetos in the Council of Ministers.

Still, both champions and opponents of the EEC tended to agree that it had been meant to develop into a federal-style polity, and that it was likely to do so. (This is why de Gaulle felt so strongly about modifying the provisions of an organisation whose powers at the time were fairly modest.) To cut a long story short, it eventually did – though not by any sort of linear, simple path. After de Gaulle's assaults and the economic chaos of the 1970s, the story of European federalisation was woven from two threads. One was comprised of a series of further bargains between national governments. As of the mid-1980s, a combination of Europe-wide economic challenges and the arrival of pro-supranational leadership – most notably French President François

Mitterrand, German Chancellor Helmut Kohl, and Commission President Jacques Delors – led to an expansion of EEC activities. In the Single European Act (SEA) of 1986, the member states renewed and broadened the community's liberalising mandate, limited their national vetos, allowing more majority voting in the Council of Ministers, and assigned new responsibilities to the long-powerless EP. The same leaders accelerated this agenda after the fall of the Berlin Wall, using the Maastricht Treaty to signal the enduring commitment of a reunified Germany to integration with its neighbours. Besides upgrading the community's title to 'European Union', the treaty further extended majority voting, strengthened the EP's powers and committed the signatories to the creation of a single currency by 1999 (with opt-out clauses for the British and the Danes). It also broadened the scope for EU legislation well beyond strictly economic affairs (to consumer protection, education, health, trans-European energy and transport networks, and some aspects of social policy), and formalised co-operation in internal security (policing, judicial affairs, border control, immigration) and foreign and security policy. The member states isolated the latter areas in new 'pillars' of the union, assigning them rules of more classic inter-governmental co-operation that preserved national vetoes and limited ECJ, Commission and EP involvement. But despite a complex list of exceptions to its authority, the European project had taken on a range and depth of policy responsibilities that resembled a weak federal government much more than any international organisation.

Much of the rise of a federal-style EU order, then, followed from conscious and explicit decisions by national leaders to create such an order. But a less politically salient thread of the EU story is at least as important for the constitutional status of their creation. During the 1960s, the ECJ used individual cases to resolve broader ambiguities in the treaties about the relationship between European and national law. In the 1963 *Van Gend & Loos* decision the court proclaimed the 'direct effect' of community law, making it justiciable in national courts even before its passage into national legislation:

> The Community constitutes a new legal order ... for the benefits of which the states have limited their sovereign rights, albeit in limited fields, and the subjects of which comprise not only Member States but also their nationals. Independently of the legislation of the Member States, Community law therefore not only imposes obligations on individuals but is also intended to confer upon them rights which become part of their legal heritage.[3]

A year later in *Costa v. ENEL*, the court affirmed the supremacy of community law over national statutes:

> By contrast with ordinary international treaties, the EEC Treaty has created its own legal system ... the law stemming from the Treaty, an independent source of law, could not, because of its special and original nature, be overridden by domestic legal provisions, however framed, without being deprived of its character as Community law and without the legal basis of the Community itself being called into question.[4]

In 1970 the court underscored that EEC law trumped not just statutes but national constitutions as well.[5] These judgments amounted to a clear, aggressive assertion of complete European legal primacy. Their timing was also striking, strengthening the legal underpinnings of supranationality just as de Gaulle and economic troubles weakened the community project politically. It was not until the early 1990s, though, that these developments received much attention beyond specialists in European and international law. As the more overtly political 'relaunch' of the European project in the SEA and Maastricht attracted broader attention, politicians and scholars discovered that the communities had established a uniquely powerful system of international law.[6]

Around the same time, several legal cases resolved the main remaining ambiguities about national acceptance of the EU legal order. In Britain, the key step came with the *Factortame* case in 1990.[7] Earlier British court rulings had largely side-stepped the issue of how fully they accepted European supremacy. The language in the UK's act of EEC accession (the European Communities Act 1972) was ambiguous. Its statement that 'any enactment, passed or to be passed . . . shall be construed and have effect subject to' community law could be interpreted as requiring just that any UK statute be read – wherever possible – as consistent with EEC law. Advocates of the dominant 'pure parliamentary sovereignty' conception of British constitutional law, in the tradition of A. V. Dicey, argued that a post-1972 statute would still prevail in a case of clear inconsistency.[8] Until *Factortame* the courts tacitly accepted this view, finding ways to interpret UK statutes as consistent with community legislation.[9] But when placed before a clear conflict involving statutory discrimination against British-registered but Spanish-owned fishing vessels, the Appellate Committee of the House of Lords ruled that community law trumped UK law and that British courts had the power to review domestic law for European compliance.[10] By the mid-1990s, even

British industrial tribunals – from their modest place in the judicial hierarchy – had taken to invoking the supremacy of EU laws over national statutes.

In the early 1990s the two threads of the story inter-laced into a narrative of constitutional federalism. The quasi-formal consolidation of legal supremacy and new formal delegations of authority in the Maastricht Treaty led many observers to begin using 'federal' and 'constitutional' to describe the EU. John Major managed to strike the word 'federal' from the Maastricht document (as would Tony Blair in subsequent treaty revisions), but, as the *Economist* commented shortly thereafter, 'Call it what you will: by any other name it is federal government.'[11]

Legal scholars raised the notion of a 'transnational constitution' in the EEC as early as 1981, and by the early 1990s such a description was commonplace.[12] The EU also received growing attention in nationally focused legal scholarship. By the mid-1990s, not only did experts on British constitutional law tend to present the EU order as constitutional in its own right, they commonly characterised its domestic impact as 'by far the most significant constitutional innovation undertaken by any government in the twentieth century.'[13] For a British constitution ostensibly built on pure parliamentary sovereignty, it was difficult to imagine a change more drastic than embedding the domestic system in a superior constitutional order.

The EU constitutional settlement of the 1990s is admittedly an odd one, and not without ambiguities. Aside from anything else, its textual basis is unclear: the 300-page treaty makes it difficult to separate out constitutional features from a wealth of less fundamental points. Substantively, it is narrow if compared to national constitutions. EU commitments are broad and detailed relative to any other international agreement, but the EU remains focused mostly on constructing a transnational market. It is true that market regulations comprise the largest sub-set of modern governance – and EU rules run to over 80,000 pages – but the EU framework is selective relative to the full range of public and private issues covered by national law.[14] In the less strictly economic areas to which its legislation has expanded, such as the environment, cultural policies or education, EU activity tends to focus on how transnational market-making impinges on these issues rather than on their governance in a broader sense. Even on issues of economic regulation, it tends to leave wide margins for national manoeuvre. British and other national courts still avoid 'disapplying' national laws by creatively interpreting them as compatible with EU legislation. At the most abstract level, the EU's ultimate supremacy remains contested. All national courts accept EU primacy over domestic statutes, but many continue to object – if mostly in hypothetical terms – to its claim of primacy over constitutions. In several countries ratification of the Maastricht Treaty required constitutional amendments, and these became vehicles for showdowns between national constitutional courts and the ECJ. The latter proclaimed its 'Kompetenz-Kompetenz': the authority to decide the limits on how far EU rules could alter national constitutions. No national court accepted this claim, and the German, Danish, and French constitutional courts explicitly rejected it.[15] In Britain, the parallel discussion concerns what British courts would do if Parliament passed an Act that specifically claimed to trump EU commitments. British judges would be hard pressed to declare such a statute invalid.

But these are still qualifications, not fundamental objections, to the description of the EU treaty of the 1990s as a constitution.[16] The ambiguities it retains are similar to the perennial questions about the precise contents and sanctity of the British constitution. Just as many elements of Britain's constitution rest on tacit convention, so the EU order is partly built on political acceptance rather than the letter of written law.

Rise and fall of the European 'constitution'

If the EU had a constitution by the early 1990s, politicians shied away from the term. Characterising the union as constitutional would invoke language about legitimacy and authority that was sure to be poorly received by some Europeans, especially in Britain. But three political developments around the turn of the millennium led to an attempt to recognise the EU's constitutional status.

First was the prospect of EU enlargement into eastern Europe and the Mediterranean. The addition of ten new countries (with more waiting in line) required renegotiation of the EU's careful allotments of votes, seats and offices. It involved twenty-five governments in enormously complex bargaining. The basic haggling was accomplished in the treaties of Amsterdam and Nice in 1997 and 2000 respectively. The Nice deal was so acrimonious, complex and asymmetrical, however – with votes and seats allocated by 'late night horse trading rather than any mathematical or demographic formula' – that it included a provision for a further round of treaty revision in an inter-governmental conference (IGC) in 2004.[17] Some politicians began to suggest that a rapidly changing union of twenty-five members called for a more fundamental revisiting of basic principles. Undertaking such a deep discussion might also require a new kind of bargaining format. As Tony Blair remarked after the Nice meeting, 'As far as Europe is concerned, we cannot do business like this in the future.'

Second was a fall in public support for the EU after the early 1990s. The proportion of Europeans who saw EU membership as a 'good thing' peaked at 72 per cent in 1991, between the SEA and Maastricht, but then fell steadily to a low of 46 per cent in 1997. These numbers partly reflected an economic downturn, but they were also widely interpreted as representing the replacement of the EU's long-standing 'permissive consensus' in public opinion with a new level of public scrutiny. The slide was also paralleled by a growing chorus of complaints from intellectuals about the Union's 'democratic deficit.'[18] In a variety of ways they argued that delegation of power to the EU had outstripped the development of mechanisms of accountability. Many called for a more open and participatory modification of the treaties to redress the deficit and legitimate the union with the public.

Third was the completion of the historical blueprint for the EU project: the success of monetary union in 1999 realised the most ambitious plans of the post-war founding fathers. The political generation of early post-war Europeanists had passed from the scene. Besides vague and hotly contested plans for a stronger European voice in foreign policy and defence, no one was sure what exactly the EU should do next in a substantive sense.

In this context a broad debate about the union appealed to many of its supporters and even to some of its critics. In May 2000, even before the debacle at Nice in December, the German Foreign Minister, Joschka Fischer, called for a fundamental rethinking of the EU architecture.[19] Few European leaders were ready to endorse his vision of 'full parliamentarisation as a European federation', but French President Jacques Chirac and Blair responded with their own calls to make the treaties clearer, more transparent to citizens and more effective.[20] Chirac mentioned an idea that was circulating around Brussels: that a widely participatory 'convention' might make proposals to the IGC scheduled for 2004. At the end of 2001 the member states endorsed this plan in the Laeken Declaration and accepted language that the result might be called a European 'constitution.' The British and several other governments were slow to accept the notion of a convention and the language of constitutionalisation, fearing the combination would provide a soapbox for Euro-federalists. But eventually even the more sceptical leaders allowed that a discussion with limited ambitions could be useful, especially if it could better codify the bounds of EU competences and so prevent creeping federalisation. The UK's Minister for Europe, Peter Hain, captured the spirit of this acquiescence after the Laeken meeting in December 2001: 'If it is a question of clarifying a tangled web of treaties which are unintelligible, then we are up for that.'

Unlike the British reform agenda, then, the EU constitutional programme did not emerge from specific calls for major change. Much of its justification focused on issues of process, calling for an open, legitimating discussion of the EU project. The Convention on the Future of Europe that opened in Brussels in February 2002 was itself seen as part of the reform effort. An elaborate website allowed citizens to follow and give input to the debates of the 105 delegates from national governments and parliaments, EU institutions and elsewhere. Some 160 organisations across Europe registered as regular partici- pants in the web-based forum. Civil society was also welcomed physically into the convention, with special working groups and plenary sessions scheduled for input from non-governmental organisations.[21] In keeping with this tone, the main substantive themes were the Laeken Declaration's priorities of 'democracy, transparency and efficiency'. Conventioneers were tasked with rendering the EU simpler and more comprehensible, encouraging more bottom-up access to its decision-making, and streamlining or strengthening its cumbersome procedures to generate more effective action.

Though there was no shortage of ideas about how to do so, powerful players both inside and outside the convention constrained its ambitions from the start. As president of the convention the member states chose ex-French President Valéry Giscard d'Estaing. Unlike his erstwhile Gaullist ally and rival Chirac, Giscard was a long-standing champion of strong EU institutions. Yet he held a somewhat idiosyncratic notion of what a strong EU meant – supporting the subordination of national sovereignty to EU processes of majority voting on the one hand, but generally distrusting the independent supranational institutions of the Commission, EP and ECJ on the other.[22] Famous for his brilliance and for his imperious manner, he also inclined much more towards strong leadership than bottom-up transparency. Outside the proceedings, the participants knew that their plans would be realised only if they could be accepted in the subsequent IGC talks between the national governments. National governments also increased their scrutiny of the convention as it advanced, with France and Germany in particular replacing early delegates with their own foreign ministers in late 2002. Throughout the process the British government worked to restrain the convention's ambitions.[23]

In the absence of a mandate for major change and the presence of powerful actors to block it, the convention's arrival at a coherent draft constitution in June 2003 was hailed by many Europhiles as a surprising success. From the viewpoint of EU elites, Giscard had assembled some important innovations. In the name of simplification and transparency the draft abolished the Maastricht pillar structure, uniting EU decision-making in one 'ordinary' procedure with majority voting in the Council of Ministers and an equal bicameral role for the EP (with all legislation requiring majority votes in both bodies). Taxation, defence and foreign policy remained exceptions with unanimity rules, but national vetos would disappear in some sensitive areas (agriculture and fisheries, immigration and asylum, structural and cohesion funds). Another simplification replaced the council's messy 'weighted voting' rules with a 'double majority' of 50 per cent of states and 60 per cent of the EU population. The number of commissioners and MEPs would also be slimmed down. To foster more effective leadership, member states would now select a president of the European Council rather than rotating the presidency among themselves, and a new European Foreign Minister would coordinate external action. For citizens' rights, the draft gave legal force to a Charter of Fundamental Rights drawn up in the late 1990s. Still more impressive was that almost all of the convention draft survived the IGC talks among national governments in autumn 2004 and spring 2005. The bargaining broke down briefly in December 2004, as Spain and Poland rejected the double majority rules that would replace a Nice formula that had disproportionately benefited them.[24] With a watering-down of the double majority to 55 per cent of states and 65 per cent of the population, the governments ultimately accepted most of the convention's work in the final constitution text.

But if the convention and the IGC rejigged the EU rules in ways that mattered to insiders, they did little to change how EU policy-making would relate to its citizens or its broader environment. Indeed, at a broad level it was difficult to see how the constitution would make any real difference for democracy, transparency or effectiveness in Europe. The basic structure of the EU remained as impenetrable as ever. As Paul Craig commented dryly, 'An informed citizen, reading the text of the Draft Constitution assiduously, would still find it difficult to understand the locus and distribution of executive power within the EU.'[25] It was far from clear that more majority voting and a stronger EP role would produce more transparent or effective majoritarian decisions, since the watered-down council double majority actually demanded larger majorities than the previous rules. The new EU Foreign Minister would only represent a slight centralisation of authority in that field. Nor had the convention format secured its goal of attracting wide citizen participation in the process. Peter Norman cites a convention official who 'described the efforts at consultation as a "gallant failure", which pleased the lobbies but failed to get through to the general public'.[26] Three quarters of British citizens had not heard of the convention at the time of its conclusion.

Legal commentaries generally found that the constitution brought 'no relevant structural change' to the legal order.[27] Since law scholars had been emphasising the constitutional nature of the EU for more than a decade, they tended to portray the new text as 'a sensible but far from radical amendment to the institutional architecture and decision-making processes of the Union; some meaningful but equally non-radical nods towards further democratisation of the above; the Charter . . . and some sensible cleaning up of language' – overall a 'Treaty of Nice *bis*'.[28] Expert testimony before the House of Lords European Union Select Committee similarly argued that the constitution had few implications for British law.[29] The Charter of Fundamental Rights seemed likely to impact future discussions of rights, but uncertainty over how far national courts would ultimately allow for extra-national interpretation of basic rights – the 'Kompetenz-Kompetenz' ambiguities – left such effects hard to predict (and this uncertainty was increased by changes to the language on the applicability of the charter during the IGC process). When it came to core constitutional issues – fundamental rights, obligations and relations between citizens and public authorities – the constitution primarily codified a pre-existing order much more than it changed it.

In broad political terms, the novelty of the constitution lay not in its institutional fixes but in its provocative use of the symbolic word 'constitution', and in the decision of many member states to hold referendums to approve it. If citizens generally showed little interest in the convention process or the finer points of the text, in many countries they did mobilise to express a yea or a nay on the EU overall. In France, a poll shortly before the May 2005 referendum found that 80 per cent of respondents had discussed the issue privately in the preceding two weeks. Unfortunately for the EU, however, this grandiose declaration of a 'constitutional' discussion around a largely consolidated constitutional settlement mobilised opposition more than support. Many Europhiles were lukewarm about a treaty modification that contained no new substantive ambitions for the EU and did little to address the Laeken goals of transparency, democracy and efficiency. Making a case for a pro-

European 'no' was neither difficult nor uncommon.[30] Critics, by contrast, leapt at the opportunity to complain about many different aspects of the EU. Tellingly, they focused practically all their attention on broader EU features – market liberalisation, openness to eastern European competition and immigration, questionable accountability – that the constitutional text itself did nothing to alter.[31]

The rejection of the constitution by substantial French and Dutch majorities (54.7 per cent and 61.6 per cent respectively) brought an end to the EU's explicitly constitutional episode. Hopes for revival of the text persist today in some corners of Brussels, but most observers agree that its solid rejection by two core member states makes this politically impossible (especially with leadership changes looming in France and Britain and a grand coalition in place in Germany). On the one hand, the fall of the constitution is a political development of the first order. It leaves the agenda of EU reform stalled. On the other hand, since the constitution did little to alter the main lines of the de facto EU constitution, its demise is not a fundamental constitutional development in the EU arena, let alone in Britain. Once we see that the EU's constitutional episode was an odd, truncated debate in which the word 'constitution' was invoked more to mobilise citizens than to designate an active programme of change, it is easy to understand why neither its rise nor its fall resonated in British constitutional discussions.

Still, this conclusion just drives the chapter's questions back one step. A quick summary of the saga of the EU constitution can explain its isolation from this book's subject. But if, as Ian Loveland argues, the earlier consolidation of the de facto EU constitution amounts to Britain's 'most significant constitutional innovation', how did that development relate to the New Labour reform agenda launched in 1997? And to the extent that there is a relationship between this deeper constitutional EU narrative and British domestic reform, why have they remained discrete in political discourse and as policy domains?

The European context and the 1997 reform agenda

In Chapter 2, Peter Riddell echoes the common description of EU legal supremacy as 'the major constitutional change of the past half-century'. But he then sets EU-related developments aside from a domestic story of constitutional change, as a 'background [that] seldom impinged directly' on national processes and debates. Rather than exhibiting any grand paradox, these two observations simply point to a distinction between legal or institutional principle and concrete political effects. For a polity traditionally understood to be based upon unlimited parliamentary sovereignty, acceptance of a superior federal legal order represents a particularly sharp break in principle. Yet the EU has not surged through this breach to put significantly greater pressure on other domestic constitutional rules. It has had a wide and deep range of concrete effects in regulatory affairs – in everything from financial services to agriculture to labour markets to environmental policy – but its impact on national constitutional rules has been much less striking. Nonetheless, the notion of the EU as background to domestic constitutional reform implies that we may find at least some indirect ways in which the EU context has contributed to this book's story. The connections between the two agendas are most apparent if we focus on three themes: judicial empowerment, citizens' rights and devolution.

The links between the two processes of reform have most commonly been identified in changes to the authority of the British judiciary. Domestic developments have fostered more assertive courts since the mid-1960s but consolidation of the EU order has given them a new claim on power and influence. Historically, British judicial review has been weak relative to the authority of many other countries' courts. To the extent that courts set any constraints on other branches of government, the common-law principles of lawfulness, procedural regularity and reasonableness provided the basis for review of public action and rules.[32] In the 1970s and 1980s judges began to review administrative action more aggressively along these lines. Their new activism was at least partly a response to the general crisis of confidence in Britain's institutions in the 1970s, and reflected generational shifts in the judiciary. More active review also followed simply from the expanding tasks of government, as state administration reached deeper into social issues and immigration – the subjects of most of the key cases of judicial assertiveness.[33] Still, domestic sources ultimately offered limited bases for judicial empowerment. Most obviously, common law without a codified constitution or Bill of Rights limited courts' role to reviewing the implementation of statutes, not statutes themselves. Even in reviewing implementation, British courts have been greatly disadvantaged by a political system with largely unchecked single-party governments and relatively strong party organisations. As Martin Shapiro notes, 'An English reviewing court knows that should it find a piece of delegated law-making [or administrative action] unlawful under the primary law, the government will probably order parliament to change the primary law to fit the secondary one.'[34] British governments find it easier to 'correct' a judicial interpretation than does any other European executive. Given these domestic features, links to external sources of law or rights that were not easily manipulable by the British government took on a special significance for potential judicial power.

The European Communities Act 1972 provided the first statutory tether to such an external anchor. We have seen that it created the possibility – eventually realised in *Factortame* – that judges would move into the business of disapplying Acts of Parliament. More important for judicial power in practice, however, was that it inter-laced many cases of lower-level review with a body of EU legislation that cannot be routinely altered by a simple majority in the House of Commons. While disapplication of statutes remains exceptional, two observations suggest that EU law has emboldened British courts at the much more common level of administrative review. In broad patterns, traditionally un-English and relatively expansive doctrines of review such as proportionality, purposive interpretation and legitimate expectations have increasingly been invoked not just in EU-related cases but in domestic review more broadly.[35] More specifically, a few EU-related cases have led to traceable 'spillover' of new claims of judicial authority.

A secondary aspect of the *Factortame* cases provides one example. While the case waited for a ruling from the ECJ, Factortame Ltd sought an interim injunction against the British policies that were harming its fishing business. Initially the Law Lords rejected this idea. Since British courts on their own could not hold legislation invalid, argued the court, they could not issue any injunction until the ECJ had ruled. The ECJ then ruled against the UK statute, and added that in future national courts must decide on their own whether to grant interim injunctions. In *Factortame (No. 2)*, the Law Lords accepted that British courts could grant such interim relief in cases raising points of EU law. Just a few years later they allowed interim injunctions more generally in a high-profile immigration case of *M. v. Home Office* – creating a widely recognised 'spillover of the holding of [*Factortame*] to a purely domestic situation'.[36] *Factortame*'s rather abstract assertion of EU legal primacy may, in time, have encouraged British courts to claim a more general kind of authority.

Another example carries our exploration of the EU background a step closer to recent constitutional reform. In *Thoburn v. Sunderland City Council*,[37] fresh produce traders objected to being prosecuted for using imperial weights rather than the metric measures required by the EU Metrication Directive of

1979. Not until 1994 did the UK use secondary legislation, under the European Communities Act 1972, to require metric measures and thereby revoke the Weights and Measures Act 1985 that allowed for both systems. The produce traders suggested that the 1985 Act, in contradicting an EU directive, had effectively repealed part of the 1972 Act, thereby invalidating the secondary legislation based upon the latter in 1994. Not only did the court reject this argument in 2003, it built its defence of the 1972 Act around the new notion of a 'constitutional statute'. Such a statute 'conditions the legal relationship between citizen and state in some general, overarching manner' and has an entrenched quality: 'Ordinary statutes may be implicitly repealed. Constitutional statutes may not.'[38] In the leading judgment Lord Justice Laws went further: 'The conditions of Parliament's legislative supremacy in the United Kingdom necessarily remain in the UK's hands. But the traditional doctrine has in my judgment been modified. It has been done by the common law, wholly consistently with constitutional principle.'[39]

Here, Laws endorsed a change in the overarching narrative of British constitutional law. It reflected what Shapiro calls a 'modified parliamentary sovereignty' view of the British constitution, as opposed to the 'pure parliamentary sovereignty' interpretation that remained the orthodoxy into the 1990s. The 'modified' view holds that Parliament and the courts have always been partners in making laws. Parliamentary self-restraint meant that the shifting limits to parliamentary sovereignty (and the courts' potential enforcement of them) simply tended to be tacit in the past, with the majority generally refraining from passing laws that could be seen as undercutting basic conventional rights.[40] Shapiro argues that the advocates of this interpretation (such as Laws or legal theorists Paul Craig or Mark Elliott) see the EU as an important part of the rising influence of this 'modified' view of domestic constitutional law: parliamentary action has connected the UK constitution to rights 'grounded' in the European Convention on Human Rights (ECHR) and the EU treaties, but these rights are '*independently* interpreted by English judges who are part of a European community of independent judges which itself transcends national sovereignties'.[41]

In other words, the anchoring of elements of British judicial review in the external system of the EU has encouraged judges to reinterpret their political role more broadly. As Kate Malleson details in Chapter 6, this reinterpretation has in turn encouraged members of the judiciary to express greater concerns about judicial independence. Again, the EU-related mechanisms in these changes in judicial attitudes – let alone in the subsequent reforms of the Lord

Chancellor's office and plan for a Supreme Court – are at most secondary and indirect. As Damian Chalmers argues, distinct domestic changes preceded the main instances of EU influence: 'It was only after the judiciary repositioned itself, in disputes that did not involve EC law, vis-à-vis the other arms of government that the incidence of [more aggressive judicial action] involving EC law increased.'[42] Nor did the recent reforms flow in any direct way from the judiciary itself, instead emerging rather suddenly from the government and provoking complaints from the legal community about a lack of consultation. Still, Malleson stresses that the reforms were essentially 'intended to secure the independence of the judiciary' and were bolstered by a rising sense in judicial circles that the British system was 'out of step with the rest of Europe'.[43] Once British judges began to seek stronger powers of review, the EU context provided an external legal anchor for review, a string of cases as opportunities for new precedents and an excuse for comparison to other legal systems where judicial independence was more distinctly institutionalised.

Factortame also helped embolden the proponents of a British Bill of Rights and facilitated implementation of the Human Rights Act 1998, at least on the margins. While Britain had taken a prominent role in negotiating the ECHR after the Second World War and subsequently allowed its citizens access to the Strasbourg ECHR court, it had not translated the convention into domestic law. The chief objection to such legislation from both major parties was parliamentary sovereignty. Any Bill of Rights would effectively mean constitutional review of statutes and so might bring with it restrictions on the sovereignty of future Parliaments. Although the ECHR has no direct organisational or legal relationship with the EU (which is based in wholly separate treaties), the Law Lords' acceptance of the possibility of constitutional review in *Factortame* was not lost on advocates of ECHR incorporation. 'Now that Britain's highest judicial authority had permitted the 1972 Parliament to bind its successors,' writes Danny Nicol, 'there was pressure to use similar provisions to entrench Convention rights.'[44] In the early 1990s both Paul Craig and William Wade predicted that *Factortame* would facilitate the passage of a Bill of Rights.[45] As with judicial review, this is not to deny the mainly domestic impetus to ECHR incorporation. It enjoyed both old philosophical roots and newer momentum as a reaction to the long period of Conservative rule. Nor did the EU's legal breach of parliamentary sovereignty fully sweep away all constitutional objections to the ECHR. The Human Rights Act 1998 bowed to Diceyan tradition, leaving to Parliament the decision on how to respond to any judicial finding on domestic law that contradicted the convention. But without the earlier changes arising from EU law, the legislation would have been regarded as even more threatening to the established order. Instead, the few cases where courts have issued declarations of incompatibility have appeared less as novel constitutional challenges and more as modest additions to a broader process of judicialisation.[46]

The EU context has also provided encouragement to advocates of devolution. They gathered force in the 1980s mainly in reaction to Margaret Thatcher's combination of market liberalisation and state centralisation, but from the early 1980s they increasingly pointed to the European project as supportive of their agenda. Both the Scottish National Party (SNP) and Plaid Cymru in Wales shifted from anti-EEC positions to more Europeanist discourse in the mid-1980s. The SNP officially endorsed EEC membership in 1983, and by 1988 had taken 'Independence in Europe' as its main slogan. Labour politicians in both nations followed suit, reflecting and contributing to the Labour move to a more pro-European position in the 1980s.[47] As one of the architects of the SNP shift explained in 1986, the EEC provided a framework that would facilitate a transition to independence, limiting economic dislocation and political isolation as Scotland separated from the UK.[48] More moderate advocates of devolution, such as Labour's John Smith, echoed this thought in suggesting that Europe's model of 'multi-level government' legitimated domestic decentralisation.[49] On the basis of opinion polls that show strong support for 'independence in Europe', an option that MORI began including in its regular surveys in 1988, Michael Keating concludes that 'there is no doubt about the importance of this [European] reassurance factor' in the rise of support for devolution in the 1980s.[50] Domestic political concerns drove this rise, but the European framework helped people to perceive and present devolution as forward-looking reform rather than regional separatism.

Further contributing to a sense of European support for regionalism was rising EC funding for regional development (on top of substantial funding that Scotland and Wales already received from the Common Agricultural Policy and European fisheries policies). Scotland would receive a cumulative £2.6 billion from the European Regional Development Fund from 1975 until 1988, and more from 1989 until 1999.[51] The launch of Jacques Delors's Social Charter initiative at the end of the 1980s was also received by many Scots and Welsh (as well as by Labour MPs across the UK) as a sign that the European project could support their socio-economic priorities.[52] Overall, whether in terms of broad institutional models, regional subsidies or supportive policy priorities, pro-devolution actors in Britain have consistently and explicitly seen the EU order of the early 1990s as providing a safety net for greater regional autonomy. It helped them to imagine how modest-sized regions could safely take more responsibility for their own affairs without risking isolation on the margins of Europe.

The EU has continued to offer modest support for devolution in the implementation of the 1997 reforms. To some degree it has bolstered the devolved authorities by giving them a greater policy role outside the UK than would have been probable if the EU had not existed. This dynamic was already visible before 1997, pulling the Scottish Office in particular into many EU policy discussions. It held formal responsibility for ensuring respect of EU legislation in Scotland, and three quarters of its divisions interacted with the EU in some way (in agriculture, fisheries, environmental protection, electricity, water, rural affairs, roads, vocational education and so on).[53] These external interactions sometimes strengthened the hand of Scottish Office officials in intra-UK networks:

> The Scottish Office was one of those departments ... which, due to having built up their own expertise, did not have to over-rely on the European Secretariat's advice and support functions [in EU-related policy issues]. From the perspective of the Scottish Office, the fact that lower grade officials had developed direct EU-level contacts over time meant that there was less need to depend upon Whitehall channels for information provision.[54]

The post-devolution authorities gained more formally recognised roles in UK policy-making vis-à-vis the EU, and some new direct connections to the EU arena as well.[55] In the approach to each six-month EU presidency, ministers from Whitehall and the devolved administrations discuss the agenda in a joint ministerial conference for European affairs. In 2002 the Joint Ministerial Committee on Europe even produced a UK–Scottish–Welsh paper for submission to the Convention on the Future of Europe.[56] Official Scottish and Welsh offices for direct representation in Brussels were opened in 1999 and 2000. Scottish and Welsh elites also show signs of broader-based involvement in EU policy making, not just a slightly deeper and more formal role in intra-UK negotiations. The Holyrood Parliament and the Welsh Assembly quickly created European Union committees to track EU issues. The Scottish committee has been particularly active, meeting frequently and publishing thirty major reports between November 1999 and June 2004.[57]

This scrutiny in the new legislatures represents a heightened level of formal discussion on international matters in the Scottish and Welsh arenas – at least creating the potential for the development of distinct regional positions and for the prosecution of local interests beyond the UK's borders. The Scottish Executive has also aggressively pursued relationships with other 'constitutional regions' across the EU, attempting to emphasise its state-like status alongside powerful entities such as Catalonia or the German *Länder*.[58]

If the Labour government's programme of constitutional modernisation flows mainly from domestic political considerations, its fit with 'Europeanisation' is not just a coincidence. As Tony Wright and Peter Riddell point out, Thatcher deserves the title of 'the real architect of constitutional reform in Britain'.[59] The diverse elements of the reform agenda have multiple motivations, but a common theme is that all are ways to anchor the British polity in obstacles to executive – and especially Conservative – dominance. The EU project too has multiple motivations, but it was intended first and foremost to put constraints on the nation-state in order to prevent war within Europe. Many of its features and consequences were not foreseen by its founding fathers, of course, and like the domestic reform agenda they do not form any sort of seamless political model. Still, we should hardly be surprised that the EU order brought with it modest encouragement for a similar list of constraints on national government action. Thatcher's hostility to the EU's political dimension – which became extreme after she left power and the EU order consolidated in the 1990s – reflects some of the same debates over shared authority that we see around domestic reform. Despite the enduring separation in political practice between the two constitutional agendas, the enemy of their enemy has been their friend.

On the isolation of EU issues

The EU is the source of Britain's 'most significant constitutional innovation' and yet the Blair government's programme of constitutional change has paid very little attention to it. Especially if we ask this book's main question – what is the overall story of constitutional reform under New Labour? – the EU appears to be relevant only in piecemeal, secondary ways. But to observe this separation is not to explain it. The EU has had deep and widespread effects on British policies, and one claim of classic political-science wisdom is that 'policy determines politics.'[60] We typically expect patterns of political mobilisation and discourse to follow shifting flows of policy-making power and money. Indeed, the core expectation of the founders of the EU was precisely that integration of policy-making would lead to a deeper fusion of political loyalties, polities and identities. Why have the emergence of a constitutional EU order and British constitutional politics remained separate in political action?

At one level the book's question slightly exaggerates the apparent separation. Andrew McDonald and Robert Hazell stress that there is not actually much of an overall story or 'single narrative' of domestic constitutional reform for EU developments to relate to. New Labour's constitutional actions consist of a package of fairly distinct proposals bundled into a programme by complex party politics. The EU played no role in how that package came together. When we disaggregate the domestic reforms, though, we find experts on each point paying more attention to the EU and the ECJ. Legal theorists and judges writing on judicial empowerment rarely fail to mention the EU. For a scholar of international law it is now commonplace to set the Human Rights Act alongside the institutional and legal development of the EU as parallel strands in a broad expansion of international governance. The notion that the EU encourages and legitimates regional autonomy and 'multi-level government' is standard fare in political and academic discussions of devolution. In other words, the EU looks more distant and isolated from the rather thin discourse of 'constitutional reform' as a package than it does from its component parts.

But if the EU makes some appearances in discussions of the separate pieces of the domestic reform agenda, it remains separate from the main patterns of domestic politics. Not only have EU issues been largely absent from the explicit conception and management of New Labour's constitutional reforms, but they remain strikingly isolated from domestic politics and policy-making more broadly. As one recent study concludes, Britain has a 'Europeanised government in a non-Europeanised polity'.[61]

The EU has effected a 'quiet revolution' in central government and policy-making since the 1970s.[62] The border between domestic policy-making and the international arena became progressively more porous at all levels as EU expertise and connections spread across departments. The Foreign and Commonwealth Office (FCO) gradually lost its monopoly on international diplomacy. It also lost power to Downing Street as successive Prime Ministers took leading roles in EU policy. At the same time, major decision-making in EU-related areas gradually centralised in 'an informal, yet powerful elite comprising No. 10, the FCO, the Cabinet Office and the UK permanent representation'.[63] Thus the FCO's loss of its international 'gatekeeper' role was compensated by its retention of the leading departmental role in this new nexus of policy making.[64] British central government emerged both more internationalised and more centralised.

In the shape of these policy-making shifts to a 'Europeanised government' we find one reason for the 'non-Europeanised polity'. Decision-making in the EU is still steered by officials who are categorised as diplomats and who manage relations with the outside world. They are located institutionally in a separate conceptual realm from domestic politics. The nebulous policy network between Downing Street, the FCO and diplomats in Brussels is also difficult to chart in familiar organisational terms. The sheer complexity and geographic scope of EU affairs would keep them relatively distant from public discussion no matter how they were organised, but the current policy-making configuration does little to facilitate transparency or bottom-up mobilisation.

Yet the deeper foundations of the wall between the EU and the domestic polity lie away from the corridors of Whitehall. They are built on mutually reinforcing features of political party organisations and public opinion. The definition of Britain's main political parties (like those almost everywhere else in Europe) around socio-economic debates of right and left make them into obstacles to coherent representation and debate on EU issues. As has long been obvious in Britain and is now well documented across Europe, political divisions over sovereignty and supranationality tend to cross-cut right and left.[65] Political parties constructed on right or left platforms have thus tended to divide over major EU decisions. When they have not appeared divided, this has more often reflected leadership with strong popularity on other issues or tight control of party discipline than spontaneous agreement.[66] Whatever their views of the European project, party leaders have generally seen strong incentives to avoid explicit discussion of EU issues – focusing on the more familiar right/left issues around which their organisations, discourses and networks of funding and recruitment are constructed.

Patterns of voting behaviour greatly amplify the organisational disincentives to broader politicisation of the EU. The low resonance of EU debates with voters has left little ambiguity about where electoral incentives lie in the choice of issues for party campaigning. Even in Britain, with its special sensitivity to sovereignty and a media that treats EU issues with remarkable hyperbole, EU issues have never had a decisive impact on national elections. In the 2001 elections, with the Conservatives campaigning heavily on anti-EU themes, Europe only registered as the tenth most important issue in polls. In the 2005 elections only 5 per cent of voters even mentioned Europe as an important issue. Though a clear majority of British voters consistently say they dislike supranationality and oppose federalising steps such as monetary union, there are few votes to be gained on these themes. Citizens continue to vote mainly on the basis of past party identification, perceptions of economic policies and parties' or leaders' economic competence and social issues.[67]

The British Conservatives since the 1990s constitute the main exception that proves these rules: the only major party in a large European country to make the EU a central campaign theme in recent years. Under John Major the Tories were riven by internal debate over the EU and squeezed by New Labour's move to the socio-economic centre. The pro-European wing was considerably weakened within the smaller parliamentary party that emerged from the 1997 landslide. Under William Hague the party consolidated around a platform that put anti-EU themes front and centre, leaving pro-EU heavyweights such as Kenneth Clarke, Michael Heseltine, Leon Brittan and Chris Patten isolated and 'spitting tacks'.[68] But in spite of most voters' sympathy for anti-supranational views, this brought the party no electoral benefit in 2001 – a result that was so foreseeable that electoral analysts still puzzle over the choice of strategy.[69] More recently, part of David Cameron's increasingly successful renovation of the party has been a studious avoidance of EU issues. He effectively acknowledged, as have most of his predecessors in Britain and most mainstream party leaders in the rest of Europe for decades, that attention to the EU generates elite-level tension without electoral reward.

The failure of the EU constitution, and the broader crisis of the EU that it represents, seem likely to maintain the isolation of EU issues from domestic politics. The French and Dutch spared the British the trial of their own referendum. Britain's recent economic success relative to the Continent also moved debates on the pound and EMU off the political radar. The one track on which the EU does seem to be moving forwards – enlargement – has generally been welcomed by both pro- and anti-EU British politicians. Immigration concerns have complicated British views about enlargement, but at a broad level British elites have seen a double benefit in 'widening' the EU to Romania and Bulgaria in 2007 and then to the rest of the Balkans and Turkey. Not only will enlargement consolidate markets, democracy and law in these countries, it will also obstruct federal-style EU 'deepening' with a larger number of more heterogeneous members. Yet even as the advocates of a more federal EU see their hopes fading, their earlier accomplishments settle more deeply into the Continent's foundations. The EU constitutional order is strongly entrenched.

In future the EU will remain an important but distant part of the background to domestic constitutional debates. Constitutional politics in Britain will still be most comprehensible as a tale of two constitutions, not as a single federal order. Domestic advocates of further reform will continue to draw mainly on national-level discourses, precedents and resources to advance their agendas. In electoral campaigns they will pay little public attention to connections to EU themes, even when EU principles or resources support their cause, because of the divisive ramifications for party politics. Beyond the electoral spotlight, however – inside the judiciary and legal community, in Scottish and Welsh policy networks, among proponents of more expansive codified rights – the evolving EU will subtly influence the arguments and resources which domestic reformers use in pursuing institutional change. The EU has transformed the legal and political context for member states. Despite all appearances, Britain's constitutional debates no longer take place on an island.

9

Constitutional reform and British political identity

Jack Citrin[1]

Introduction

Two successive revolutions have transformed the textbook version of the British political system. First, the Thatcher regime elevated the market over the state, ending the post-war consensus of nationalised industries and a generous welfare state. Privatisation and competition became the new watch-words of social policy, but, paradoxically, the reduction in the power of economic monopolies was accompanied by the centralisation of administrative authority.

What largely made Labour 'New' in the 1990s was its acceptance, however resignedly, of the main principles of Margaret Thatcher's reforms. To be sure, New Labour promised a kinder and gentler version of capitalism than Thatcher had pursued, but when in 1997 the newly elected Blair government immediately ceded control over monetary policy to the Bank of England, it was clear that there would be no counter-revolution.

Instead, the Labour government embarked on a second revolution: a programme of constitutional reform that substantially altered the structure of government in Britain. The purpose, in Lord Irvine of Lairg's words, was 'to develop a maturer democracy with different centres of power, where individuals enjoy greater rights and where government is carried out closer to the people'[2] and in so doing to overcome the 'crisis of confidence' in British institutions.[3] Irvine's description of the reform programme's goals repeatedly stressed the need to change the culture of government and the importance of flexibility. The constant mantra was that one administrative suit does not fit all parts of the British body politic.

Reviewing New Labour's actions towards the end of the first Blair government, Anthony King concluded that the unifying theme and emerging outcome of constitutional reform was a shift from 'power-hoarding' to 'power-sharing.'[4] A partial list of proposals makes this clear: devolution of power to Scotland, Wales and Northern Ireland; more autonomy and less uniformity for local government; a Freedom of Information Act to limit official claims to secrecy; making the European Convention of Human Rights (ECHR) enforceable in domestic courts; the use of referendums on important questions such as devolution or a new constitution for the European Union; and modernisation of procedures in the House of Commons to give committees a more prominent role.

The totality of these reforms has undeniably encroached upon parliamentary sovereignty, unitary government and the fusion of executive and legislative power, the core elements of the distinctive British political system. New Labour's constitutional reforms look suspiciously like Americanisation. Devolution exudes the odour of federalism; the Human Rights Act strengthens judicial review; referendums introduce direct democracy; the Freedom of Information Act limits executive privilege. Openness, accountability, minority rights and popular consent are the ambitious goals for New Labour's new British constitution.[5]

Justified as a necessary response to public discontent, New Labour's constitutional revolution in reality was a top-down affair. Scottish nationalism aside, there was no mass movement for devolution or regional government. Indeed, after the overwhelming defeat of the proposal for a regional assembly for the north-east of England, the government cancelled other planned referendums. There was also no great public clamour for incorporating the ECHR, passing the Freedom of Information Act or proposals for electoral and legislative reform. New Labour's programme of constitutional reform has been an endeavour of elites. Public opinion about the programme is best described as permissive rather than engaged one way or another.

Nevertheless, one ingredient vital to the successful institutionalisation of New Labour's reforms and to its remaining hopes for future change is public acceptance of what already has been achieved. In a democracy, public opinion ultimately constrains what actions elected leaders can safely contemplate. More significantly, the institutional legitimacy of institutions enhances voluntary compliance with what governments decide. When allegiance to prevailing constitutional arrangements cuts across social classes, interest groups and political parties, the incentives to mobilise opposition and turn back the clock of reform are diminished.

This chapter concentrates on the view from below. It analyses how the British public feels about the main components of New Labour's constitutional reforms. It concentrates on the national question – on how New Labour's constitutional reforms and other contemporary developments are shaping Britons' political identities. Political structures both reflect and shape popular identifications and loyalties. New Labour's reforms assumed the existence of strong sub-national identities in Scotland and Wales, and the move towards regional assemblies in England reflected the belief, or perhaps the hope, that an equivalent sense of group consciousness existed there.

The chapter will consider public attitudes towards the nation in the light of three of the principal changes to have affected Britain: devolution; European integration; and the more diverse ethnic composition of the country arising from migration in a globalised world. Since devolution was central to New Labour's constitutional reform agenda, an obvious place to begin is by asking how this has affected Britons' sense of national identity – their sense of who belongs to their political community and what attributes define their shared 'Britishness.'

The constitutional reform agenda after 1997 did not address European integration. Yet the United Kingdom's continued membership of the EU is arguably the most significant constitutional change to have happened over the past fifty years; Craig Parsons demonstrates in this volume that the courts came to confirm beyond any doubt that European law had primacy over Westminster statutes. How Britons reconcile their national identity with attachment to Europe is important to know, since these attitudes affect the government's freedom of manoeuvre in the continuing negotiations over the future of the EU.

New Labour's constitutional reforms similarly ignored the dilemmas of multiculturalism, although Lord Irvine did proclaim confidently that 'devolution will forge a new Britain – a strong multi-national, multicultural, multi-ethnic country where our strength will come not from uniformity but from our diversity; not from a flattening process of programmed assimilation, but from democratic renewal through mutual toleration and respect'.[6] One out of many, as the Americans put it.

September 11 and its aftermath caused old anxieties about the loyalties of immigrants to resurface and put the issue of national cohesion back on the political agenda. Gordon Brown, in particular, has called for a renewal of British patriotism defined by inclusive democratic values, not ancestry or place of birth.[7] How Brown's concern may affect a new phase of constitutional reform is unclear, but it is important to understand the prevailing public conceptions of who should belong to Britain and on what terms.

To explore British attitudes towards the constitutional reform agenda and the implications for national identity, I review the results of surveys conducted between 1995 and 2005, building on important earlier studies by John Curtice and Anthony Heath.[8] Wherever data are available, comparisons are made over time and across respondents grouped by region, party affiliation and age in order to speculate about the likely trajectory of future preferences.

The acceptance of devolution for Scotland and Wales

Public opinion about separate legislatures for Scotland and Wales suggests that New Labour's programme of devolution for these nations is here to stay. In 1997, the British General Election Study found that a plurality of 42 per cent of the British public favoured an arrangement in which Scotland remained part of the UK but had its own parliament with the power to tax. Table 9.1 shows that support for a Scottish Parliament with tax-raising powers was the most popular position in England as well as in Scotland. Labour and Liberal Democrat supporters were more strongly in favour of devolution than Conservatives.

Between 1997 and 2003, acceptance of devolution grew across the UK and among all party supporters and age groups. The most notable shifts were in England and among Conservative partisans. For example, the proportion of English respondents favouring a strong Scottish Parliament within the UK rose from 42 to 57 per cent. Among Conservatives there was a 19-point increase in those choosing this position, resulting in a new majority for the strong form of devolution. In the light of such shifts, it is fair to conclude that devolution is for the moment a psychological as well as a legal done deal.

Table 9.2 shows a similar (albeit weaker) trend in opinion about devolution for Wales. Enthusiasm for devolution was less intense among the Welsh than the Scottish. Indeed, in both 1997 and 2003 support for Welsh independence was stronger among Scots than the Welsh themselves. Still, preferences for devolution for Wales grew among all groups. Whatever their nation, party affiliation or age, more respondents favoured either independence or a strong Welsh Parliament in 2003 than 1997.

To echo Curtice, there now is strong majority support for the principle of devolution for Scotland and Wales among all three national sub-groups.[9]

Nationalist sentiment is most intense in Scotland, but the current settlement of an autonomous Parliament with some taxing power is the dominant preference throughout Britain. At the same time, Curtice sounds a warning note about the stability of current preferences. He points out that in both Scotland and Wales, assessments of the effects of devolution reflect disappointment, with the majority believing in 2003 that the existence of separate parliaments had made no real difference in giving ordinary people more influence in government or improving local education. The perceived benefits of devolution were more symbolic than real, and if the gap between expectations and achievements persists, the present consensus on the proper scope of authority for the regional legislatures could crumble.

Table 9.1: Trends in opinion about Scottish devolution

Scotland should be . . .

	fully independent of UK★		*part of UK, with own Parliament and tax-raising powers*		*part of UK, with own Parliament but no tax-raising powers*		*part of UK, without own Parliament*	
	1997	*2003*	*1997*	*2003*	*1997*	*2003*	*1997*	*2003*
Total	18	23	42	54	16	8	24	14
England	15	20	42	57	18	9	25	15
Scotland	27	27	44	51	10	7	19	14
Wales	13	N/A	33	N/A	24	N/A	30	N/A
Conservative	7	14	33	52	20	10	40	24
Labour	20	21	48	60	15	9	18	10
Lib Dem	15	13	50	67	15	6	20	14
17–34	24	24	41	58	16	9	19	9
35–54	19	25	44	54	16	8	22	13
55+	13	21	41	52	16	9	30	18

★ This category combines two responses: Scotland should be independent from the UK but part of the EU, and Scotland should be independent of both the UK and the EU.

Table entries are percentages.

Number of respondents: in total there were 3,341 and 3,102 in 1997 and 2003 respectively. There were 2,345 English respondents in 1997 and 1,689 in 2003; 832 Scottish respondents in 1997 and 1,413 in 2003; 164 Welsh respondents in 1997 and none in 2003.

Source: 1997: British General Election Study; 2003: British National Identity and Constitutional Change Survey 2001–2003. The question wording was identical in both surveys.

Table 9.2: Trends in opinion about Welsh devolution

Wales should be . . .

	fully independent of UK★		*part of UK, with own Parliament and tax-raising powers*		*part of UK, with own Parliament but no tax-raising powers*		*part of UK, without own Parliament*	
	1997	*2003*	*1997*	*2003*	*1997*	*2003*	*1997*	*2003*
Total	16	19	41	42	18	21	26	18
England	14	19	40	43	19	21	28	17
Scotland	22	22	47	44	14	15	18	17
Wales	10	14	36	37	20	27	34	22
Conservative	7	11	33	37	21	23	39	29
Labour	17	18	46	45	16	23	20	15
Lib Dem	14	12	46	50	20	24	20	15
17–34	20	21	40	44	18	22	22	13
35–54	16	21	44	42	17	20	24	17
55+	12	16	40	40	18	21	31	23

★ This category combines two responses: Wales should be independent from the UK but part of the EU, and Wales should be independent of both the UK and the EU.
Table entries are percentages.
Number of respondents: in total there were 3,196 and 3,722 in 1997 and 2003 respectively. There were 2,333 English respondents in 1997 and 1,674 in 2003; 691 Scottish respondents in 1997 and 1,105 in 2003; 172 Welsh respondents in 1997 and 843 in 2003.
Source: 1997: British General Election Study; 2003: British National Identity and Constitutional Change Survey 2001–2003. The question wording was identical in both surveys.

The example of devolution in Scotland and Wales failed to generate demand for similar institutions in England. Surveys conducted between 1999 and 2003 consistently showed majority support for England to be governed as 'it is now', with its laws being made solely by the UK Parliament. Table 9.3 shows that between 1999 and 2003, those favouring the existence of regional assemblies to 'run services' such as healthcare did increase from 15 to 24 per cent among English respondents, but at the same time, support for the option of a separate English Parliament on Scottish lines did not grow at all. Predictably, Conservatives were most favourable to the status quo, but throughout the period under study a majority of the followers of all three main parties favoured sticking with things as they are. One possible reason that the example of devolution in Scotland and Wales has had no great effect on support for regional government among the English is the widespread belief that this reform would have no significant impact on improving political or economic outcomes.[10]

Table 9.3: Trends in opinion on regional devolution in England

	The ideal method for governing England would be . . .					
	as now, with laws by UK Parliament		*for each region of England to have its own assembly that runs services such as health*		*For England as a whole to have its own new Parliament with law-making powers*	
	1999	*2003*	*1999*	*2003*	*1999*	*2003*
Total	65	56	15	24	18	18
Conservative	69	60	10	20	20	18
Labour	66	59	16	24	16	17
Lib/Dem	62	53	19	30	19	16
17–34	61	52	18	22	20	25
35–54	63	55	18	22	18	21
55+	70	65	11	20	18	14

Table entries are percentages.

Only respondents living in England were asked this question. Number of respondents: 2,623 in 1999 and 923 in 2003.

Source: 1999: British Social Attitudes Survey; 2003: British National Identity and Constitutional Change Survey 2001–2003. The question wording was identical in both surveys.

As for the ready acceptance of devolution among the English, one likely explanation is that the reform so far has been costless. Implemented during a time of growing public expenditure in all parts of the UK, the net fiscal gains for Scotland and Wales have not required a visible sacrifice for taxpayers in England. Devolution has yet to generate a debate equivalent to the persistent argument in the United States about how federal revenues are distributed to the states. If it should happen that English voters have to pay a steeper price for devolution and come to see themselves as subsidising 'separate' nations who can tax themselves, then preferences regarding devolution and the need for an England-only Parliament could change.

Devolution and political identity

Identity is a slippery concept, simultaneously referring to sameness and difference. A group identity unites one with some people while dividing one from others. On the other hand people do have multiple identities, belonging to several groups, and some are more overarching or inclusive than others. The Scots, Welsh and English all can be categorised as British, just as Britons, French and Germans all can be categorised as European and call themselves such. Identifying *as*, however, is not the same as identifying *with*. The strength of one's emotional attachment to a particular group varies, of course, and it can be critical to know how people prioritise their several identities, as shown by concern about the loyalty of British Muslims after the London bombings of 7 July 2005.

The attributes defining membership of a particular identity group are malleable and often contested. Is being Scottish, Welsh or English – which I, for purposes of shorthand, will call national identities – a matter of descent, place of birth or mere residence? And if ancestry determines this identity, then what makes all these groups British is a more inclusive quality, although this too may be bounded by descent or place of birth.

New Labour assumed the existence of separate Scottish and Welsh nations, defending devolution as a sensitive response to differences in cultures and desires. Ernest Gellner famously asserted that a multi-ethnic nation is an oxymoron, on the grounds that a substantial dose of cultural unity is a necessary condition for feelings of mutuality in modern society.[11] More recently, Samuel Huntington has worried that the changing ethnic composition of the United States is challenging that country's tradition of national identity.[12]

By definition, the common identity of a multi-national, multicultural Britain (or Europe) must be civic rather than ethnic. This recognition under-lines Gordon Brown's conception of a value-based Britishness, a distinctive identity based on a tradition of individual liberties, civic engagement, and fairness and decency to neighbours and the less fortunate.[13] As long as these values guide conduct, Brown argues, it matters not that Britons of Pakistani origin root for their ancestral home in Test matches or that Scots cheer for 'anyone who beats England' in the Word Cup. In a similar vein, Jürgen Habermas has advocated 'constitutional patriotism' – a principled commit-ment to egalitarian and democratic values – as the only possible foundation for a common European identity.[14] Whether such abstractions provide a strong enough emotional glue to bind together people of different languages, religions and histories remains problematic.

Surveys conducted between 1997 and 2005 have asked respondents where they perceived their identity on a spectrum from only British on the one hand to only English, Welsh or Scottish on the other. Table 9.4 shows that in all three nations between 1997 and 2006 there was a rise in the share of the public opting for an exclusively national identification. In Scotland, the proportion saying they felt only Scottish and not British grew from 23 percent to 41 percent; in England, those feeling exclusively English rose from 7 to 17 percent. As these figures suggest, prioritising 'ethnic' over British identities was much more widespread in Scotland and Wales than in England.[15] Curtice has pointed out that a sense of being British is pervasive in England; as the overwhelming majority in the UK, the English are more likely to equate their national and British identities. Accordingly, how a person balances national and British identifications has less of an influence on preferences regarding independence or devolution in England than in Scotland or Wales. For the Scots and Welsh, the stronger one's sense of ethnic consciousness the more likely one is to favour independence or a stronger variant of devolution.[16]

Table 9.4: Trends in 'ethnic' and 'British' identities

Which, if any, of the following best describes how you see yourself?	England			Scotland			Wales		
	1997	2003	2005	1997	2003	2005	1997	2003	2005
'Ethnic' not British	7	17	16	23	31	34	17	21	17
More 'ethnic' than British	17	19	14	38	34	31	26	27	20
Equally 'ethnic' and British	45	31	50	27	22	27	34	29	35
More British than 'ethnic'	14	13	9	4	4	4	10	8	12
British not 'ethnic'	9	10	11	4	4	4	12	9	15

Table entries are percentages.
1997 and 2003 figures taken from John Curtice, 'Public Opinion and the Future of Devolution', in Alan Trench (ed.), *The Dynamics of Devolution: The State of the Nations 2005* (Exeter: Imprint Academic, 2005), pp. 117–36. 2005 figures obtained from the 2005 British General Election Study. For sample sizes in 1997 and 2003 see Curtice, 'Public Opinion and the Future of Devolution'. The total number of respondents in the 2005 sample is 3,797. Of these, 2,123 respondents were living in England, 960 in Scotland and 714 in Wales.

More recent data on the balancing of 'ethnic' and British identities comes from the 2005 British General Election Study. English respondents make up more than 80 per cent of this sample; nevertheless, 40 per cent of the electorate said they felt only or mainly English, Scottish or Welsh rather than British, slightly more than the 35 percent in the 1997 British General Election Study. The 2005 British General Election Study also shows that the connection between party affiliation and preferences for a regional (or 'ethnic') identity differs between England, where Conservatives are more likely to prioritise their English over their British identity, and Scotland or Wales, where Labour and Liberal Democrat supporters elevate the national over the British. Ironically, to the extent that devolution has had a consciousness-raising effect among the English, a stronger national identity seems to be more attractive to Conservatives, providing the opposition party with a possible basis for mobilising electoral support.

Table 9.5: Pride in Union Jack and regional flags 2003

	When you see the (flag), does it make you feel...			
	very proud/a bit proud	a bit hostile/very hostile	very proud/a bit proud	a bit hostile/very hostile
	Union Jack		St George/Saltire/Red Dragon	
Total	48	5	70	1
England	62	2	48	3
Scotland	38	7	77	1
Wales	44	4	80	0
Conservative	72	1	70	1
Labour	48	5	72	1
Lib Dem	50	4	65	2
17–34	33	9	69	1
35–54	35	6	66	2
55+	55	3	73	1

The 'Union Jack' and 'St. George/Saltire/Red Dragon' items were asked separately, though with identical wordings apart from the flag mentioned. For the former question, the number of respondents is 3,426, of whom 967 were living in England, 1,485 in Scotland and 974 in Wales. For the latter question, the total number of respondents is 3,428, of whom 962 were living in England, 1,490 in Scotland and 976 in Wales.
Source: British National Identity and Constitutional Change Survey (2003)

Further confirmation about the greater intensity of national identities among the Scots and Welsh comes from their reactions to the Union Jack, a symbol of British identity. The British Social Attitudes Survey in 2003 asked about feelings of pride in 'seeing' the Union Jack on the one hand and the St George's Cross, the Saltire or the Red Dragon flags on the other. Table 9.5 presents the results and shows that positive feelings about the Union Jack were significantly more widespread among the English, Conservatives, and people over fifty-five years of age. By contrast, pride in the national flag was much more intense and pervasive in Scotland and Wales. A simple way to capture this result is to subtract the proportion expressing pride in their national (or 'ethnic') flag from the equivalent response to the Union Jack. Among the English, pride in the Union Jack was more common (although it would be worthwhile reviewing this in the aftermath of the 2006 World Cup when the English, not the British, flag was waved). In Scotland and Wales, the common British flag was *less* likely to evoke feelings of pride by large margins. How much devolution will further accentuate this pattern of ethnic consciousness remains to be seen.

The strength of Scottish and Welsh identities does not imply that Britain is breaking apart. Group identities necessarily separate 'us' from 'them', but the specific 'other' depends on the context. The Scots (or Welsh) are more likely to prioritise their Britishness if asked 'Do you feel more British than European?' rather than 'Do you feel more British than Scottish (or Welsh)?'

British patriotism remains strong. In both 1995 and 2003, the International Social Survey Programme (ISSP) asked national samples in the United States, Britain, Austria, Germany, Ireland and Spain to say how proud they felt (on a scale of 1 to 4) about ten aspects of their country.[17] These answers were summed to create a score on a national pride index with a range of 4 to 40. The mean scores for the British public were 28.2 in 1995 and 28.5 in 2003, well towards the high end of the range, and more patriotic than all the other countries included in both ISSP surveys save the United States and Austria.

In 2003, 72 per cent of English respondents, 67 per cent of those in Scotland and 69 per cent of those in Wales agreed that 'I would rather be a citizen of the United Kingdom than any other country in the world'. It is true that patriotic feeling was far more pervasive among those over fifty-five than those under thirty-five years of age, a difference that also appears in most other countries. Similarly, a 2000 national survey found that Britons over fifty-five were much more likely than those under thirty-five to agree that 'the government should do everything possible to keep all parts of Britain together in a single state'. These cohort differences in opinion suggest a slow waning of intense feelings of British identity, with potential policy consequences. Patriotism, the love of and pride in one's country, is correlated with less support for devolution within the UK and with more opposition to European integration.[18]

Nation over Europe

New Labour has made a number of rhetorical bows to Britain's European identity. Tony Blair's colleague Robin Cook called him Britain's most pro-European Prime Minister ever, even though this outlook has not resulted in concrete action in favour of greater political integration. But Britain's continued membership of the EU has consequences for its political institutions and so this chapter – and Chapter 8 – will examine trends in national attitudes towards European integration during New Labour's reign. The unmistakeable evidence is that Euroscepticism, always more widespread in Britain than in most other EU members, has grown even stronger.

The Eurobarometer, a cross-national survey of public opinion conducted every two years since 1970, provides a number of measures of popular attitudes towards European integration. Previous analyses of public opinion have distinguished between the utilitarian and affective bases of identification with the European Union.[19] One simple measure of support is the question 'Do you think that your country's membership in the European Union has generally been a good thing or a bad thing?' Figure 9.1 shows the trend in net support for the EU between 1980 and 2004 by subtracting the proportion saying bad from those saying good. The figure compares the British public to those in the original six members of the European Community. British opinion about EU membership was strongly negative in 1980 but by 1992 had moved towards convergence with the consistently more favourable views of continental publics. After Maastricht, however, scepticism about Europe grew across the board, with British opinion moving more sharply in the negative direction.

Conservatives were more positive than Labour voters about the worth of British membership in the EU in 1980, just after the nationalistic Margaret Thatcher was elected Prime Minister. In that year the net good minus bad score for Conservatives was plus 6 per cent, compared to minus 50 per cent among Labour voters. By 1992, this pattern was reversed; both parties' voters

Figure 9.1: Trends in support for membership of the European Union

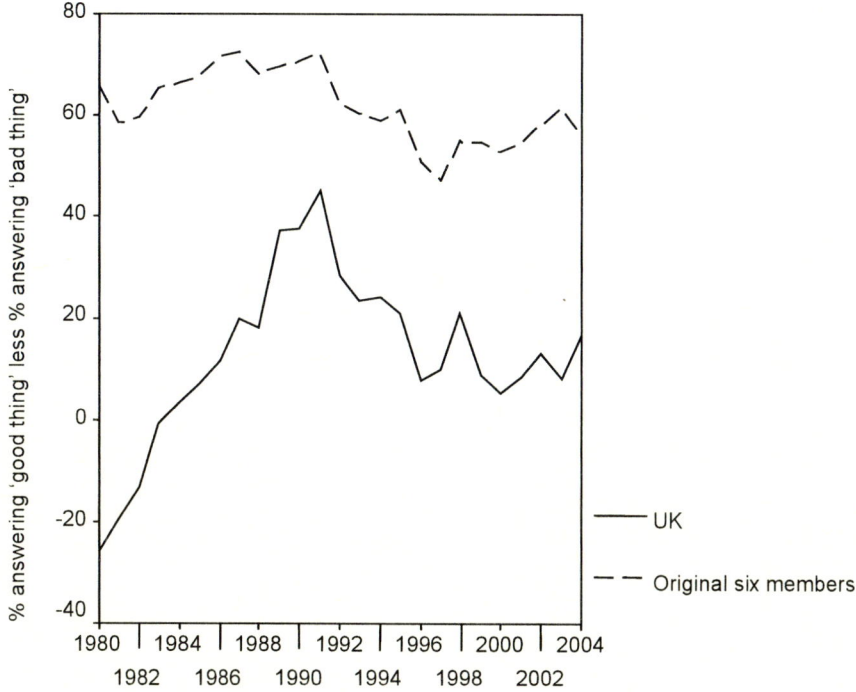

Question text: Generally speaking, do you think that [your country's] membership of the European Community is a good thing, a bad thing, or neither a good thing nor a bad thing? 'Original six members' refers to an aggregate of the following countries: Belgium, France, Germany, Italy, Luxembourg and the Netherlands.
Sources; *Mannheim Eurobarometer Trend File 1970–2002*; *Eurobarometer* 60.1 and 62.

had become more pro-European, with Labour voters having a slightly higher net worth score. The trajectory between 1992 and 2000 was downward among both sets of partisans, but far steeper among Conservatives. In 2000, their net worth score was minus 20 per cent compared to plus 14 per cent among Labour voters, who are on balance younger than Conservatives. Age is negatively associated with support for European integration. More important than the pattern of partisan differences is the fact that the trend in opinion was the same across the board – increasing support for the EU between 1980 and 1992 followed by a sharp decline thereafter.

Figure 9.2: Support for national–joint European authority by policy domain: the UK versus the original six EU members 1992–7

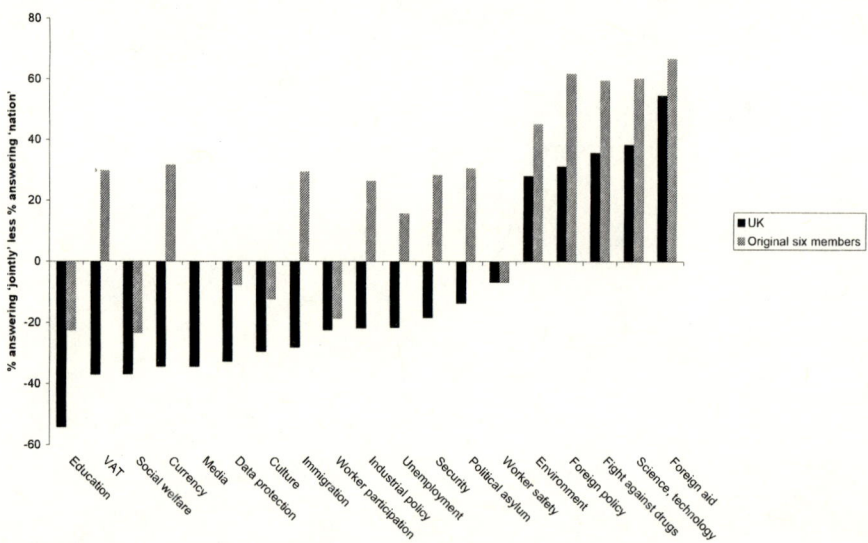

Question wording: Some people believe that certain areas of policy should be determined by the [national] government. Which of the following areas of policy do you think should be determined by the [national] government, and which should be decided in common with the European Community as a whole?

'Original six members' refers to the aggregate of opinion in France, Italy, Germany, Belgium, Luxembourg and the Netherlands. Some policy areas (VAT, Worker participation, Industrial policy, Worker safety, Data protection) were not the subject of questions during the 1998–2002 period.

Source: *Mannheim Eurobarometer Trend File 1970–2002.*

A similar trend appears for preferences about how control over policy-making should be divided between the nation and the European Union. Eurobarometer asked whether the nation should be wholly sovereign or share policy-making powers in domains ranging from foreign and defence policies to cultural and educational policies. Following a recent analysis by political scientists Richard Eichenberg and Russell Dalton,[20] Figures 9.2 and 9.3 chart the public's willingness to cede some authority to the EU's institutions in fifteen of these specific policy domains from 1992 until 2004, once again comparing Britain to the original six members. This figure aggregates public

Figure 9.3: Support for joint national–European authority by policy domain: the UK versus the original six EU members 1998–2002

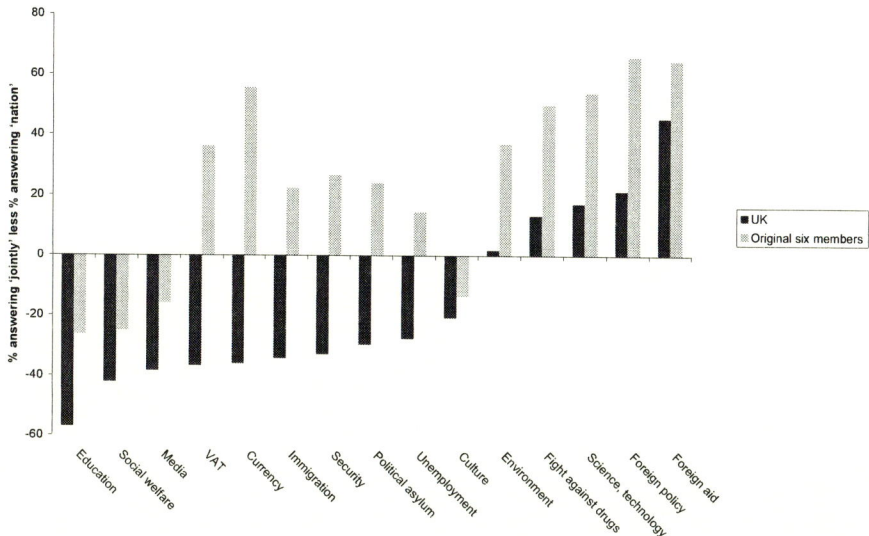

Question wording: Some people believe that certain areas of policy should be determined by the [national] government, while other areas of policy should be determined in common with the European Community. Which of the following areas of policy do you think should be determined by the [national] government, and which should be decided in common with the European Community as a whole?

'Original six members' refers to the aggregate of opinion in France, Italy, Germany, Belgium, Luxembourg and the Netherlands. Some policy areas (VAT, Worker participation, Industrial policy, Worker safety, Data protection) were not the subject of questions during the 1998–2002 period.

Source: *Mannheim Eurobarometer Trend File 1970–2002.*

opinion into two periods: the pre-Blair period between 1992 and 1997 (Figure 9.2) and the subsequent Blair years (Figure 9.3). In both periods the British public has been more hostile to sharing power than their counterparts on the Continent. Between 1992 and 1996, the British public preferred solely national to joint control in ten out of fifteen cases, compared to five out of fifteen on the Continent. The comparable figures for the Blair era are ten out of fifteen and four out of fifteen respectively. The gap in support for joint decision-making is consistently large and Britons are particularly concerned about ceding power to European institutions when it comes to issues touching on national identity such as education, immigration, media, currency and culture. Despite Blair's pro-European rhetoric, between 1997 and 2002 Britons became less, rather than more, favourable to joint authority over policy-making.

Figures 9.4 and 9.5 track the trends in opinion on the same set of questions, but this time focus on comparisons among Conservative, Labour and Liberal Democrat supporters within the UK. Conservatives are consistently more resistant to ceding authority to European institutions, but among all three groups of party identifiers, the balance of opinion tilts strongly towards a preference for national sovereignty. There is also consensus on which domains of policy should be sacrosanct. Although the full set of data is not included here for reasons of space, there is a shift towards limiting the authority of European institutions in both Britain and the original six EU countries after 1992. For example, in 1992, 42 per cent of the British public was prepared to share control over the national currency; by 2002 only 30 per cent felt this way.

Eichenberg and Dalton argue persuasively that the rise in public support for European integration between 1970 and 1992 was based on rational economic calculations.[21] Both at the aggregate and individual level, perceptions of economic gain were associated with increased support for the EU. Citizens responded to the distribution of benefits through the EU budget, to perceptions of how further integration would influence their personal standard of living, and on trends in growth, inflation, and unemployment.[22]

After Maastricht, however, the calculation of costs and benefits seemed to change. The EU was no longer simply an economic enterprise, but was moving in the direction of political integration. Maastricht expanded the number of policy domains for which the EU had some responsibility, limiting the fiscal autonomy of member nations by insisting on the reduction of budget deficits, and expanding the coverage of majority voting in the European Council. The move towards a quasi-federal Europe with an ever stronger 'central' government continued in the treaties of Amsterdam in 1997 and Nice in 2003.

These top-down actions of elites overwhelmingly committed to political integration sharply diverged from mass opinion, as the close votes on the euro in Denmark and France and the defeat of the new constitution in France and the Netherlands showed. The decline in citizen support for integration in Britain and elsewhere reflected public recognition that a stronger European mega-state had consequences for both social welfare policies and cultural identities. Eichenberg and Dalton report that the stronger desire for national

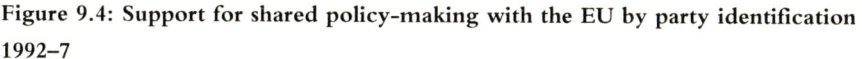

Figure 9.4: Support for shared policy-making with the EU by party identification 1992–7

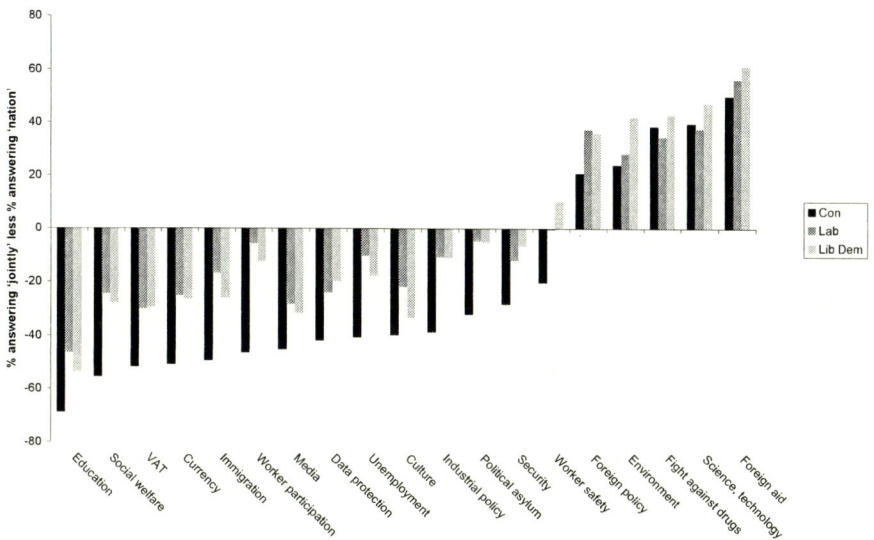

Question wording: Some people believe that certain areas of policy should be determined by the [national] government, while other areas of policy should be determined in common with the European Community. Which of the following areas of policy do you think should be determined by the [national] government, and which should be decided in common with the European Community as a whole?
Source: *Mannheim Eurobarometer Trend File 1970–2002.*

control of policy-making was most evident in policy domains related to transfer payments and policies related to the nation's culture and identity.[23] Citizens tend to favour European integration when it is perceived as important for preserving, rather than eroding, the national welfare state, one core element of the post-war political consensus in most countries. Yet it is increasingly apparent that national identities remain potent and the strength of these attachments is an obstacle to the political elite's dream of constructing a pre-eminent European identity.

Additional evidence of the staying power of the nation-state, particularly in Britain, lies in answers to a Eurobarometer question asking: 'In the near future,

Figure 9.5: Support for shared policy-making with the EU by party identification 1998–2002

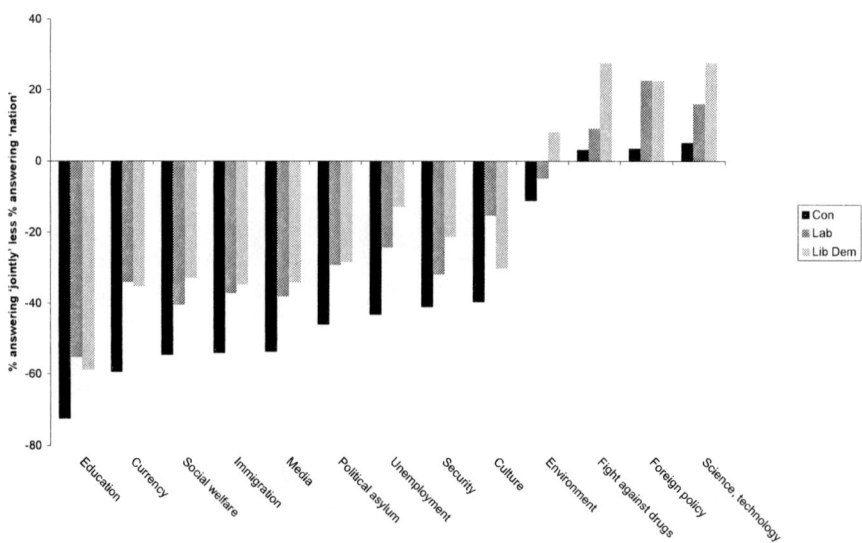

Question wording: Some people believe that certain areas of policy should be determined by the [national] government, while other areas of policy should be determined in common with the European Community. Which of the following areas of policy do you think should be determined by the [national] government, and which should be decided in common with the European Community as a whole?

'Some policy areas (VAT, Worker participation, Industrial policy, Worker safety, Data protection) were not the subject of questions during the 1998–2002 period.

Source: *Mannheim Eurobarometer Trend File 1970–2002.*

do you think you will see yourself as only a national, only a European, a national first and then a European, or a European first and then a national?' In 2000, more than 90 percent of the British public said they see themselves either as exclusively British or as British first.

Another Eurobarometer question asked how attached people felt to their country and to Europe respectively. Respondents may express a dual identity. Between 1991 and 2004, the period during which perceptions of the EU as a 'good' thing and support for joint policy-making declined, there was an increase in the segment of the public, in Britain and elsewhere, saying that they were attached to both their country and Europe. Figure 9.6 shows that an

Figure 9.6: Trends in attachment to the nation and Europe, 1991–2004

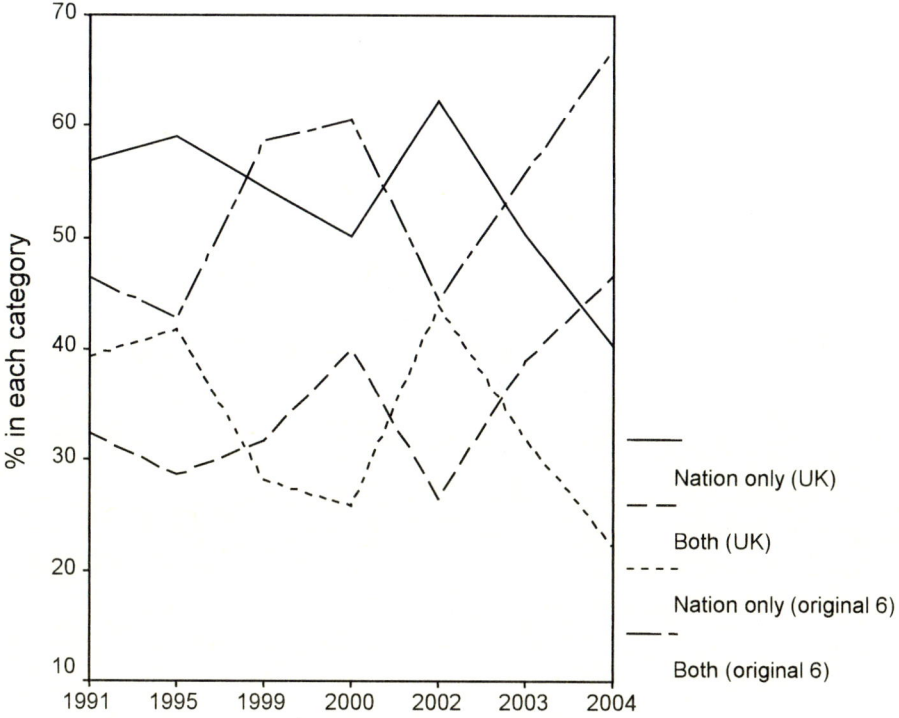

Question text: People may feel different degrees of attachment to their town or village, to their region, to their country or to Europe. Please tell me how attached you feel to . . .
'Original 6' refers to an aggregate of the following countries: Belgium, France, Germany, Italy, Luxembourg and the Netherlands.
Source: *Mannheim Eurobarometer Trend File 1970–2002*; *Eurobarometer* 60.1 & 62.

exclusive attachment to the nation always was more pervasive in Britain than in the original six EU members, but by 2004 'country first, but Europe too' had become the most frequently chosen position in Britain as well.[24] Throughout the 1990s and beyond, attachment to their country and to Europe were positively associated in the public mind. People seem to accept that they can belong to two overlapping political communities, perhaps because at least up to the implementation of the Maastricht Treaty, many viewed the European Union as protecting rather than threatening their economic well-being and national identities. In Britain, the Eurobarometer question asking about attachment to Europe and the belief that membership in the EU was a good thing for Britain correlated 0.46 in 1999. The more one regarded membership in the EU as providing benefits, the more strongly one expressed an emotional attachment to Europe. By 2004, this link had frayed and the correlation among these responses was substantially lower, 0.30. This indicates that those with an exclusive attachment to their country had moved farther from those with a dual attachment to both Britain and Europe in how they viewed the benefits of integration. But even if a sanguine view of the compatibility of national and supranational identities has eroded in recent years, the greater attachment to Europe among the young and well-educated segments of the public, in Britain and elsewhere, makes it difficult to envisage a successful movement to unravel the European Union even if the drive for greater political integration comes to an end.

Multiculturalism and national identity

One question raised by New Labour's programme of constitutional reform is whether institutional changes leading to the sharing, if not fragmentation, of power will engender greater disunity and social conflict. The evidence reported in this chapter suggests that devolution after 1997 has reinforced feelings of Scottish and Welsh nationalism while nurturing similar feelings in England. Critics thus might assert that devolution gnaws at British national identity from within. On balance, however, there is little evidence of increasing demands for Scottish or Welsh independence, and patriotism in Britain remains strong.

Europeanisation threatens British national identity from without. If the project of One Europe – in which Britons feel as much at home in Vienna or Athens as in London or Manchester – were to succeed then Europe, the birthplace of modern nationalism, would also be the place of its demise. Yet even as the idea that one can accommodate attachment both to the nation and the larger European entity is more widely accepted, particularly among younger and well-educated citizens with presumably more cosmopolitan values, European publics are questioning the benefits of membership and the wisdom of ceding power to EU institutions and reasserting nationalist feelings.

A more potent threat to British national identity than either devolution or European integration might be seen in multiculturalism – the growing presence in Britain of people of different races and religions, most notably

Muslims. New Labour's programme of constitutional reform has not as yet engaged this problem, although it is one factor leading Gordon Brown to call for the regeneration of British patriotism. Is it possible for the immigrants from India, Pakistan, Afghanistan, the Middle East, the West Indies, Hong Kong, and Eastern Europe to feel British and be accepted as such? If so, what is the unifying glue, the ideological cement that binds people together in an imagined community? Will the newly constructed British identity be acceptable to the native population? The final section of this chapter plumbs public opinion towards cultural diversity, a problem confronting governments throughout Europe in the wake of immigration and asylum-seeking.

Whatever its excesses, nationalism, in the sense of a people's right to self-determination, has global legitimacy as the basis for democratic politics. The criteria used to demarcate a nation's identity designate insiders from outsiders and separate the 'we' from the 'they'. The philosopher David Miller argues that a strong sense of national identity underpins feelings of social solidarity and reciprocity among citizens.[25] Human psychology is such that people tend to favour members of their in-group and are more willing to share with, and sacrifice for, people regarded as national kin. Over time, a politics of difference that stresses the unique, irreducible identities of sub-national ethnic or religious groups is likely to reduce a willingness to share or redistribute. Put crudely, people may increasingly question the obligation to provide the benefits of social citizenship to groups proclaiming themselves to be hostile to dominant values. Of course, if the duties of citizenship have narrowed and if the nation-state has diminished authority and control over economic and social policies, the contribution Miller attributed to national identity may be less relevant.

The debate over multiculturalism in Britain and elsewhere centres on the desirability of official support for the maintenance of cultural differences through education, the acceptance of religious symbols and practices in public life, or, more generally, the politicisation of ethnicity through various forms of group representation. Multiculturalism as a fact merely denotes the presence of people of different ethnicities in a single polity. Multiculturalism as an ideology takes many forms, ranging from a simple appeal to tolerance and openness to diverse food, literature, music and arts through to an insistence that each ethnic group has a distinct identity and derivative set of interests that supersedes all other affiliations. Advocates of multiculturalism hold that since a positive sense of ethnic identity is essential to personal dignity and self-realisation, recognising the worth of minority cultures and assuring their survival are necessary objectives of humane, liberal governments.[26]

Faced by demographic multiculturalism that has placed diverse cultures side by side, governments have three main choices in how to define and sustain a sense of a common national identity. One approach is exclusionary and ethnocentric. This ideological solution defines a nation in ethnic terms, by its common culture if not purity of blood. Immigration is discouraged and when newcomers are allowed, preference is given to immigrants with the same language and religion as the native born. In addition, rapid assimilation must be the goal of government policy. Immigrants should shed their original customs and adopt the customs, values and habits of Britain.

An alternative vision of the nation is more inclusive. Brown's formula for British identity in membership in the national community rests not on ancestry but on core values and modes of conduct. This means that there are no inherent ethnic barriers to becoming British. What is required is adherence to the values of liberty, civic responsibility, fairness and decency. To be sure, a common language is an important asset for understanding and assimilating these British qualities, but language can be learned.

Cultural unity is an element of national identity in this liberal nationalist approach, but the scope of such unity – the content of Britishness – is relatively narrow. A common religion is not required; nor are there prescribed dress codes or musical tastes. If anything, multiculturalism helps the popular culture evolve. Amartya Sen recently noted that chicken tikka masala has become a marker of British cuisine, along with fish and chips and Yorkshire pudding.[27] He also points out that a genuinely pluralistic education would include learning about the global contributions to modern civilisation as well as the nation's history and traditions.[28] Sen argues that Britain has been largely successful in integrating immigrants from different cultures and credits the policy of non-discrimination in healthcare, schooling and social security for progress in race relations.[29] But at the same time he warns against giving automatic priority to inherited religion or tradition as this might encourage cultural apartheid at the expense of individual freedom.

Placing ethnicity above all other affiliations transforms a multicultural nation-state into a confederation of ethnic groups with equal rights. In this model – the third option open to governments of multicultural societies – there are no values or customs that are privileged and, in this context, to call for the elevation of core British values would amount to cultural imperialism. 'Live and let live', the principle of mutual tolerance for all constituent groups, whatever their principles and practices, is the model's proposed basis for social solidarity. 'Live and let live' might mean – if one were to pursue this rationale – the legitimation of illiberal practices and the erosion of the felt obligation to assist the disadvantaged or those of a different ethnicity.[30]

Writers sympathetic to multiculturalism propose a conception of national identity that would foster 'a nation at peace with its constituent groups that identify with the nation'.[31] But it seems implausible that this minimal consensus, derived from the notion that 'we live here together so let's just get along' can create a shared patriotism strong enough to overcome the attraction of religious fundamentalism, an attraction buttressed by ideologies that both define people by their ethnicity and evaluate policies according to how they affect the standing of one's ethnic group and its heritage.

There is only fragmentary evidence regarding the British public's view of these various images of national identity. A national survey conducted in 1999 did ask respondents in England, though not Scotland or Wales, about the importance of having English parents, being born in England, living most of one's life in England, and being white for making someone 'truly' English.[32] Table 9.6 shows majorities believing that being born in England, having English parents and living in England are important in defining an English identity, with this outlook significantly more pronounced among Conservatives and older residents of England than others. This finding is consistent with the greater propensity of the young and those on the political left to express less nationalistic attitudes. It is noteworthy, however, that only 26 per cent of this sample regarded being white as important for making one English and fully 45 per cent said race was not at all an important criterion of Englishness. Again, age and, to a lesser degree, party affiliation were associated with a more racially tinged definition of English identity. And although the emphasis on birth and long residence in England might be viewed as belief in a racial marker of nationhood – evidence of ethnocentrism – it is perhaps equally plausible that people simply regard time spent in England as facilitating socialisation into the dominant cultural values.

Other data suggests a willingness to accept newcomers of different races and cultures as Britons on the condition that they assimilate. In a 1995 national survey, 81 per cent of the public said that 'it is better for a country if all racial and ethnic groups adapt and blend into the larger society rather than maintaining their distinct customs and traditions'. Similarly, 63 per cent disagreed with the statement 'ethnic minorities should be given government assistance to preserve their customs and traditions', a central tenet of multiculturalism's policy agenda. In light of recent international events it seems unlikely that this perspective has changed, and in Britain as well as elsewhere the policy pendulum has swung sharply from celebrating diversity to encouraging cultural integration.

Table 9.6: Perceived contents of English national identity, 1999

Question text: 'People have different views about what it means to be truly English. Some would say that a person needs to [category] to be truly English. How much do you think this matters?' The table shows the percentage of respondents who answered 'a great deal' or 'quite a bit'.

	be born in England	live most of life in England	have English parents	be white
Total	59	64	57	26
Conservative	64	70	64	30
Labour	58	65	58	24
Lib Dem	58	62	55	24
17–34	54	57	47	14
35–54	52	58	49	20
55+	68	74	72	39

The total number of respondents was 2,700, and the sample included only respondents living in England.
Source: 1999 British Social Attitudes Survey.

The public's balance-sheet

How, then, has New Labour's programme of constitutional reform fared in the court of public opinion? Devolution for Scotland and Wales has been implemented, and the survey data reviewed above suggests that the public throughout the UK, including the English, now view the new institutions as part of the normal way of doing business. In Scotland and Wales, support for devolution rested on feelings of ethnic consciousness that the new institutions sustained and arguably enhanced. The germ of a specifically English identification exists, but in such a muted form that proposals for regional assemblies or an England-only assembly receive a negative reception. The majority of the English continue to view themselves as British and to express pride in this national identity. As long as this psychological outlook prevails, political as opposed to administrative regionalism in England is unlikely to win a popular vote.

There is only scattered evidence about public reactions to the Freedom of Information Act or the Human Rights Act. However, Chapter 4 in this volume documents the emergence of a 'rights' culture that implies support for more individual liberties, political voice and minority rights, and so a reasonable conclusion is that these important components of the constitutional reform programme also have popular legitimacy.

Opinion about the complex issue of electoral reform, on the other hand, is uncrystallised. A 2001 national poll found that by a margin of 59 to 41 per cent the public agreed that 'the voting system should be kept the same as it is to produce more effective government' rather than changed to 'allow smaller political parties to get a fairer share of MPs'. Yet 55 per cent of the same sample – 46 per cent in England, 51 per cent in Scotland and 62 per cent in Wales – agreed that 'Britain should introduce proportional representation, so that the number of MPs in the House of Commons each party gets matches more closely to the number of votes each party gets'. In practice, proportional representation creates an incentive to form new parties. Proportional representation may be a barrier to the emergence of a nationalist majority in the Scottish and Welsh national legislatures, but the same electoral system could encourage the formation of new ethnic or religious parties in other jurisdictions.

Assessing the impact of New Labour's constitutional reforms on the effectiveness of British government is beyond the scope of this chapter. It does not appear, however, that devolution, parliamentary reform and increased opportunities to vote have increased either popular participation or public confidence in government. Instead, the trend in voter turnout has been a slide towards the notoriously lower American level of participation. As for trust in the political system, in 1997 56 per cent of the British public said that the present system of government works extremely well or that it needed only small improvements. By 2003 only 36 per cent felt that way, with the rest saying the system of government could be improved a lot. This increased sense of dissatisfaction manifested itself in all regions, political parties and age groups, though it is true that supporters of the Blair governments were less likely to complain than others. Constitutional change, however popular, was insufficient to overcome the usual impact of unfavourable political and economic events on political trust.

In looking at current trends in British national identity, one must again look beyond the limited effects of New Labour's constitutional reforms outside Scotland and Wales to the implications of European integration and immigration. Scepticism about Europe has grown: elite policies have run up against the ordinary citizen's increasing doubts about the benefits of EU membership. After Labour won power in 1997, opposition in British opinion to sharing policy-making authority with European institutions continued to increase. So although the British public has been moving towards accepting the idea that feelings of attachment to Europe and one's own country are compatible, the dominant trend in public opinion underscores the primacy and potency of national identity.

During New Labour's rule, Britain also confronted anew the discontents engendered by the inter-play of immigration, terrorism and the war in Iraq. Amid the growing fear of home-grown terrorists whose primary identity was not British but fundamentalist Islam, there has been a shift from the optimistic celebration of 'multicultural' Britain in Lord Irvine's 1998 lecture. Instead there is talk of language tests for immigrants, national identity cards and programmes to assure assimilation. The spectre of 'Eurabia' has reawakened understanding of the unifying virtues of a common national identity.[33]

In this context, Gordon Brown has proposed a civic conception of identity that centres on linguistic assimilation and the inculcation of democratic political principles. It should not be surprising that these values include fairness and decency, principles of conduct that resonate well with the socialist ethos of fraternity and with continued support for the welfare state. Both Brown and the Conservative leader, David Cameron, have hinted that they favour a written Bill of Rights for Britain and this ultimately could become an important symbol of a civic national identity, as is the case in the United States and Canada.

More significant than any specific formula for British identity in a multi-ethnic society is the recognition that patriotism and assimilation are not dirty words but positive forces for communal feeling. Britain's changed ethnic composition makes it useful to consider the relevance of the American ideal of the melting pot, in which new immigrants both blend into the dominant culture and add new spice to it, for policies aimed at reconciling unity and diversity. New Labour's constitutional reforms have transformed the British political system by diffusing authority. Whoever is in power in future faces the more formidable task of shaping identities. 'There'll Always Be an England' was a patriotic song during Britain's 'finest hour'. Will there be a 21st-century reprise and, if so, who will sing it?

About the contributors

Mark Bevir is a professor of political science at the University of California, Berkeley. He is the author of *New Labour: A Critique* (Routledge, 2005) and *The Logic of the History of Ideas* (Cambridge University Press, 1999), and co-author with R. A. W. Rhodes of *Interpreting British Governance* (Routledge, 2003) and *Governance Stories* (Routledge, 2006).

Jack Citrin is a professor of political science at the University of California, Berkeley. He is also the associate director of the Institute of Governmental Studies, Berkeley.

Joseph F. Fletcher is an associate professor in the Department of Political Science at the University of Toronto. He has written extensively on public attitudes towards political and judicial reform.

Robert Hazell is the founder and director of the Constitution Unit, and professor of government and the constitution in the School of Public Policy at University College London. The Constitution Unit has worked on almost every aspect of the UK's constitutional reforms since its foundation in 1995.

Ailsa Henderson is an assistant professor in the Department of Political Science at the University of Toronto. She is the author of *Hierarchies of Belonging: national identity and political culture in Scotland and Quebec* (Montreal & Kingston, ON: McGill-Queen's University Press, 2007) and co-editor with Colin Coates of *Scotland–Quebec: An Evolving Comparison*, a special issue of *British Journal of Canadian Studies* (2006).

Andrew McDonald is a civil servant. Between 2003 and 2005 he ran the UK government's constitutional reform programme. In 2005/6 he was a Fulbright fellow at the University of California, Berkeley. He has written on public policy and modern history.

Kenneth MacKenzie was a UK civil servant for thirty-six years, serving in all departments of the Scottish Office (now the Scottish Executive) and in the Cabinet Office. In 1997 he became head of the newly formed Constitution Secretariat, set up in the Cabinet Office to orchestrate the New Labour government's ambitious programme of constitutional reform including devolution to Scotland and Wales. He now works as a consultant in public administration and is currently advising the Office of the Prime Minister of the Provisional Government of Kosovo.

Kate Malleson is professor of law at Queen Mary, University of London. Between 2003 and 2005 she was a specialist adviser to the House of Commons Constitutional Affairs Select Committee, assisting it in its review of the provisions of the Constitutional Reform Bill. She is the author of a wide range of publications on the judiciary and the legal system, including *Appointing Judges in an Age of Judicial Power: Critical Perspectives from Around the World* (with Peter Russell; Toronto University Press, 2006), *The Legal System* (Oxford University Press, 2005) and *The New Judiciary: The Effects of Expansion and Activism* (Ashgate Press, 1999).

Craig Parsons is associate professor of political science at the University of Oregon. He is the author of *A Certain Idea of Europe* (Cornell University Press, 2003) and *How to Map Arguments in Political Science* (Oxford University Press, 2007). He has had articles published in *International Organization, Journal of Common Market Studies, European Journal of International Relations* and other journals, and is a co-editor of recent books on European Union politics and immigration in Europe.

Peter Riddell is chief political commentator of the *Times*. He has written six books on British politics, including *Parliament under Blair* (Politico's, 2000), *Hug Them Close: Blair, Clinton, Bush and the 'Special Relationship'* (Politico's, 2003) and, most recently, *The Unfulfilled Prime Minister: Tony Blair's Quest for a Legacy* (Politico's, 2005). He has also written for academic journals. He is a fellow of the Royal Historical Society and an honorary fellow of Sidney Sussex College, Cambridge.

Notes

Chapter 1

1. Since one of the authors is a civil servant, it is worth noting here that this chapter does not make any use of information which is not already in the public domain.
2. London: Vintage, 1997.
3. All the more extraordinary in that Cranborne made the deal without involving his party leader, William Hague. Cranborne lost his job, but the deal remained.
4. The European Parliament Elections Bill found its place in the programme after pressure from the Liberal Democrats.
5. But by now it was to be a single equality and human rights commission – bringing human rights together with the other anti-discrimination commissions.
6. 'A Heath Robinson constitution', Bagehot, *Economist*, 18 April 1998, p. 34.
7. Lord Irvine, *Government's Programme of Constitutional Reform* (London: Constitution Unit, University College London, 1999), p. 8.
8. Ibid.
9. At the time of writing (July 2006) the Northern Ireland Assembly is suspended, pending an accommodation between the two largest parties, the Democratic Unionists and Sinn Fein.
10. Jack McConnell, interview in the *Observer*, 29 January 2006; Rhodri Morgan, speech to the National Centre for Public Policy, Swansea, November 2002.
11. Barnett has not seriously been challenged in Wales either, but the Welsh have been successful in securing funding over and above Barnett; see Iain MacLean, 'The National Question', in Anthony Seldon (ed.), *The Blair Effect* (London: Little, Brown, 2001), pp. 429–48, esp. 443–6.
12. The derogation was lifted in 2005 following the passage of the Prevention of Terrorism Act.
13. In practice, the government has favoured the second course.
14. Five of the declarations were overturned on appeal; two appeals are still pending at the time of writing. And in the cases where incompatibility was found, the government has taken action to amend the offending statute.
15. *Review of the Implementation of the Human Rights Act* (Department for Constitutional Affairs, 2006).
16. The annual figure relates to the forty-two central government organisations

whose FoI requests are subject to monitoring by the Department for Constitutional Affairs. Of the total, 19,717 requests were made of Departments of State. Further details are in the annual report on the first year of FoI: see *Freedom of Information Annual Report 2005: Operation of the FoI Act in Central Government* (Department of Constitutional Affairs, 2006).

17. Additionally, the Good Friday Agreement was endorsed by votes north and south of the border in Ireland.

18. Paddy Ashdown, *The Ashdown Diaries, vol. 2: 1997–1999* (London: Allen Lane, 2001), pp. 257–8.

Chapter 2

1. Professor J. G. Griffith, 'This Bill should have no rights', *Spectator*, 15 February 1987.

2. Tony Wright (ed.), *The British Political Process: An Introduction* (New York: Routledge, 1999), p. 333.

3. Quite separately, the judiciary was drawn into the political arena in ruling, from time to time, on whether British law and the decisions of British ministers were in conflict with European Community law, which was superior.

4. Robert Blackburn and Raymond Plant (eds), *Constitutional Reform: The Labour Government's Constitutional Reform Agenda* (London: Longman, 1999), pp. 66–81.

5. Labour manifesto, in Alan H. Wood and Roger Wood (eds), *The Times Guide to the House of Commons April 1992* (London: Times, 1992), pp. 340–2.

6. David Butler and Dennis Kavanagh, *The British General Election of 1992* (London: Macmillan, 1992), pp. 129–30.

7. Mark Stuart, *John Smith: A Life* (London: Politico's, 2005), p. 293.

8. John Smith, 'A Citizen's Democracy', lecture to Charter 88, 1 March 1993.

9. John Morrison, *Reforming Britain: New Labour, New Constitution?* (London: Pearson Education, 2001), p. 35. Morrison's underappreciated book provides a full and balanced account of this whole period.

10. This reflected a paper on pre-legislative scrutiny from the Constitution Unit, which had been set up in 1995 under Robert Hazell, a former Home Office civil servant and lawyer, to provide expert analysis rather than to campaign.

11. Morrison, *Reforming Britain*, pp. 40–1.

12. Blackburn and Plant, *Constitutional Reform*, pp. 9–11.

13. Labour's election manifesto, in Tim Austin (ed.), *The Times Guide to the House of Commons May 1997* (London: Times, 1997), p. 326.

14. Paddy Ashdown, *The Ashdown Diaries, vol. 1: 1988–1997* (London: Allen Lane, 2000), pp. 311–14.

15. Report of the Joint Consultative Committee, in Blackburn and Plant,

Constitutional Reform, pp. 468–80.

16. Peter Riddell, *The Unfulfilled Prime Minister: Tony Blair's Quest for a Legacy* (London: Politico's, 2005), p. 160.

17. Peter Mandelson and Roger Liddle, *The Blair Revolution: Can New Labour Deliver?* (London: Faber and Faber, 1996), pp. 209–10.

18. Labour's election manifesto, in Austin, *Times Guide to the House of Commons May 1997*, pp. 326–8.

19. Riddell, *Unfulfilled Prime Minister*, p. 159.

20. Some Labour MPs became enthusiasts for the alternative-vote system of elections, which would preserve single-member constituencies, but this is not a proportional system.

21. Paddy Ashdown, *The Ashdown Diaries, vol. 2: 1997–1999* (London: Allen Lane, 2001), p. 446.

Chapter 3

1. James Ramsay MacDonald, *Socialism and Society* (London: Independent Labour Party, 1905), p. 70.

2. G. D. H. Cole, 'Conflicting Social Obligations', *Proceedings of the Aristotelian Society* (1914–15), vol. 15, p. 159.

3. G. D. H. Cole, *Guild Socialism Re-stated* (London: Leonard Parsons, 1920), p. 9.

4. The Welsh proposals only just got the 50 per cent vote required.

5. Although the latter two were moved to the Cabinet Office in 1998, they, like all these units, rarely seem to stay still. The Social Exclusion Unit was moved to the Office of the Deputy Prime Minister (ODPM) and then replaced in June 2006 by the Social Exclusion Task Force, which is back in the Cabinet Office. For its part, the Women's Unit, now the Women and Equality Unit, has gone to the Department for Communities and Local Government, the successor to the ODPM, via the Department of Trade and Industry.

Chapter 4

1. Mark Bevir and Kenneth MacKenzie each make a similar point in their chapters in this volume.

2. Lord Irvine, Constitution Unit lecture, December 1998. See also *A New Agenda for Democracy: Labour's Proposals for Constitutional Reform*.

3. Michael Ignatieff, *The Rights Revolution* (Toronto: House of Anansi Press, 2000); Mark Tushnet, *Taking the Constitution Away from the Courts* (Princeton: Princeton University Press, 1999); Ron Hirschl, 'The Political Origins of

Judicial Empowerment through Constitutionalization: Lessons from Four Constitutional Revolutions', *Law and Social Inquiry* (2000), vol. 25, no. 1, 91–149.

4. For details, see William L. Miller, Annis May Timpson and Michael Lessoff, *Political Culture in Contemporary Britain: People and Politicians, Principles and Practice* (Oxford: Clarendon Press, 1996). I thank Bill Miller for his generosity in making the data from the British Rights Survey available for secondary analysis.

5. All question wordings are contained in Appendix B.

6. That the survey succeeded on both counts will become evident in the high level of coherence in the results, discussed in the latter portion of this chapter. The interviews lasted forty-five minutes on average.

7. Miller et al. report contacting 'all the County, District, Metropolitan and Borough Councils in England and Wales plus the Regional and District Councils in Scotland' (p. 466) to identify the leader of each political group on the council. More than 85 per cent of the leaders identified in this way were interviewed. In the present analysis results for only those leaders affiliated with the Conservatives, Labour and the Liberal Democrats are included. The resulting sample offers an opinion portrait of a well-informed and experienced group of politicians affiliated with each of the three major political parties.

8. The difference reported in Table 4.1 between Labour and the Liberal Democrats can be regarded as statistically significant at .022. Naturally, other comparisons are also significant.

9. A similar pattern of results occurs for Welsh devolution, where popular opposition, though always in the minority, is greatest in Wales, with no national differences among the politicians.

10. Although there is a question about Northern Ireland, it was not included in the sample.

11. Differences between Liberal Democrats and Labour would be regarded as statistically significant regarding Wales and Northern Ireland but not for London or the English regions.

12. Labour's 1997 and 2001 manifesto commitment to regional devolution in England was qualified by the proviso that it would first test the local demand for elected regional chambers.

13. See Appendix A for question wording. Moreover, the reliability analysis confirms that the House of Lords item fits well within the three-item citizen rights index both for politicians ($\propto$=.72) and for the general public ($\propto$=.57). Nevertheless, as we will see shortly, this is only one of several measurement issues concerning democratic reform that will receive further attention in note 31 below.

14. Standard errors and the confidence interval allow one to take sampling error into account in interpreting mean scores. The upper and lower bounds presented in the two rightmost columns in the panels of Table 4.2 present the likely range (or confidence interval) of mean scores in the population.

According to probability theory, scores lower or higher than these lower and upper bounds will occur only 5 per cent of the time. More specifically, in 95 out of 100 samples, the mean score may vary by as much as ± 1.96 standard errors (calculated using sample size and variation in observed scores).

Confidence intervals are useful in determining whether two groups differ by more than chance. Thus, noting that the range in mean scores for the Conservatives does not overlap that for Labour indicates that, taking sampling error into consideration, there is less than a 5 per cent chance (or probability) that these two groups do not differ.

15. Meg Russell and Mark Sanford identify not only the attitudes of the Labour government but also public opinion as barriers to Lords reform. See 'Why Are Second Chambers So Difficult to Reform?', *Journal of Legislative Studies* (2002), vol. 8, no. 3, 79–89. Consistent with this perspective, a survey conducted in February 2004 by CommunicateResearch for the Constitution Unit of University College London shows more opposition than support among Labour MPs for a fully elected House of Lords. Additional UCL data collected in May 2005 find the public to be more sceptical than either Labour or Conservative MPs in assessing the increased legitimacy of the reformed House of Lords.

16. Between 1993 and 1996, Labour adopted candidate quotas in the form of all-women shortlists. Research by the Equal Opportunities Commission concludes that such positive measures are decisive in increasing women's representation. See *Women in Parliament: A Comparative Analysis* (Manchester: Equal Opportunities Commission, 2001).

17. As Appendix A shows, the BRS used two versions of the referendum question. The results do not differ substantively due to this wording difference. Accordingly, the results of the two questions have been combined.

18. The skewed distributions here, in which the views of Conservative and Liberal Democrat politicians essentially form mirror-image constants, present formidable obstacles in the further analysis of this question among these two groups. See note 31.

19. These results correspond closely to those obtained in a 1996 survey of candidates for Parliament which finds support for proportional representation at 4 per cent among Conservative candidates, 56 per cent among Labour candidates and 100 per cent among Liberal Democrats. See Pippa Norris, 'Political Elites and Constitutional Change', in *Understanding Constitutional Change*, special issue of *Scottish Affairs* (1998), 93–109. The correspondence suggests that at least concerning proportional representation, political leaders in the local context share the perspective of their parliamentary counterparts.

20. See Appendix A for the details on question wording.

21. Pippa Norris's 1996 survey of parliamentary candidates again found similar results for Conservative and Labour candidates with Liberal Democrats essentially divided down the middle. See Pippa Norris, 'Breaking the Barriers: Positive Discrimination Policies for Women', in Jytte Klausen and Charles S.

Maier (eds), *Has Liberalism Failed Women?: Assuring Equal Representation in Europe and the United States* (New York: Palgrave, 2001), pp. 89–110.

22. A 1997 MORI poll, 'Political Attitudes in Great Britain', shows a clear plurality in favour of an elected House of Lords and proportional representation just as New Labour took office.

23. Ronald Inglehart, *Modernization and Postmodernization: Cultural, Economic, and Political Change in 43 Societies* (Princeton: Princeton University Press, 1997).

24. Paul M. Sniderman, Joseph F. Fletcher, Peter H. Russell and Philip E. Tetlock, *The Clash of Rights: Liberty, Equality, and Legitimacy in Pluralist Democracy* (New Haven: Yale University Press, 1996).

25. The most common measure of consistency among a set of questions is Cronbach's reliability coefficient alpha. It is based upon the average correlation among the responses to the questions. A more fully specified version of the model appears in Appendix B.

26. The respective reliability coefficients for the politicians and the public for each of these measures are as follows: Liberty α =.49/.43; Authority α = .81/.74; Equality α =.77/.66.

27. The reliabilities are devolution α =.90/.80; rights protection α =.76/.57; democratic restructuring α =.51/.32; and judicial reform α =.79/.71. A number of measurement issues are discussed in note 31.

28. A structural equation model (SEM) using AMOS 6.0 is employed to estimate the interconnections specified in Figure 4.1. SEMs combine the strengths of a path analytic strategy with those of factor analysis. They use an iterative approach to derive from sample data the most likely estimates for the hypothesised linkages in the theoretical structure. Before examining estimates of the relationships among the elements of the model, overall fit of the model is assessed with a variety of measures. These include a chi-square statistic with related degrees of freedom. With large samples other measures less sensitive to sample size have been developed. The oldest of these is the ratio of chi-square to degrees of freedom. A cut off of 3:1 is often used. The most highly regarded of these is the root mean square error of approximation (RMSEA). It expresses discrepancy between the model and data per degree of freedom (Barbara M. Byrne, *Structural Equation Modeling with AMOS: Basic Concepts, Applications, and Programming* (Mahwah, NJ: Lawrence Erlbaum Associates, 2001). For a model to be considered a relatively good approximation of the data, RMSEA should be less than 0.6 (L. Hu and P.M. Bentler, 'Cutoff criteria for fit indexes in covariance structure analysis', *Structural Equation Modeling* (1999), vol. 6, 1–5). Another widely used measure of fit is the comparative fit index (CFI) indicating proportion of fit improvement of the estimated model relative to a model in which the observed variables are assumed to be uncorrelated. It should exceed 0.9.

29. The presentation here highlights the influence of values on support for constitutional reforms within each party and among citizens. It provides a rigorous look at the influence of values on attitudes towards the four themes of

reform by controlling for the partisan effects discussed earlier. An alternative approach is to a use a two-group SEM, gathering the politicians from the three major parties together into one group and the British public into a second group. Although the explained variation of this alternative model is markedly higher, its fit to the data is markedly worse (with a higher chi-square despite having fewer degrees of freedom). Nevertheless, it does offer direct estimates of partisan differences on both the values and reforms available only through comparison of latent mean in the current approach. Both approaches indicate that Labour and the Liberal Democrats do not differ significantly on any of the three values. The Conservatives, however, score substantially lower on liberty and equality and higher on authority. Moreover, consistent with Tables 4.1–4.4, the Conservatives are substantially less supportive of all four themes of reform than either Labour or Liberal Democrat politicians. The Liberal Democrats are slightly more likely to favour devolution and rights protection instruments and substantially more in favour of democratic restructuring than Labour. Labour, however, is more supportive of judicial reform. Last but not least, attitudes on all four themes of reform are influenced by value differences as anticipated, as well as by partisanship. All reported differences are significant.

30. As discussed in note 28, the fit of a model to the data can be assessed using a variety of measures. Here all the measures indicate a good fit: chi-square = 1829.2; degrees of freedom (DF) = 839; chi-square/DF ratio = 2.2; CFI = 0.94; RMSEA = 0.020 (0.019–0.021); p (close) = 1.0.

31. Models specifying fewer themes provide a significantly worse fit to the data. In constructing the model a number of measurement issues bearing upon the composition of the themes have to be addressed, almost all of which concern the theme of democratic restructuring. Foremost among these is where to place the House of Lords reform item in the model. As mentioned previously, the question wording is formulated in terms of protecting rights and, as such, it seems to belong in the citizen rights theme along with the items about a Bill of Rights and a freedom of information Act. Conceptually, however, as McDonald and Hazell indicate, it seems appropriate to place House of Lords reform together with the questions on referendums and proportional representation in the democratic restructuring theme. The factor analytic aspect of SEM allows this question to be addressed empirically, to see how the respondents themselves view the House of Lords item. As it turns out, the four sample groups viewed it somewhat differently. Its placement in the model was therefore settled for each group in accordance with how that group saw the item. For the public and Liberal Democrat politicians, the House of Lords item fits relatively smoothly within the citizen rights theme. For Conservative and Labour politicians, however, it partakes of both the citizen rights and democratic restructuring themes. Accordingly, for Conservative and Labour politicians the House of Lords reform item is treated as part of both citizen rights and democratic restructuring themes. In technical parlance, it is allowed

to cross-load onto both latent variables for these groups.

A second measurement issue concerns the referendum question. For Labour politicians it is perceived more as a citizen rights protection device and is treated accordingly. In all other groups it is viewed as, and hence treated as, part of the democratic restructuring theme as theorised by McDonald and Hazell. A third issue in the democracy theme concerns the proportional representation item. As evident in the second panel of Table 4.3, for Liberal Democrat politicians, and to a lesser degree Conservatives, there is very little variation in responding to this question. This adversely affects the model's capacity to estimate the effect that value differences may have on the democratic reform theme. The difficulty is so acute in the case of the Liberal Democrats that an alternative measure of support for proportional representation with some variation to it is required. This leads to a fourth issue involving democratic reform. It concerns the question about minority representation in Parliament. In point of fact, this is a not a reform that has been effected. Moreover, including this item in the model for all four groups skews some of the results. Therefore, it is included in the model only for the Liberal Democrats, for whom it provides a measure of support for proportional representation on which there is some variation. A final measurement challenge concerns the European-versus-British courts measure. Although it conceptually fits the theme of judicial reform well, it sharply reduces the reliability coefficient for the latent variable. As it turns out, its inclusion or exclusion makes virtually no difference in the estimates of the influence of values of views of the judiciary. So it is eliminated from the final model.

32.   Estimates from the first panel are derived from a partial model relating to only the four constitutional reforms. Its fit statistics are: chi-square 463.2 with DF 195; ratio of chi-square:df = 2.4; CFI = 0.94; RMSEA = 0.020 (0.019–0.021); p (close) = 1.0. The figures in the second and third panel are derived from the full model described in note 30.

33.   The magnitude of correlation coefficients, ranging from a low of 0 to a high of 1 corresponds to the strength or predictability of the association between two variables. A coefficient of 0 indicates a completely unpredictable relationship in that to know the support for one variable, in this case one theme of reform, tells us nothing about the degree of support for another reform theme. A coefficient of 1 is rarely, if ever, attained as it indicates a perfectly predictable relationship. Correlations over 0.2 are generally considered to be of moderate predictability while those over 0.4 are considered to be strong. The direction of the relationship is indicated by either a positive (typically implied) or negative sign. A positive sign means that an increase in support for one theme of reform is associated with an increase in the other corresponding theme. A negative sign means an increase in support for one theme of reform corresponds to a decrease in the other theme.

34.   The two negative estimates are not significant and hence essentially zero.

35.   Compare the results for the Conservatives in Tables 4.1 and 4.2.

36. Compare the results for Labour in Tables 4.1 and 4.3.

37. Interestingly, it is only the British public that connects, albeit weakly, attitudes towards the judiciary with support for rights instruments beyond what one would expect by chance.

38. For a similar finding see Neil Nevitte and Christopher Cochrane, 'Value Change and the Dynamics of the Canadian Partisan Landscape', in Alain-G. Gagnon and A. Brian Tanguay (eds), *Canadian Parties in Transition*, 3rd ed. (Peterborough, ON: Broadview Press, 2007).

39. The larger the coefficient the larger the effect is estimated to be. The magnitude indicates the amount of change in attitudes towards the relevant theme of reform associated with a one-unit change in the relevant value. Standardised rather than unstandardised coefficients are presented to facilitate comparisons within groups. A positive coefficient indicates that greater support for the value is associated with greater support for the reform. Negative coefficients indicate an inverse relation. Comparisons between groups should properly use unstandardised coefficients, though in this instance the results are largely similar in either case. Appendix C includes sample output of the fully specified model with complete estimates of the measurement of variables as well as their interconnections, which is the focus of attention here. The output is for British public, on which the entries of the fourth set of columns in the second and third panels of Table 4.5 are based. The fit statistics provided are for the four-group model.

40. These differences also shed some light on the patterns observed in the first panel of Table 4.5. For example, democratic and rights reforms are more tightly connected in part because they share a similar root in equality. And democratic and judicial reform share a common basis in the value of authority.

41. In every instance the coefficient fails to reach significance. This negligible effect of liberty is consistent with findings in Canada that the value of liberty has no influence on Canadians' assessments of the Charter of Rights and Freedoms despite its considerable impact on police action, the administration of justice and civil liberties generally. See Paul Howe and Joseph F. Fletcher, 'The Evolution of Charter Values', in Harvey Lazar and Hamish Telford (eds), *Canada: The State of the Federation 2001: Canadian Political Culture(s) in Transition* (Montreal: McGill-Queens University Press, 2002). It also corroborates Canadian findings that views on Supreme Court cases involving important civil liberties showed little correlation with opinions on the Supreme Court or the Charter. See Joseph F. Fletcher and Paul Howe, 'Public Opinion and Canada's Courts', in Paul Howe and Peter H. Russell (eds), *Judicial Power and Canadian Democracy* (Montreal: McGill-Queens University Press, 2001), pp. 255–96. See also Joseph F. Fletcher and Paul Howe, 'Supreme Court Cases and Court Support', *Choices* (2000), vol. 6, no. 3, 30–56.

42. While the Human Rights Act has attracted criticisms as contrary to British traditions, based on this evidence, this was apparently not the view of the British public in 1992. A similar result was found for the citizens of Canada in

their early years of experience with the Charter of Rights, though the effect soon waned. See Howe and Fletcher, 'Evolution of Charter Values'.

43. This is again fully consistent with the Canadian results, where evaluations of the charter are based nearly exclusively on questions of equality (ibid.).

44. In viewing these findings, though, it is well to keep in mind that a positive relation here not only implies that high levels of support for equality are related to high levels of support for the rights instruments, but also that low is associated with low. This may be particularly important in considering the results for the Conservatives, where the relationships between equality and rights protection are strongest. It is useful to note that the results here obscure some differences of emphasis in the value basis of support for the different rights instruments. Examining support for each innovation separately reveals that while the pattern whereby equality is the leading predictor holds in predicting views on all three rights protection instruments, liberty plays a secondary role among politicians and a primary role among the public in predicting support for a Freedom of Information Act.

45. In fact, to the extent that liberty is engaged at all by the theme of citizen rights, Conservatives who place a greater value on liberty are more likely to oppose the new rights instruments. Not too much should be made of this, however, as the coefficient does not reach conventional levels of statistical significance.

46. See Sniderman et al., *Clash of Rights*.

Chapter 5

1. Bagehot, 'A Heath Robinson Constitution', *Economist*, 18 April 1998.

2. The Labour Party in Scotland, *New Labour: Because Scotland Deserves Better*, pp. 32–5.

3. Composition and terms of reference were published in HC Deb, Written Answers, 9 June 1997, vol. 295, cols 302–8.

4. Green Papers are consultative; White Papers contain proposals on which the government intends to act.

5. Sewel's name has subsequently become associated with an amendment to enable either Parliament to allow the other to legislate on its behalf. This has been increasingly used in circumstances in which Holyrood is depicted as passing the buck to Westminster on controversial measures such as recognition of single-sex partnerships.

6. *Memorandum of Understanding and Supplementary Agreements*, Cm 5240, December 2001.

7. The Labour Party. *Ambitions for Britain*, p. 35.

8. *Parliament and the Legislative Process*, Fourteenth report, Session 2002/3, HL 173, ch. 3.

9. Seventeen declarations were made in the first five years. Five were overturned on appeal and two appeals are outstanding at the time of writing.

10. The Chancellor of the Exchequer spoke on the government's reasons for developing a new constitutional settlement between the state, the individual and the community at a Charter 88/*Economist* constitutional conference in July 1997.

11. The Rt Hon. Lord Irvine of Lairg, Annual Constitution Unit Lecture, December 1998, paragraphs 16–17.

12. Professor Peter Hennessy, 'Re-engineering the State in Flight: A Year in the Life of the British Constitution, April 1997–April 1998', unpublished lecture at Lloyds TSB Forum, the Burrell Collection, Glasgow, 28 April 1998.

13. Ibid.

Chapter 6

1. See K. E. Malleson, 'Modernising the Constitution: Completing the Unfinished Business', *Legal Studies* (2004), vol. 24, 119–33.

2. Lord Chancellor's Department Select Committee, minutes of evidence, HC 903-i, 30 June 2003.

3. Lord Irvine commented when Lord Chancellor: 'We are a nation of pragmatists, not theorists, and we go, quite frankly, for what works.' Lord Chancellor's Department Select Committee, minutes of evidence, HC 611-i, q. 28, 2 April 2003.

4. O. Hood Phillips, 'A Constitutional Myth: Separation of Power', (1977) 93 LQR 11.

5. The Cabinet reshuffle involved the removal of Lord Irvine, who opposed the proposals, and his replacement by Lord Falconer, who later admitted that the first he had heard of them was on the day he was appointed.

6. Lord Hailsham, 'The Problems of a Lord Chancellor', 1972 presidential address, Holdsworth Club, Faculty of Law, University of Birmingham, quoted in Lord Steyn, 'The Weakest and Least Dangerous Branch of Government', [1997] PL 89.

7. Steyn, 'Weakest and Least Dangerous Branch of Government', p. 93.

8. HC 611-i, q. 29.

9. The statutory qualifications for the post holder require only experience as a minister, member of either House of Parliament, certain types of lawyer, legal academic or such 'other experience that the Prime Minister considers relevant' (Constitutional Reform Act 2005, Section 2(2)).

10. Constitutional Reform Act 2005, Section 3(1).

11. Parts 2 and 4 of The Constitutional Reform Act include the arrangements set out in the concordat. The full text of the concordat can be found in the government paper *Constitutional Reform: The Lord Chancellor's Judiciary-Related Functions: Proposals*, which was reproduced in Constitutional Reform Bill

Committee, First Report, Session 2003/4, HL 125-I, Appendix 6.

12.   This long private conversation was described by Woolf in his valedictory speech in 2005 as one of 'almost continuous dialogue' over two years.

13.   Falconer commented that the Concordat 'lays down the right kind of partnership between the executive and the judiciary, with clear roles for each within the framework of the separation of powers of both' (HL Deb, 12 February 2004, vol. 657, col. 1216). Woolf similarly noted: 'A spirit of partnership between the judiciary, the legislature and the executive is essential if the judiciary are to meet the changing needs of society' (Squire Centenary Lecture, Cambridge University, 3 March 2004). See also speech of the senior presiding judge, Lord Justice Thomas, 'The Judicial and Executive Branches of Government: A New Partnership' (Institute of Advanced Legal Studies, London, 10 November 2005).

14.   Woolf, Squire Centenary Lecture, p. 11.

15.   Constitutional Reform Act 2005, Section 108(2).

16.   From a speech at the London School of Economics, 27 July 1993.

17.   See Lord Woolf's comments on the resuscitation of the Judges' Council from being a 'semi-moribund institution'. 'Current Challenges in Judging', 5th Worldwide Common Law Judiciary Conference, Sydney, 10 April 2003.

18.   1994 F. A. Mann Lecture, published in [1995] PL 57, 68–9.

19.   Steyn, 'Weakest and Least Dangerous Branch of Government', p. 85.

20.   *R v. Secretary of State for the Home Department ex parte Simms* [1999] WLR 328.

21.   See for example Jeffrey Jowell, 'Immigration wars', *Guardian*, 2 March 2004; 'A constitutional crisis of the Government's making', *Daily Telegraph*, 5 March 2004.

22.   See n. 12 above.

23.   Lord Steyn, *Jackson and Others v. Her Majesty's Attorney General,* [2005] UKHL 56, para. 102.

24.   Lord Justice Sedley, for example, talks about the bipolar sovereignty of courts and Parliament: 'Human Rights: A Twenty-First Century Agenda' [1995] PL 389.

25.   A. M. Slaughter, 'A Global Community of Courts', Harvard International Law Journal (2003), vol. 44, 191.

Chapter 7

1.   I would like to thank Nicola McEwen, Stephen Tierney, Kenneth MacKenzie and Andrew McDonald for helpful comments and suggestions.

2.   Stephen Howe, 'Internal Decolonization?: British Politics since Thatcher as Post-Colonial Trauma', *Twentieth Century British History* (2003), vol. 41, no. 3, 286–304.

3.   Federalism was rejected previously in 1707 and 1801. See Michael Keating,

'The United Kingdom as Post-Sovereign Polity', in Michael O'Neill (ed.), *Devolution and British Politics* (Harlow: Longman, 2004), pp. 319–24.

4. Paul Chaney, Tom Hall and Andrew Pithouse, 'Introduction', in Paul Chaney, Tom Hall and Andrew Pithouse (eds), *New Governance – New Democracy?: Post-Devolution Wales* (Cardiff: University of Wales Press, 2001), p. 9.

5. Charles D. Tarlton, 'Symmetry and Asymmetry as Elements of Federalism', *Journal of Politics* (1965), vol. 27, pp. 861–74; Ronald L. Watts, *A Comparative Perspective on Asymmetry in Federations* (Kingston, ON: Institution for Intergovernmental Relations, Queen's University, 2005); Arthur Benz, 'From Unitary to Asymmetric Federalism in Germany: Taking Stock after 50 years', *Publius* (1999), vol. 29, no. 4, pp 55–78.

6. Martin Laffin, 'Constitutional Design: A Framework for Analysis', *Parliamentary Affairs* (2000), vol. 53, 532–41; Martin Laffin and Alys Thomas, 'The United Kingdom: Federalism in Denial?', *Publius* (1999), vol. 29, no. 3, 89–108.

7. Archie Brown, 'Asymmetrical Devolution: The Scottish Case', *Political Quarterly* (1998), vol. 69, no. 3, 217.

8. Richard Wilson, 'Constitutional Change: A Note by the Bedside', *Political Quarterly* (2005), vol. 76, 281.

9. Michael O'Neill, 'Reforming the British State', in O'Neill, *Devolution and British Politics*, p. 177. See also Michael O'Neill, 'Great Britain: From Dicey to Devolution', *Parliamentary Affairs* (2004), vol. 53, no. 1, 69–95.

10. Johan P. Olsen, 'Institutional Design in Democratic Contexts', *Journal of Political Philosophy* (1997), vol. 5, no. 3, 203–29. See also Johan P. Olsen, 'Modernization Programs in Perspective: Institutional Analysis of Organizational Change', *Governance* (1991), vol. 4, no. 2, 125–49.

11. Quoted in David Baker, 'Intra-Party Relationships of British State-wide Political Parties within the Developing Territorial Agenda', in O'Neill, *Devolution and British Politics*, pp. 207–30.

12. Richard Wyn Jones and Roger Scully, 'A "Settling Will"?: Public Attitudes to Devolution in Wales', *British Elections and Parties Review* (2003), vol. 13, 86–106.

13. Lynn Bennie and Alistair Clark, 'Towards Moderate Pluralism: Scotland's Post-Devolution Party System 1999–2002', *British Elections and Parties Review* (2003), vol. 13, 144.

14. David Marquand, *The Progressive Dilemma: From Lloyd George to Blair*, 2nd ed. (London: Phoenix, 1999); Peter Mair, 'Partyless Democracy: Solving the Paradox of New Labour', *New Left Review* (2000), no. 2, 21–35.

15. Michael Keating, 'Reforging the Union: Devolution and Constitutional Change in the United Kingdom', *Publius* (1998), vol. 28, no. 1, 217–34; Ross McKibbin, 'Treading Water?', *New Left Review* (2000), no. 4, 69–74.

16. James Mitchell, 'The Evolution of Devolution: Labour's Home Rule Strategy in Opposition', *Government and Opposition* (1998), vol. 33, no. 4; Keating, 'Reforging the Union'.

17. Anthony Barnett, 'Corporate Populism and Partyless Democracy', *New Left Review* (2000), no. 3, 80–9.
18. Brigid Hadfield, 'Devolution in the UK and the English and Welsh Questions', in Jeffrey Jowell and Dawn Oliver (eds), *The Changing Constitution*, 5th ed. (Oxford: Oxford University Press, 2004), p. 252. Or, as Mitchell and Bradbury note, 'the development of devolution in its various settings simply echoes longstanding pragmatic features of UK constitutional development: flexible and instrumentalist in its response to perceived empirical needs rather than formal and generative in its assertion of ideals'. James Mitchell and Jonathan Bradbury, 'Devolution: Comparative Development and Policy Roles', *Parliamentary Affairs* (2004), vol. 57, no. 2, 345.
19. *Nations and Regions: The Dynamics of Devolution: Quarterly Monitoring Programme, Scotland* (London: Constitution Unit, University College London, May 2002), p. 11.
20. *Nations and Regions: The Dynamics of Devolution: Quarterly Monitoring Programme, Scotland* (London: Constitution Unit, University College London, August 2000), p. 10.
21. Ian Budge, Ivor Crewe, David McKay and Ken Newton, *The New British Politics*, 3rd ed. (Harlow: Longman, 2004), p. 248.
22. Charlie Jeffery, 'Uniformity and Diversity in Policy Provision', in John Adams and Peter Robinson (eds), *Devolution in Practice* (Newcastle: IPPR North, 2002), pp. 176–97.
23. See also David Judge, 'Whatever Happened to Parliamentary Democracy in the United Kingdom?', *Parliamentary Affairs* (2004), vol. 57, 682–701.
24. Labour dual-mandate MSPs in the Scottish Executive included First Minister Donald Dewar, Henry McLeish (who later became First Minister) and Sam Galbraith. A fourth dual-mandate member, John Home Robertson, was deputy Minister for Rural Affairs. Liberal Democrat leader and deputy First Minister Jim Wallace was also a dual-mandate member.
25. Ailsa Henderson, 'Forging a New Political Culture: Plenary Behaviour in the Scottish Parliament', *Journal of Legislative Studies* (2005), vol. 11, 275–301; Ailsa Henderson and Amanda Sloat, 'New Politics in Scotland: A Guide to Scotland's MSPs', *Talking Politics* (1999), vol. 12, no. 1, 243–7.
26. 'Blair's wild bunch: deep divisions in the Scottish Labour Party threaten the success of a future Scottish parliament', *Economist*, 8 February 1997, p. 32.
27. John Curtice, 'Bending with the wind', *Scotland on Sunday*, 31 January 1999, p. 17.
28. See, for example, Jonathan Bradbury and James Mitchell, 'Devolution: Between Governance and Territorial Politics', *Parliamentary Affairs* (2005), vol. 58, 287–302; Kevin Morgan, 'The New Territorial Politics: Rivalry and Justice in Post-Devolution Britain', *Regional Studies* (2001), vol. 35, 344; Rhys Jones, 'Institutional Identities and the Shifting Scopes of State Governance in the United Kingdom' *European Urban and Regional Studies* (2001), vol. 8, 290; Barry K. Winetrobe, 'Scottish Devolution: Aspirations and Reality in Multi-

Layer Government', in Jowell and Oliver, *Changing Constitution*, p. 173.

29.   Baker, 'Intra-Party Relationships of British State-wide Political Parties within the Developing Territorial Agenda', p. 217.

30.   The short-lived tenures of Henry McLeish in Edinburgh and Alun Michael in Cardiff were improvements on the electoral failure of Frank Dobson, New Labour's preferred candidate for the London mayoral position.

31.   Baker, 'Intra-Party Relationships of British State-wide Political Parties within the Developing Territorial Agenda', p. 220.

32.   Executive member Wendy Alexander, for example, was the Scottish political campaign head for Labour during the UK election.

33.   See for example, Barry Winetrobe, *The Executive: The Dynamics of Devolution: Quarterly Monitoring Programme, Scotland* (London: Constitution Unit, University College London, 2003).

34.   Keating, 'Reforging the Union'.

35.   'The Sewel Convention is named after Lord Sewel (then Minister of State in the Scottish Office), who stated during Lords Committee stage of the Scotland Bill that the Government expected "a convention to be established that Westminster would not normally legislate with regard to devolved matters in Scotland without the consent of the Scottish Parliament"' (*Sewel Motions: Session 1* (Edinburgh: Scottish Parliament, 2006)).

36.   Keating, 'United Kingdom as Post-Sovereign Polity', p. 322.

37.   Neil McGarvey, 'Intergovernmental Relations in Scotland Post-Devolution', *Local Government Studies* (2002), vol. 28, no.3, 29–48.

38.   Whether this stems from support for devolution (and thus complacency) or dissatisfaction is up for debate. See, for example, Catherine Bromley and John Curtice, 'The Lost Voters of Scotland: Devolution Disillusioned or Westminster Weary', *British Elections and Parties Review* (2003), vol. 13, 66–85.

39.   See, for example, Robert Ingram, 'First or Second Order?: Will the Scottish and Welsh Elections Deliver Devolution?', *British Elections and Parties Review* (2003), vol. 13, 107–33; John Curtice, 'Turnout, Electoral Behaviour and Fragmentation of the Party System', in Ross Burnside, Stephen Herbert and Stephen Curtis, *Election 2003* (Edinburgh: Scottish Parliament, 2003) pp. 12–13.

40.   Mitchell and Bradbury, 'Devolution'.

41.   Ruaridh Nicoll and Lorna Martin, 'Actually, I am in charge,' *Observer*, 29 January 2006.

42.   Jonathan Bradbury and Neil McGarvey, 'Devolution: Problems, Politics and Prospects', *Parliamentary Affairs* (2003), vol. 56, 219–36.

Chapter 8

1.   Joseph Raz, 'On the Authority and Interpretation of Constitutions: Some Preliminaries', in Larry Alexander (ed.), *Constitutionalism: Philosophical*

Foundations (Cambridge: Cambridge University Press, 1998), pp.152–176; Paul Craig, 'Constitutions, Constitutionalism, and the European Union', *European Law Journal* (2001), vol. 7, 125–150.

2. I use 'federal' in its simplest sense, meaning a polity with at least two territorial levels of government which each enjoy some degree of autonomous, constitutionally guaranteed authority. Federations vary widely in how much power is lodged with the federal government. In political practice the connotation of 'federal' depends on the comparative context (which is often implicit). British politicians often use 'federal' in the EU context to mean 'centralised' – by contrast to less supranational international agreements. In comparative government, however, 'federal' typically contrasts to 'unitary' states and connotes relative decentralisation.

3. *NV Algemene Transporten Expeditie Onderneming van Gend en Loos v. Nederlandse Administratie der Belastingen*, ECJ Case 26/62, [1963] ECR 1; [1963] CMLR 105.

4. *Costa v. Ente Nazionale per L'Energia Elettrica (ENEL)*, ECJ Case 6/64, [1964] ECR 585; [1964] CMLR 425.

5. *Internationale Handelsgesellschaft mbH v. Einfuhr- und Vorratsstelle für Getreide und Futtermittel*, ECJ Case 11/70, [1970] ECR 1125.

6. Joseph Weiler, 'The Transformation of Europe', *Yale Law Journal* (1991), vol. 100, 2403–83; Anne-Marie Burley and Walter Mattli, 'Europe before the Court: A Political Theory of Legal Integration', *International Organization* (1993), vol. 47, 41–76.

7. *R. v. Secretary of State for Transport ex parte Factortame Ltd*, [1990] 2 AC 85, was the key step in what was actually a series of cases from 1989 to 1998.

8. A. V. Dicey, *Lectures Introductory to the Study of the Law of the Constitution* (London: Macmillan, 1885); Sir William Wade and Christopher Forsyth, *Administrative Law*, 7th ed. (Oxford: Clarendon, 1994).

9. In this period any apparent conflicts, writes Damian Chalmers, 'were to be interpreted away under the fiction that [the European Communities Act] was merely an extension of the practice of interpreting British statutes in the light of its international treaty obligations' ('The Positioning of EU Judicial Politics within the United Kingdom', in Simon Hix and Klaus H. Goetz (eds), *Europeanised Politics?: European Integration and National Political Systems* (London: Frank Cass, 2001), pp. 169–210). See also Danny Nicol, *EC Membership and the Judicialization of British Politics* (Oxford: Oxford University Press, 2001).

10. The case invalidated the Merchant Shipping Act of 1988. Paul Craig, 'Sovereignty of the United Kingdom Parliament after *Factortame*', *Yearbook of European Law* (1991), vol. 11, 221–55.

11. 14 December 1991.

12. Eric Stein, 'Lawyers, Judges, and the Making of a Transnational Constitution', *American Journal of International Law* (1981), vol. 75, no. 1, 1–27; Craig, 'Constitutions, Constitutionalism, and the European Union'.

13. Ian Loveland, 'Britain and Europe', in Vernon Bogdanor (ed.), *The British*

Constitution in the Twentieth Century (Oxford: Oxford University Press, 2003), pp. 663–88.

14. Chalmers, 'Positioning of EU Judicial Politics within the United Kingdom'.

15. Karen Alter, *Establishing the Supremacy of European Law: The Making of an International Rule of Law in Europe* (New York: Oxford University Press, 2001).

16. Craig, 'Constitutions, Constitutionalism, and the European Union'; Otto Pfersmann, 'The New Revision of the Old Constitution', *International Journal of Constitutional Law* (2005), vol. 3, 383–404.

17. Peter Norman, *The Accidental Constitution: The Story of the European Convention* (Brussels: Eurocomment, 2003).

18. Vivien A. Schmidt, *Democracy in Europe: The EU and National Polities* (Oxford: Oxford University Press, 2006).

19. Joschka Fischer, 'From Confederacy to Federation: Thoughts on the Finality of European Integration', speech at the Humboldt University in Berlin, 12 May 2000. Available in English at http://www.auswaertiges-amt.de.

20. Jacques Chirac, 'Our Europe', speech at the Bundestag, Berlin, 27 June 2000; Tony Blair, 'Superpower – Not Superstate?', speech in Warsaw, October 2000. Both available in English at http://www.fedtrust.co.uk.

21. Norman, *Accidental Constitution*.

22. Craig Parsons, *A Certain Idea of Europe* (Ithaca, NY: Cornell University Press, 2003).

23. Paul Magnette and Kalypso Nicolaidis, 'The European Convention: Bargaining in the Shadow of Rhetoric', *West European Politics* (2004), vol. 27, 381–405.

24. Simply through aggressive bargaining at Nice, Spain and Poland, with roughly forty million people each, had received twenty-seven weighted votes in the Council, almost as many as the EU's largest countries, Germany (eighty million), France, the UK, and Italy (each roughly sixty million), which had twenty-nine.

25. Paul Craig, 'European Governance: Executive and Administrative Powers under the New Constitutional Settlement', *International Journal of Constitutional Law* (2005), vol. 3, 407–39.

26. Norman, *Accidental Constitution*, p. 50.

27. Pfersmann, 'New Revision of the Old Constitution'.

28. J. H. H. Weiler, 'On the Power of the Word: Europe's Constitutional Iconography', *International Journal of Constitutional Law* (2005), vol. 3, 173–90; but see Damian Chalmers, 'Judicial Authority and the Constitutional Treaty', *International Journal of Constitutional Law* (2005), vol. 3, 448–72.

29. House of Lords Select Committee on European Union, *The Future Role of the European Court of Justice*, Sixth Report, Session 2003/4, HL 47, Written Evidence, Takis Tridimas and Karen Alter.

30. Henry Milner, '"YES to the Europe I want; NO to this one": Some Reflections on France's Rejection of the EU Constitution', *PS: Political Science and Politics* (2006), vol. 39, 257–60.

31. Pascal Perrineau, (ed.), *Le Vote européen 2004–2005: De l'élargissement au référendum français* (Paris: Presses de Sciences Po, 2005); Kees Aarts and Henk van der Kolk, 'Understanding the Dutch "No": The Euro, the East, and the Elite', *PS: Political Science and Politics* (2006), vol. 39, 243–6.

32. Lawfulness concerns whether public actors or administrative rules meet or exceed their statutory basis. Appeals to procedural regularity invoke some requirement for consultation and deliberation in public decision-making. Reasonableness concerns whether actions and lower-level rules follow in some reasonable way from statutory mandates.

33. Susan Sterett, *Creating Constitutionalism?: The Politics of Legal Expertise and Administrative Law in England and Wales* (Ann Arbor: University of Michigan Press, 1997).

34. Martin Shapiro, 'Judicial Delegation Doctrines: The US, Britain and France', *West European Politics* (2002), vol. 25, 173–99.

35. Proportionality principles allow public actions to impinge on individual rights only to the extent necessary – as the court sees it – to realise legitimate public aims; purposive interpretation authorises courts to seek the purpose of a statute beyond its written language; and legitimate expectations suggests that individuals may hold certain expectations that enjoy legal protection despite not qualifying fully as rights. All three were generally seen as foreign principles in England before the 1980s. See Gordon Anthony, *UK Public Law and European Law* (Portland, OR: Hart, 2002); Joseph Jupille and James Caporaso, 'The Second Image Overruled: European Law, Domestic Institutions and British Sovereignty', unpublished MS, 2006.

36. *M. v. Home Office*, [1994] 1 AC 377; [1992] QB 270. The ruling required the administration to provide benefits to an immigrant during a case about his access to benefits, arguing that otherwise he might starve to death in the interim. Patrick Birkinshaw, *Does European Public Law Exist?* (Belfast: Institute for European Studies, Queen's University, 2001).

37. QB 151 (Admn. Ct 2003).

38. QB 151, para. 63 (Admn. Ct 2003). See Mark Elliott, 'Parliamentary Sovereignty under Pressure', *International Journal of Constitutional Law* (2004), vol. 2, 545–54.

39. QB 151, para. 59 (Admn. Ct 2003).

40. Elliott, 'Parliamentary Sovereignty under Pressure'.

41. Shapiro, 'Judicial Delegation Doctrines', 190, his emphasis.

42. Chalmers, 'Positioning of EU Judicial Politics within the United Kingdom', p. 203.

43. See Chapter 6, pp. 134 & 135 of this volume.

44. Nicol, *EC Membership and the Judicialization of British Politics*, p. 236.

45. Craig, 'Sovereignty of the United Kingdom Parliament after *Factortame*', 253; H. W. R. Wade, 'Sovereignty – Revolution or Evolution?' *Law Quarterly Review* (1996), vol. 112, 568–75.

46. D. Bean, 'The Human Rights Act Four Years On', paper presented to the

Australian Bar Association Conference, Paris, 10 July 2002.

47. Philip Daniels, 'From Hostility to "Constructive Engagement": The Europeanisation of the Labour Party', *West European Politics* (1998), vol. 21, 72–96.

48. Jim Sillars, *Scotland: The Case for Optimism* (Edinburgh: Polygon, 1986).

49. Stephen Tindale, 'Learning to Love the Market: Labour and the European Community', *Political Quarterly* (1992), vol. 63, 276–300.

50. Michael Keating and Barry Jones, 'Nations, Regions, and Europe: The UK Experience', in Barry Jones and Michael Keating (eds), *The European Union and the Regions* (Oxford: Clarendon Press, 1995), pp. 89–114.

51. Alex Wright, *Who Governs Scotland?* (London: Routledge, 2005), p. 36. Until the establishment of EU controls in 1988, the funds basically replaced national funding and so added little to Scottish spending. Even since 1988 the 'additionality' of the funding, compared to what Scotland would receive from the UK government without the EU, is a subject of debate. But as Keating points out, political actors in Scotland generally seem to believe that the EU funds are additional (or wilfully pretend that they are so they can appear to claim credit for 'winning' them) (Michael Keating, *The Government of Scotland: Public Policy Making after Devolution* (Edinburgh: Edinburgh University Press, 2005, p. 154)).

52. Tindale, 'Learning to Love the Market.'

53. Kelly B. Shaw, 'The European Union, Britain, and Scotland: Conflict, Cooperation, or Compromise?', paper presented at European Union Studies Association conference, Nashville, TN, 27–29 March 2003.

54. J. Smith, 'Government in Scotland', in Ian Bache and Andrew Jordan (eds), *The Europeanization of British Politics* (Basingstoke: Palgrave Macmillan, 2006), pp. 67–81.

55. Simon Bulmer, Martin Burch, Patricia Hogwood and Andrew Scott, 'UK Devolution and the European Union: A Tale of Cooperative Asymmetry?' *Publius* (2006), vol. 36, 75–93.

56. Keating, *Government of Scotland*, p. 133.

57. Smith, 'Government in Scotland', p. 77.

58. Janet Mather, 'The Impact of European Integration', in O'Neill, *Devolution and British Politics*, pp. 269–94.

59. Tony Wright (ed.), *The British Political Process: An Introduction* (New York: Routledge, 1999), p. 333.

60. Theodore Lowi, 'American Business, Public Policy, Case Studies, and Political Theory', *World Politics* (1964), vol. 16, 677–715.

61. David Allen, 'The United Kingdom: A Europeanised Government in a Non-Europeanised Polity', in Simon Bulmer and Christian Lequesne (eds), *The Member States of the European Union* (New York: Oxford University Press, 2005), pp. 119–41.

62. Simon Bulmer and Martin Burch, 'Central Government', in Bache and Jordan, *Europeanisation of British Politics*, pp. 37–51.

63. Randall Smith, 'European Union Policies and Funds: The Role of Urban Government in England', in Bernhard Blanke and Randall Smith (eds), *Cities in Transition: New Challenges, New Responsibilities* (Basingstoke: Macmillan, 1999).

64. D. Allen and T. Oliver, 'The Foreign and Commonwealth Office', in Bache and Jordan, *Europeanisation of British Politics*, pp. 52–66.

65. Paul Taggart and Aleks Szczerbiak (eds), *Opposing Europe?: The Comparative Party Politics of Euroscepticism* (Oxford: Oxford University Press, forthcoming).

66. Parsons, *Certain Idea of Europe*.

67. Harold D. Clarke, David Sanders, Marianne C. Stewart and Paul Whiteley, *Political Choice in Britain* (Oxford: Oxford University Press, 2004); John Bartle and Anthony King (eds), *Britain at the Polls 2005* (Washington, DC: CQ Press, 2006).

68. David Baker, 'Britain and Europe: The Argument Continues', *Parliamentary Affairs* (2001), vol. 54, 276–88.

69. Pippa Norris and Joni Lovenduski, 'Why Parties Fail to Learn: Electoral Defeat, Selective Perception and British Party Politics', *Party Politics*, (2004), vol. 10, 85–104.

Chapter 9

1. I am indebted to Andrew McDonald for many useful suggestions, corrections and sources of information. I am also grateful to Matthew Wright for invaluable assistance in the discovery, analysis and preparation of the public opinion data.

2. Lord Irvine of Lairg, 'Government's Programme of Constitutional Reform', annual Constitutional Unit lecture, 8 December 1998.

3. Ibid.

4. Anthony King, *Does Britain Still Have a Constitution?* (London: Sweet and Maxwell, 2001).

5. Ibid., p. 7.

6. Irvine, 'Government's Programme of Constitutional Reform'.

7. I am again indebted to Andrew McDonald for directing me to Brown's speeches on the topic of national identity. See his Hugo Young Lecture, 13 December 2005.

8. See John Curtice, 'Public Opinion and the Future of Devolution', in Alan Trench (ed.), *The Dynamics of Devolution: The State of the Nations 2005*, pp. 117–36 (Exeter: Imprint Academic, 2005); Anthony Heath, Bridget Taylor, Lindsay Brook and Alison Park, 'British National Sentiment', *British Journal of Political Science* (1999), vol. 29, 155–75.

9. See Curtice, 'Public Opinion and the Future of Devolution', pp. 119, 134.

10. Ibid., p. 129.

11. Ernest Gellner, *Nations and Nationalism* (Oxford: Blackwell, 1983).

12. Samuel Huntington, *Who Are We?: Challenges to American National Identity*

(Cambridge, MA: Harvard University Press, 2004).

13. Gordon Brown, Fabian Lecture, 14 January 2006.

14. Jürgen Habermas, 'Citizenship and National Identity', in Bart van Steenbergen (ed.), *The Condition of Citizenship* (London: Sage, 1994).

15. Curtice, 'Public Opinion and the Future of Devolution', pp. 126, 131.

16. Ibid., p. 126.

17. These features were: how well democracy is working, economic achievements, scientific achievements, sporting achievements, cultural achievements, artistic achievements, political influence in the world, social security system, history, and equal treatment of all groups in society.

18. See Heath et al., 'British National Sentiment'.

19. See notably Martin Gabel, *Interests and Integration: Market Liberalization, Public Opinion, and European Union* (Ann Arbor: University of Michigan Press, 1998); Jack Citrin and John Sides, 'Can Europe Exist without Europeans?: Problems of Identity in a Multinational State,' in Margaret Hermann (ed.), *Advances in Political Psychology, vol. 1* (Amsterdam: Elsevier, 2004), pp. 41–70.

20. Richard Eichenberg and Russell Dalton, 'Post-Maastricht Blues: The Transformation of Citizen Support for European Integration 1973–2002,' unpublished paper available from the authors, p. 16.

21. Ibid., pp. 22–23. See also, Gabel, *Interests and Integration*.

22. Eichenberg and Dalton, 'Post-Maastricht Blues', p. 23.

23. Ibid., p.22.

24. Those saying that they are attached to Europe only or attached to neither are always a small minority of less than 20 per cent combined in both Britain and the original six EU countries and so these trends are omitted from the chart.

25. David Miller, *On Nationality* (Oxford: Clarendon Press, 1995).

26. For a similar discussion, see Christian Joppke and Stephen Lukes (eds), *Multicultural Questions* (Oxford: Oxford University Press, 1999).

27. Amartya Sen, 'The Uses and Misuses of Multiculturalism,' *New Republic*, 26 February 2006, p. 3.

28. Ibid., p.6.

29. Ibid., p.1.

30. This problem is posed in Susan Moller Okin, *Is Multiculturalism Bad for Women?* (Princeton: Princeton University Press, 1999).

31. T. Alexander Aleinikoff, 'A Multicultural Nationalism', *American Prospect* (1999), vol. 36, 80–7.

32. The response options were 'a great deal', 'quite a bit', 'not much' and 'not at all'. Table 9.6 reports the proportion saying 'a great deal' or 'quite a bit'.

33. The term 'Eurabia' is taken from 'Tales of Eurabia: The West and Islam', *Economist*, 24 June 2006. A recent expression of this point of view is found in Bruce Bawer, *While Europe Slept: How Radical Islam Is Destroying the West from Within* (New York: Doubleday, 2006).

Chapter 1, Appendix A

	1997 Cook–Maclennan Agreement	1997 manifesto	Delivery in 1997 parliament
House of Lords (hereditary peers)	End right of hereditaries to sit in Lords	End right of hereditaries to sit in Lords	Done (for all but 92 hereditaries) in House of Lords Act 1999
House of Lords (crossbench and life peers)	Crossbenchers valuable and should remain at around 20% of Lords (after hereditaries excluded). Life peers should not be forced out	Review system of appointment of life peers	Appointments Commission for crossbench life peers established in 2000
House of Lords (long-term solution)	Joint committee to put forward proposals for long-term structure, functions and composition. No one party to seek a majority in Lords	Committee of both Houses to propose Stage 2. No one party to seek a majority in Lords	Wakeham commission reported, giving options for reform

Labour's delivery of its manifesto commitments on constitutional reform

2001 manifesto	Delivery in 2001 parliament	2005 manifesto	Delivery as at July 2006
Remove remaining hereditaries	White Paper 2001 (hereditaries out; 20% elected). Inconclusive February 2003 vote on composition. White Paper July 2003 (hereditaries out; strengthen Appointments Commission; no consensus on elected component). March 2004 reform Bill dropped before introduction	Remove remaining hereditaries	Initial focus was on powers, not composition; see 'House of Lords (long-term solution)' *below*
Put Appointments Commission on statutory footing	No progress	No direct reference in the manifesto, but see 'House of Lords (long-term solution)' *below*	N/A
Committed to making the Lords more representative and democratic. Supports implementation of Wakeham. Favours modernisation of Lords procedures	See summary under 'House of Lords (hereditaries)' *above*. Procedures reformed following report of the Leader's Group on Working Practices	Reformed Lords should be effective, legitimate and more representative, and no challenge to Commons. Review by committee of both Houses of the powers and procedures of Lords. Free vote on future composition of Lords	Joint Committee on Conventions established May 2006 – to consider powers of House of Lords but not composition

	1997 Cook–Maclennan Agreement	1997 manifesto	Delivery in 1997 parliament
House of Commons	Select committee to modernise; programming of business; better pre-legislative scrutiny; improve PM's Questions; better scrutiny of European legislation; stronger select committees	Select committee to modernise; PM's Questions to be more effective; ministerial accountability to be reviewed; better scrutiny of European legislation	Modernisation Committee appointed; led to modest changes. Westminster Hall debates introduced. PM's Questions format changed
Elections (PR)	Referendum in first term to choose between first-past-the-post and a PR system (to be selected by a commission)	Early appointment of commission to recommend PR. Referendum (presumably subsequently)	Jenkins commission appointed and reported, favouring modified version of the alternative vote
Elections (process and funding)	Improve registration and voting processes – including independent oversight	Reform of party funding to end sleaze: parties to declare source of all donations above a threshold; foreign funding to be banned; Committee on Standards in Public Life to be asked to consider reform of funding of political parties	Political Parties, Elections and Referendums Act 2000 to establish Electoral Commission; Representation of the People Act 2000 to introduce rolling registration and to facilitate experiments in voting methods
Elections (European)	Regional-list PR system to be introduced	Manifesto notes long-standing support for PR for European elections	Regional-list PR introduced by European Parliamentary Elections Act 1999

2001 manifesto	Delivery in 2001 parliament	2005 manifesto	Delivery as at July 2006
Continued modernisation so that Commons can effectively carry out representation and scrutiny functions	Hours of sittings reformed. Payment introduced for select committee chairs. Bills allowed to carry over from one session to the next. Programming of Bills made permanent. PM questioned regularly by Liaison Committee	Continued support for Modernisation Committee	Modernisation Committee's first report into legislative process
Review experience of new voting systems and Jenkins report to determine whether to reform. Referendum needed for any proposed change	Review began, but did not report by time of election	Remain committed to reviewing experience of new electoral systems. Referendum remains right way to agree any change for Westminster	Review continuing
No reference to party funding in manifesto	N/A	Will work with Electoral Commission to explore how best to support political parties, but their campaigning must be self-funded	Electoral Administration Act to reform voter registration and tighten voter security
No reference in manifesto	N/A	No reference in manifesto	N/A

	1997 Cook–Maclennan Agreement	1997 manifesto	Delivery in 1997 parliament
Democratic engagement	Not addressed	No reference in manifesto	N/A
Openness	Freedom of Information (FoI) Act; (by implication) stronger rights of access to personal information; and independent National Statistical Service	FoI Act and independent National Statistical Service	FoI Act passed 2000 to introduce right of access; Data Protection Act 1998 strengthens access to personal information; and Statistics Commission established 2000 to provide independent advice on official statistics
Devolution (Scotland)	1. Pre-legislative referendum backed by Labour but not Liberal Democrats 2. Scottish Parliament with tax-raising powers (along lines of Scottish Constitutional Convention model) 3. Additional-member system (AMS) for Scottish parliamentary elections	1. Referendum on proposals 2. If referendum approved, Scottish Parliament with tax-raising powers	Referendum Act 1997 paves way for devolution through the Scotland Act 1998 (including provision for tax-raising powers). Parliament elected by AMS in May 1999.
Devolution (Wales)	1. Referendum on devolution of Welsh Office functions 2. If referendum approved, Welsh Assembly; and 3. AMS for Welsh Assembly elections	Referendum on devolution of Welsh Office functions. Assembly to have secondary legislative powers. To be elected by AMS.	Referendum Act 1997 paves way for devolution through Government of Wales Act 1998. Welsh Assembly elected under AMS in May 1999.

2001 manifesto	Delivery in 2001 parliament	2005 manifesto	Delivery as at July 2006
No reference in manifesto	N/A	Will continue to explore new ways of engaging citizens in decision-making	Electoral Administration Act authorises electoral officers to promote participation; with government funding to support this and other activity (including registration drives)
No reference in manifesto	FoI Act fully implemented from January 2005	No reference in manifesto	Government announces its intention to legislate to bolster the independence of official statistics; consultation document March 2006 on how to establish direct accountability of the statistical service to Parliament
No additional commitment in manifesto	N/A	No additional commitment in manifesto	N/A
No additional commitment in manifesto	N/A	Enhanced legislative powers and reformed structure for Welsh Assembly; changes to Welsh electoral system	White Paper June 2005: three-stage move to full legislative powers. End to dual candidacy in constituencies and top-up list. Government of Wales Act passed July 2006

	1997 Cook–Maclennan Agreement	1997 manifesto	Delivery in 1997 parliament
London	1. Referendum 2. If referendum approved, strategic authority and elected mayor	1. Referendum 2. If referendum approved, strategic authority and elected mayor	Greater London Authority Referendum Act 1998 leads, after popular approval, to Greater London Authority Act 1998
English local government	No specific commitments	Proportion of local councillors to be elected annually and pilots of elected mayors in cities	Local Government Act 2000 requires local authorities to abandon the committee system and to choose cabinet system, city manager or directly elected mayor
English regions	Establish regional chambers and, if approved in referendums, directly elected regional assemblies should follow	Establishment of regional development agencies (RDAs) to co-ordinate economic development; create regional chambers; and, in time, referendums to test desire for elected regional assemblies	Eight RDAs established April 1999 after Regional Development Agencies Act 1998; regional chambers created as voluntary, non-statutory bodies. No progress on referendum legislation
Rights	Incorporation of European Convention on Human Rights (ECHR) into UK law; Joint Committee on Human Rights and Human Rights Commission/ Commissioner to supervise	Incorporation of ECHR into UK law	Human Rights Act 1998 incorporates ECHR rights. Joint Committee established early 2001
Justice	No specific commitments	Review of civil justice system and legal aid	Access to Justice Act 1999 to establish Legal Services Commission and reform legal aid

2001 manifesto	Delivery in 2001 parliament	2005 manifesto	Delivery as at July 2006
No additional commitment in manifesto	N/A	Review of the powers of Greater London Authority	Review approved new powers in housing, skills, planning, culture and waste management
Greater freedoms for local authorities through local public service agreements (LPSAs)	LPSAs were developed governing the delivery and funding of service targets; supplemented by local area agreements, giving greater scope to local authorities over their delivery	New powers for local neighbourhoods; greater freedoms for local authorities	Speeches by David Miliband (then a minister at the Office of the Deputy Prime Minister) on the new localism and on 'double devolution'
Repeat commitment to referendum provision to test desire for regional assemblies	Regional Assemblies (Preparation) Act 2003; trial referendum in NE England decisively rejected	Further devolution of authority to regions on planning, housing, economic development and transport	Proposals to regionalise police forces in England and Wales initially under consideration but not pursued
No additional commitment in manifesto	N/A	Establish a Commission on Equality and Human Rights; and a Single Equality Act to rationalise anti-discrimination legislation	Equality Act 2006 to establish a Commission for Equality and Human Rights (to begin operations in October 2007); discrimination law review under way as a preliminary to a single equality Bill
Unification of the magistrates' and crown courts	Courts Act 2003 unifies magistrates' and crown courts	No additional reforms in manifesto	N/A

	1997 Cook–Maclennan Agreement	1997 manifesto	Delivery in 1997 parliament
Civil service	Tighten up code and put into statutory form, to strengthen impartiality	No reference in manifesto	N/A

This table tracks the progress of the constitutional reform commitments made in Labour's election manifestos of 1997, 2001 and 2005. The party's constitutional agenda was shaped in discussion with the Liberal Democrats and their agreed programme was published in March 1997 (here called the Cook–Maclennan agreement for short).

Reforms not prefigured in the Cook–Maclennan agreement or in manifestos do not appear here. The principal omissions are the two great surprises of the reform agenda: greater freedom for the Bank of England, which was announced shortly after the 1997 election; and the government's announcement in June 2003 that it planned to abolish the office of Lord Chancellor, to appoint judges in a new way and to create a Supreme Court.

The commitments (and their mode of implementation) are necessarily described here in shorthand. Some simplification of the principles – and of action – is unavoidable.

Commitments with respect to Northern Ireland are not included in this table because they fall outside the scope of this book.

2001 manifesto	Delivery in 2001 parliament	2005 manifesto	Delivery as at July 2006
Commitment to impartial civil service and to renewal of the service's skills	Civil service reform programme (non-statutory). Publication of draft Civil Service Bill	No reference in manifesto	N/A

Chapter 4, Appendix A

Question wordings

{Braces indicate respondent supplied information}
[Square brackets indicate randomly varied information with a stroke separating the variations]

Theme 1: Devolution
If the people living there wanted more powers of self-government, would you support or oppose giving greater powers of self-government to . . .

   . . . Scotland?
   . . . Wales?
   . . . Northern Ireland?
   . . . London?
   . . . regions of England, such as the North-West or South-East?

Theme 2: Support for rights protection instruments
A mark of 10 indicates something that you think makes an extremely important contribution to protecting rights; a mark of 0 indicates something you think does nothing at all to protect citizen rights . . .

   And now some things which have been proposed for Britain by some people, but are opposed by others. How much would our rights and liberties be protected and strengthened by each of the following? Use the same scale from 0 to 10 as before.

- a Bill of Rights, passed by Parliament and enforced by the courts?
- a Freedom of Information Act, giving more legal access to government information?
- a reformed House of Lords, whose members were elected?

Theme 3: Support for democratic reforms
Referendums
Two versions of a referendum question were posed, each to a randomly selected half of the sample. For the present analysis the results for the two

questions were combined by scoring disagreement with the first version and agreement with the second version as support for referendums.

Version 1: It would be better to let the people decide important political issues by everyone voting in a referendum, rather than leaving them to Parliament as at present.

Version 2: Important political issues are too complex to be decided by everyone voting in a referendum, and should be left to Parliament to decide.

Proportional representation

Next consider how the electoral system affects these three parties (previously identified as the three main parties, Conservative, Labour and Liberal Democrat). Should the proportion of seats for each party in the House of Commons be the same as its proportion of votes in the election, or should MPs be elected the way they are now?

Minority MPs

Ideally, should the proportion of [women/ethnic and racial minority] MPs in Parliament be as large as in the country as a whole? The question elements in square brackets were randomly varied. Those scored as answering 'no' to this question include everyone who previously replied 'no' when asked: It is important to have more [women/ethnic or racial minority] MPs in Parliament?

Theme 4: Support for judicial reform

Judges

Please give a mark out of 10 to indicate how you would rate the fairness and impartiality of British judges. If you feel they are extremely fair give them a 10, if extremely unfair, give them 0; but remember, you can use *any* mark between 0 and 10. (In the analysis a low score on this question is indicative of a greater measure of support for judicial reform.)

Courts

Please give a mark out of 10 to indicate how much you feel citizens' rights and liberties are protected by each of the following. Ten indicates something you feel is extremely important for protecting rights and liberties; while 0 indicates something you feel does nothing at all to protect them. But remember, you can use *any* mark between 0 and 10. [A list of items followed, including the one examined here.]

- British courts

Prefer British court
Suppose we had a constitutional Bill of Rights, as some other countries do. If Parliament passed a law but the courts said it was unconstitutional, who should have the final say, Parliament or the courts?

Suppose someone in Britain objects to a law passed by Parliament and takes the case to the European Court of Human Rights. Who should have the final say, the European court or the British Parliament?

[The values for this variable were calculated as the difference in an individual's response to the two questions listed above.]

Value measures
Support for liberty
{Respondent's least-liked group as determined from a list} should not be allowed to make public speeches in my locality.

[Political organisations with extreme views should be banned/we should never ban any political organisation whatever its views.]

Right to demonstrate
Free speech is just not worth it if it means we have to put up with the danger to society from extremist views.

Should persons suspected of a [null/serious] crime have the right to refuse to answer police questions?

Support for authority
Using a number from 0 to 10, please tell me how important each of the following is for you:

- preserving traditional ideas of right and wrong
- respect for authority

Support for equality

We [have gone too far/have not gone far enough] pushing equal rights in this country.

The law should guarantee equal rights for homosexuals.

Using a number from 0 to 10, please tell me how important each of the following is for you:

- guaranteeing equality between men and women
- protecting ethnic and racial minorities

Chapter 4, Appendix B

Values and support for constitutional reform

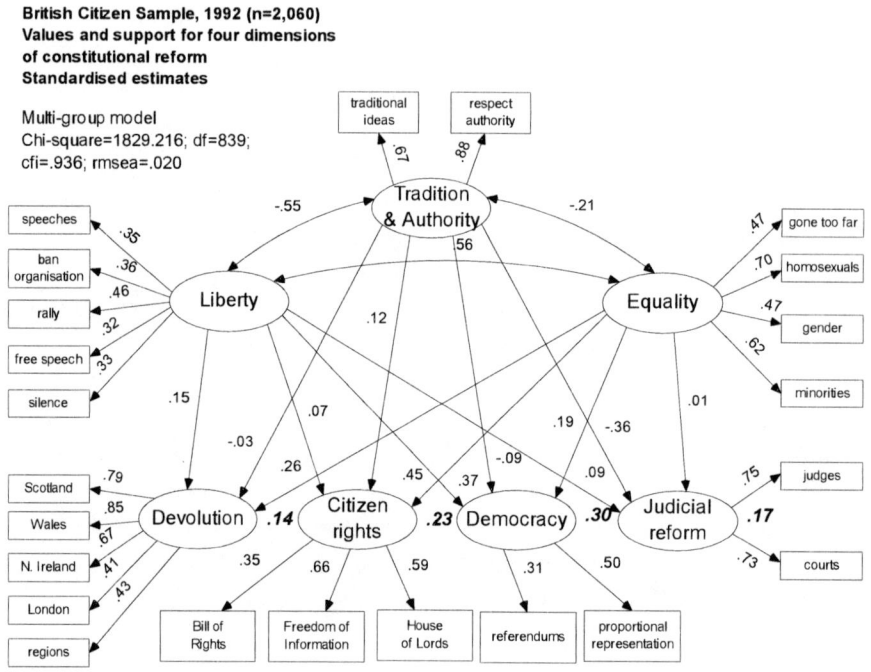

British Citizen Sample, 1992 (n=2,060)
Values and support for four dimensions
of constitutional reform
Standardised estimates

Multi-group model
Chi-square=1829.216; df=839;
cfi=.936; rmsea=.020

To reduce clutter, error terms and explained variance estimates on observed indicators have been eliminated. Observed variables are represented with rectangles or squares. Figures in **bold** indicate the percentage of explained variance in each of the four themes.

Index

The following abbreviations are used in the index:
fig – figure; *tab* – table; *n* – note